Praise for *Failed State*

"Seymour Lachman writes about Albany dysfunction as only an insider can. He knows firsthand what it is to be bullied and extorted by political bosses, to have to cast votes on massive, secretly negotiated budget deals on a few hours' notice, to be the target of nakedly partisan gerrymandering, and to watch a parade of his colleagues go to prison for corruption. *Failed State* vividly documents a sordid era of New York history and provides a practical guide to real reform."

— Bill Hammond, The Empire Center

"The unifying theme here is that New York State government is broken and is not likely to mend itself. Lachman proposes a number of reforms that he believes will restore democracy—among them, the holding of a constitutional convention, which New Yorkers will vote on in November 2017. Timely and valuable, *Failed State* will help voters understand what the stakes are when making that decision."

— Peter J. Galie, coeditor of *New York's Broken Constitution: The Governance Crisis and the Path to Renewed Greatness*

Praise for *Three Men in a Room*

"Startling: a political book that actually informs the public."

— Jimmy Breslin

"*Three Men in a Room* is a perceptive account of a state legislature in urgent need of reform, and of how to accomplish it. Senator Lachman had a front-row seat in Albany, as I once did. He also brings years of academic experience to this compelling and important book. Read it and take it seriously—for democracy's sake."

— Hugh L. Carey, New York State Governor (1975–1983)

"Required reading for any New Yorker who wants to understand what's gone wrong in Albany—and why. This book provides an invaluable dissection of Albany's dysfunction from the perspective of an idealistic insider who emerged from the experience with his principles and credibility intact."

— Edmund J. McMahon Jr., Director,
Empire Center for New York State Policy

"Both edifying and horrifying: Lachman's privileged perspective on New York's legislative practices is essential reading for would-be reformers."

— *Artvoice*

FAILED STATE

FAILED STATE

DYSFUNCTION AND CORRUPTION IN AN AMERICAN STATEHOUSE

SEYMOUR P. LACHMAN

with
Robert Polner

excelsior editions

AN IMPRINT OF STATE UNIVERSITY OF NEW YORK PRESS

Published by State University of New York Press, Albany

This new work includes revised and updated material that was originally published in 2006 as *Three Men in a Room*.

Excelsior Editions is an imprint of State University of New York Press

For information, contact State University of New York Press, Albany, NY
www.sunypress.edu

Production, Cathleen Collins
Marketing, Anne M. Valentine

Library of Congress Cataloging-in-Publication Data

Names: Lachman, Seymour, author. | Polner, Rob, author.
Title: Failed state : dysfunction and corruption in an American statehouse /
   by Seymour P. Lachman, with Robert Polner.
Other titles: Three men in a room
Description: Albany : State University of New York Press, [2017] | Series:
   Excelsior Editions | "THREE MEN IN A ROOM Revised and Updated." |
   Includes bibliographical references and index.
Identifiers: LCCN 2016032662 (print) | LCCN 2016033465 (ebook) | ISBN
   9781438465739 (hardcover : alk. paper) | ISBN 9781438465753 (e-book)
Subjects: LCSH: New York (State). Legislature—Ethics. | Political corruption—
   New York (State) | Power (Social sciences)—New York (State) | New York
   (State)—Politics and government—1951–
Classification: LCC JK3474.7 .L32 2017 (print) | LCC JK3474.7 (ebook) | DDC
   328.747—dc23
LC record available at https://lccn.loc.gov/2016032662

10 9 8 7 6 5 4 3 2 1

For Susan,
Our Children, and Grandchildren

Contents

Acknowledgments

The author would like to thank and acknowledge the following interviewees (through conversations or letters) and notes that they do not necessarily agree with the opinions expressed in this book: Ben Akselrod, Warren Anderson, Frank Barbaro, Gerald Benjamin, Preet Bharara, James Brennan, Richard Brodsky, Hugh Carey, Alan Chartock, Daniel Chill, Bill Colton, Michael Costelloe, Jeremy Creelin, Mario Cuomo, Andrew Cuomo, Michael Cusick, Dick Dadey, Thomas DiNapoli, Richard Dollinger, Robert J. Freeman, Sandy Galef, Peter Goldmark, David Grandeau, Stephen Greenwald, Blair Horner, David Jaffe, Todd Kaminsky, Abe Lackman, Marc Landis, Franz Leichter, Rachel Leon, Susan Lerner, Albert Lewis, Tarky Lombardi, Mary Louise Mallick, John Marchi, H. Carl McCall, E. J. McMahon, Manfred Ohrenstein, David Paterson, Richard Ravitch, David Reich, Felix Rohatyn, Debi Rose, Eric Schneiderman, Adam Simms, Jeffrey M. Stonecash, Robert Straniere, Tom Suozzi, and Mark Treyger.

Though much of this book is based on my personal experiences, it also relies on the following publications and organizations: the Associated Press and Bloomberg News; *Boston Globe, Buffalo* (NY) *News, City and State, City Journal, Crain's New York Business,* the *Economist, Elmira* (NY) *Star Gazette,* Gannett newspapers, *Gotham Gazette, London Telegraph, New York Daily News, New York Observer, New York Post, New York Times, Newsday, Newsweek, Politico New York, Post-Standard* (Syracuse, NY), *Democrat and Chronicle* (Rochester, NY), *Staten Island Advance, Times Union* (Albany, NY), and *Wall Street Journal;* National Public Radio, NY1 News, WNYC Radio, CUNY TV, WLIW/21 (Long Island, NY), WMHT (Albany, NY), and WNET/Thirteen (New York); the Brennan Center for Justice at New York University School of Law, the Citizens Union,

Common Cause New York, the Empire Center for Public Policy, and the New York Public Interest Research Group (NYPIRG).

My great appreciation goes to Wagner College President Richard Guarasci for this and other publications produced by the Hugh L. Carey Institute for Government Reform and his complete support for the institute since its inception. I would like to thank my present and past administrative assistants Suzanne D'Amato and Susan Rosenberg. I would also like to thank my former graduate assistants at Wagner College over the last ten years: Christopher Allen, Danielle Arena-Jacobsen, Amanda Cortese-Ainly, Alexa Marin, and Megan Marin.

Importantly, my lasting thanks to the late Norman Redlich for helping to get the project off the ground. I am especially indebted to Marc A. Rivlin, senior fellow and former interim director of the Carey Institute, and to my longtime friend and colleague Murray Polner, for their writing, editing, and research contributions. We are very grateful for the assistance of SUNY Press and its codirector James Peltz, as well as the copy editor Therese Myers.

Finally, my personal debt to Robert Polner—for his writing, research, and editing—is enormous. This book would not have been possible without him. Thanks!

1

When Poetry Met Prose

Democracy requires decades, even centuries, to take root and flourish. It is a fragile flower. My own state, New York, has learned that it takes just three men in a room to cause devastating harm to a democratic system of governance. More than the foibles of individuals, the structural fault lines that run through the legislature have made possible a cascade of corruption that shows no signs of abating.

I spent nearly a decade as an insider of sorts in the state's capital, never venturing, however, behind the closed doors where the most important deals are decided. Before first winning a special election for a vacant state senate seat in February 1996 and soon after winning a full term, I had served as a dean at the City University of New York (CUNY), at which I also taught political science and educational administration. I lectured at times on the imperfect dynamics and relative merits of the classical liberal arena so well envisioned by English political theorists of the early eighteenth century. Within that arena, conflicting interests—those of business, labor, wealthy and influential individuals, and the broader public—grappled toward compromise that one hoped would benefit the greater good and resemble at least an approximate fairness.

As my early years as a New York State senator unfolded, those lectures seemed hopeful but in some ways quite innocent. Over time, I grew surprised, distressed, and finally repelled by the routine subversion of democratic values and processes in a state that was once among America's most progressive and activist, a trailblazer in economic development and the nurturing of a middle class, workers' rights, education, public health, and poverty amelioration.

By the end of 2004, after spending nearly ten years in the senate, representing large chunks of Brooklyn and, following a redistricting,

Staten Island, I had had enough of New York State politics. I took academic positions, first at Adelphi University on Long Island, and then at Wagner College on Staten Island. My decision not to run for reelection, the result of much soul-searching, gave me time thereafter to reflect on my legislative experiences.

I was not forced by political considerations to walk away from my rather cushioned perch in the legislature. There was little chance I would have been defeated for reelection, having won at least 65 to 85 percent of the vote every two years. Even though minority-party legislators get much less support from the leadership of their house than do members of the majority, they still enjoy numerous perquisites: media attention, phone calls from the likes of Hillary Rodham Clinton and Charles Schumer, and deference from community and business leaders. Legislators also receive travel reimbursement stipends (per-diem allowances for food and lodging), staff assistants, and regular paychecks—all for a job I treated as a full-time commitment but that many of my colleagues handled as part time. To this day, many legislators who have an outside source of income in addition to their legislative salary are apt to treat their public service as a part-time responsibility; interestingly, Common Cause New York reported in December 2015 that newer members enjoy higher outside earnings than more senior members with outside earnings do.[1] For the remaining 60 percent, their public office is their only job, as it was for me.

The legislature is in session for two or three days a week between early January and the third week in June. The typical lawmaker's workday during the session lasts only a few hours, with each gathering of the state senate lasting no more than an hour or so. For much of the six-month session, legislators' schedules consist largely of meeting with interest groups and constituents, and attending receptions and community meetings within their district. In late 2015, Long Island Assemblyman Charles Lavine wrote, "My colleagues and I work shockingly few hours: Next year we are scheduled to spend just 57 days in Albany between Jan. 6 and June 16, when the legislative session ends." More than half of that time is expended on the budget, leaving just 27 days "to consider all other governmental business, including more than 10,000 bills. There is little chance we'll get to more than a handful of those. Our part-time legislature fails the needs of the public and sets the lowest of expectations for legislators."[2]

Eventually I concluded that my full-time involvement in the legislature was taking a toll on my integrity and character, and left the legislature, even with the virtual certainty of another term. The gap between my perception of myself as collaborative, law-abiding, and both ethically and independently minded, on the one hand, and the expectations for lockstep political subservience enforced by supremely arrogant legislative leaders who especially marginalize their minority-party members, had widened with each year. I did not like what was happening to me or to my state government, just as I did not like serving as a veritable puppet. I concluded that I could not possibly make an important difference—despite occasional successes of which I was proud—by continuing to work from within a greatly compromised and corrupted system.

Additionally, I determined that it did not really matter whether Democrats or Republicans controlled Albany, then or in the future, because the place was thoroughly compromised. Absent strong and sustained pressure for reform over months and years, neither the members of my party—the Democrats—nor the Republicans were going to bring a clean, transparent, and dynamic democracy back to New York State.

Fully disgusted, I left Albany and turned my attention to researching and assembling, with Robert Polner, the book *Three Men in a Room*. My hope is to help bring change to one of this country's most secretive, intractable, and misgoverned legislatures. I also want to contribute to the cause of greater democracy in state capitols around the country. *Three Men in a Room* was originally published in 2006. I subsequently founded and became director and later dean of the Hugh L. Carey Institute for Government Reform at Wagner College. The institute is named for the governor who prevented bankruptcy for New York in a previous generation. During the last years of his life, Carey was committed to and involved in the reform institute that bears his name.

The time for substantive, systemic reform of the New York legislator is, more than ever, now. Indisputably, it is well overdue. That was the case when *Three Men in A Room* was published. Now, with the publication of this revised and updated edition a decade later, the problems have not gone away. Indeed, so deeply entrenched, like a spreading cancer they have worsened.

Watching the cascade of legislative indictments and convictions that has gone on since 2006, I have felt, as an uneasy veteran of Albany, even more dismayed and disappointed. The New York legislature essentially went from being a statewide embarrassment to a disgrace of national notice. This slide was, for me, personal. One slow morning, I looked back over the recent years and assessed my former senate colleagues. I realized that nearly one in 6 of the 114 individuals who had served in the 61- to 63-member senate[3] between 2000 and 2014—including many people I know quite well and worked with closely—had gone on to indictment, trial, and very often to prison, their lengthy public service brought to a sudden and dishonorable halt, their reputations tarnished. As a state senator, I had found myself surrounded by many decent, hard-working elected representatives, but my retrospective tally of wrongdoers in the legislature confirmed that I had been working among a sizable cohort of bad actors, some of whom I had long suspected of conducting themselves unethically, and others, I was shocked to discover, harbored a criminal disposition. I wondered about the reasons for their falls—both the issues in their personal characters and, more so, the institutional provocations that makes the dysfunctional legislature susceptible to illegal behavior.

In politics, as in all professions, there will always be people who will grossly violate ethical canons, but the New York State legislature has shown itself to be especially resilient in this regard: all too willing to accept standards that are far lower than desirable, with inadequate defenses against wrongdoing, hazy parameters for appropriate behavior, and many slippery slopes. The recent years have left this untrusty trail littered with scandals. Tragically, leaders in top-tier positions of power in the upper house, the New York State Senate, have incurred charges of corruption or malfeasance, while the same fate befell more than 16 percent of the senators who served at any time between 2000 through 2014.[4]

Quite unforgettable, as I look back, was the resignation of the implacable Governor Eliot Spitzer, former state attorney general, in a sudden and dismaying prostitution scandal in 2008. Equally, if not more troubling in a way, was what happened to Alan Hevesi, another once-respected public servant. During his career in public life, Hevesi wrote the doctoral dissertation "Legislative Leadership in New York State," taught political science classes at Queens College, and served as a Queens assemblyman and then as the New York City comptroller before finally winning election as the state comptroller. A sought-after expert on corporate governance and ethics, he nonetheless headed to prison in April 2011 for a felony "pay-to-play" scheme that involved the New York State Common Retirement Fund, after earlier being forced to resign as the state comptroller when he pleaded guilty to a misdemeanor involving using state employees for personal errands. Hevesi, whose tenure as an elected official dated back forty years, saw his reputability implode in New York State Supreme Court in October 2010 when he admitted he had approved a public investment of $250 million from the state pension fund (of which the state comptroller is sole trustee) in return for almost $1 million in personal benefits from a California businessman. Those benefits included hotel and travel arrangements for him and his family during excursions to Italy and Israel, $380,000 in bogus consulting fees paid to a friendly lobbyist, and more than $500,000 in campaign contributions.

If these scandals involving major, statewide elected officials had any positive aspect, it was that they increased the public's desire for state government reform. During his campaign and on his election as governor in 2010, Andrew Cuomo, previously the state attorney general, argued strongly that the time had come to clean up Albany. He pledged "to restore honor and integrity to government," as his "New NY Agenda," a blueprint of priorities he published during his campaign, cited as his first objective if elected.[5] His initial year in office produced the Public Integrity Reform Act of 2011 (PIRA), which made several notable, albeit limited, improvements in both ethics and disclosure despite the legislature's usual intransigence.[6] Originally called the Clean Up Albany Act of 2011, PIRA created a Joint Commission on Public Ethics (JCOPE) with jurisdiction over all elected state officials and their staffs, along with all registered lobbyists. The commission superseded the state Commission of Public Integrity, which itself was a merging of the state Ethics Commission and the New York Temporary State Commission on Lobbying. The merging was part of the Public Employees Ethics Reform Act of 2007, a significant reform effort under the short-circuited governorship of Eliot Spitzer.[7] While PIRA increased financial disclosure requirements for state employees, including legislators, and made those disclosures publicly available on the JCOPE website, it gave JCOPE the power only to *investigate* members of the legislature. Enforcement remained under the purview of the Legislative Ethics Commission—controlled, problematically enough, by the leaders of both houses.[8]

When he found the legislature unreceptive to additional reforms, Governor Andrew Cuomo established a state Commission to Investigate Public Corruption in August 2013 under the Moreland Act of 1907.[9]

The commission was appointed "to probe systemic corruption and the appearance of such corruption in state government, political campaigns and elections in New York State." Armed with subpoena powers, the Moreland Commission had three cochairs and altogether twenty-five members, including many sitting district attorneys and former state and federal prosecutors. The state attorney general, Eric Schneiderman, a former state senator from Manhattan, swore in the members of the new Moreland panel as deputy attorneys general. After several months of intensive inquiry, the commission put out a preliminary report in December 2013. The report emphasized its concern over legislators' outside income as well as abuse of programmatic legislative grants known as "member items" and budget "earmarks" for special projects; unlawful use of campaign accounts and the need for campaign finance reform and possibly public financing of political campaigns; weaknesses with the state Board of Elections; and the need for additional criminal laws to fight corruption.[10]

The state Moreland Act authorizes a governor to appoint a person or persons "to examine and investigate the management and affairs of any department, board, bureau or commission of the state."[11] In recent years, though, the act has been used as a means to investigate matters outside the executive branch, such as the failed response of some public and publicly regulated utilities to the great damage wrought by Hurricane Sandy in 2012.[12] Cuomo's Commission to Investigate Public Corruption shined a light on the legislative branch (beyond the boundaries of the executive branch) by focusing on the oversight and investigative responsibilities of the state and local boards of elections (part of the executive branch) as well as JCOPE. The commission stated that its members were "tasked with, among other things, reviewing the adequacy of existing state laws, regulations and procedures involving unethical and unlawful misconduct by public officials *and the electoral process and campaign finance laws* [emphasis added]. They will also examine whether existing laws and regulations have been fairly and vigorously enforced and what changes must be made to such enforcement. The Commission is directed to make recommendations to toughen and improve existing laws and procedures."[13]

Governor Cuomo initially said that he was giving the Moreland Commission the authority to conduct the investigation as it deemed appropriate so it could ferret out corruption anywhere in state politics, calling it, at its empaneling, "totally independent," and adding, "Anything they want to look at, they can look at—me, the lieutenant governor, the attorney general, the comptroller, any senator, any assemblyman."[14]

After moving independently to illuminate the dark corners of Albany, however, the Moreland Commission ended up, as many things in the Capitol, serving merely as something used in the high-stakes negotiations in 2014 over the annual state budget among the governor and the two leaders of the assembly and senate (then Sheldon Silver and Dean Skelos). In March of that year, nearing the end of his first term, Cuomo inexplicably shuttered the commission, only halfway through the originally planned eighteen-month investigation of the state government. He insisted it had accomplished its major objectives and went on to say he was satisfied with changes in the state's bribery and financial disclosure laws to date.

If indeed the commission had become something merely to be traded in these high-stakes negotiations, the reason might have been that it issued subpoenas for all records of yearly outside income of $20,000 or more earned by assembly members and senators, and the subpoenas threatened to expose possible conflicts of interest by Assembly Speaker Silver and Senate Majority Leader Skelos themselves. Unsurprisingly enough, the leaders of the assembly and senate did not appreciate the commission's scrutiny. They retained legal representation to battle its subpoenas on behalf of the legislature as a whole.[15] Cuomo rendered the legal questions over the subpoenas moot,[16] however, in abruptly discontinuing the panel as of April 2014, just as three-men-in-a-room talks over the key content of the 2014–2015 state budget were entering their most decisive closed-door phase.

Why he opted to close down the commission, or what cooperation or concessions the sudden action might have gained for him at the negotiating table, is not known. The governor himself evidently had his own problems with the Moreland Commission as it had developed. Friction arose between the executive branch and some of the commission's investigators, with the governor's office "objecting whenever the commission focused on groups with ties to Governor Cuomo or on issues that might reflect poorly on him," according to a front-page *New York Times* article exploring the causes of the panel's premature closure.[17]

Cuomo also faced criticism for the commission shutdown during his reelection campaign. Fordham University law professor Zephyr Teachout, an expert on the pervasive problem of political corruption and the intertwining issue of campaign finance reform,[18] challenged him in the Democratic primary, drawing widespread attention and praise for her reform arguments. Nonetheless, Cuomo prevailed over Teachout and a third candidate with more than 60 percent of the vote.[19] He went on to win reelection easily.[20]

The legislative leaders must have breathed a bit easier with the Moreland Commission decommissioned, despite the public uproar over its disbandment. Speculation that Silver and Skelos each had had a personal stake in the panel's discontinuance, not merely an institutional one, was reinforced when U.S. Attorney for the Southern District of New York Preet Bharara intervened forcefully. Bharara dramatically had the files of the commission shipped to his lower Manhattan office in order to follow up on the panel's lines of inquiry.[21]

Media initially focused on alleged interference in the Moreland Commission investigations by aides to the governor, as well as possible motivations for the commission's shutdown.[22] Federal prosecutors interviewed members of the commission[23] but eventually concluded that evidence was insufficient to proceed with prosecution in connection with its shutdown.[24] Governor Cuomo maintained that there had been no wrongdoing because, as a creation and extension of the governor's office, Moreland Act commissions are subject to gubernatorial control.[25]

Whatever the principal reason or reasons for the commission's ill-starred fate, the panel's files apparently contributed to the eventual indictments of the two sitting legislative leaders in 2015, Assembly Speaker Sheldon Silver and Senate Majority Leader Dean Skelos. Even more than the Spitzer and Hevesi scandals, Bharara's intricate prosecutions of these men shook up the elaborate insider rationales and justifications for the legislature's long-standing secretive, top-down manner of operating. Though at this writing the mode remains largely intact, it came under public criticism as perhaps never before.

The longtime Democratic speaker of the assembly, who had become leader of the overwhelmingly Democratic body in 1994, was arrested and handcuffed in front of news cameras for alleged fraud and embezzlement. It was a case built on Bharara's investigation into the millions of dollars of outside income Silver received from two law firms—Weitz and Luxenberg, the prominent personal injury law firm where Silver was counsel, and Goldberg and Iryami, a relatively obscure two-attorney law firm run by Silver's longtime friend and former counsel Jay Arthur Goldberg, both of which paid referral fees to Silver.[26] While the former had appeared on Silver's annual financial disclosure filings, the latter had not.[27]

Silver was accused of steering $500,000 in state funds to a Columbia University Medical Center clinic run by Dr. Robert Taub that treated patients with mesothelioma, a rare cancer directly related to asbestos exposure. He was also alleged to have provided assistance to Taub's charity, on whose board Taub's wife sat. In return, Taub's clinic directed some of its patients to Weitz and Luxenberg, one of the leading law firms handling asbestos claims. Silver received an estimated $4 million from the firm for the referrals. At Silver's trial, Dr. Taub testified that he was surprised that the assembly speaker told him not to discuss with anyone their evolving relationship dealing with the clinic—not even with the person who introduced them.[28] Silver's concern was money. At trial, the managing partner of Weitz and Luxenberg described how Silver was annoyed by delays in payment he was drawing for the mesothelioma patient referrals to the law firm with which he was associated.[29]

Until shortly before his indictment, the public was unaware of Silver's affiliation with Goldberg and Iryami, a firm that works to secure reductions in New York City real estate taxes for property owners.[30] One of Goldberg and Iryami's major clients happened to be the largest political donor in the state—developer Leonard Litwin and his Glenwood Management, responsible for $10 million in contributions to political campaigns and party committees from 2004 to 2015. Silver was alleged to have used his power and influence to steer Glenwood Management and another developer to hire Goldberg and Iryami, for which he received 25 percent of the fees the firm earned.[31]

Given the legislature's weak financial disclosure requirements concerning the source and amount of outside income—marginally strengthened by PIRA in 2011, and again in 2014 when the Moreland Commission was shut down—just who might have been trying to influence the assembly speaker with regard to the state budget, policies, and legislation was difficult to discern. Litwin and his real estate development firm were not charged in the case, but media outlets reported that Glenwood Management was the "Developer 1" described in Silver's indictment,[32] and its lobbyist testified at Silver's trial.[33]

Silver's indictment, handed down by the grand jury in January 2015—a day after the newly reelected Governor Andrew Cuomo delivered his State of the State address and budget address—sent shockwaves through the state government. It also appeared to disrupt the three-men-in-a-room negotiations over the state's $142 billion annual budget, and it left legislators teetering from the political reverberations and public outrage. Yet the indictment of one of the state's most powerful elected representatives was not so very shocking. Over the prior fifteen years, *thirty-three* Democratic and Republican legislators in the assembly and senate had already been forced to leave office due to criminal charges, ethical lapses, and alleged wrongdoing.[34] Even before Silver resigned as assembly speaker, federal prosecutors had prevailed on a few state legislators to wear a hidden recording device to record their colleagues talking.[35] This was Albany as New Yorkers had come to know it. The surveillance was reminiscent of investigations of the mob, a sign of how far the legislature's reputation, while never one immune from scandal in its long and colorful history, had fallen in our own time, long past the days of Tammany Hall. Silver's arrest itself added to an embarrassingly lengthy streak of recent corruption cases.

After his indictment, Silver attempted to hold onto his well-consolidated power. Initially he was supported overwhelmingly by the Democratic conference he still headed, including members with reputations as progressive reformers.[36] As pressure from editorial boards and constituents built, sentiment changed and he simply had no choice but to resign the speakership. It was not something he had planned to do; he had kept such tight control over the assembly throughout his tenure that he lacked an heir apparent. Silver's majority leader (his "number two"), an upstate assemblyman with a low profile outside his district and the Capitol, had little chance of winning sufficient support because the speaker's position traditionally goes to a member from New York City (like Silver, whose district was on the Lower East Side of Manhattan). The New York City delegation comprises the majority of the chamber's Democratic conference. A contest to succeed Silver followed, which Bronx County Democratic leader and Assemblyman Carl Heastie won.[37] Heastie was elected to the post by the 150-member chamber, sailing through despite allegations and questions media reports raised about some of his past financial decisions and use of campaign funds.[38] By many accounts, he acquitted himself well in the state budget talks into which he was plunged, affording lawmakers greater consultation on major sticking points, such as the terms for renewal of rent regulations for tenants and tax breaks for real estate developers, than many had come to expect from his tight-lipped predecessor.[39] With Silver out of the speakership and the Moreland Commission out of business, Cuomo worked out a flurry of budget deals with Heastie and Skelos (prior to Skelos's indictment). The deals dealt with rent regulation and tax credits for real estate developers in New York City—both of which were then on the verge of expiring—as well as criminal justice and aid to public, parochial and charter schools. These agreements were incorporated into the massive budget package known in Albany as the Big Ugly—"the product of an expensive annual carnival of dysfunction," as Jim Dwyer wrote in the August 13, 2015, *New York Review of Books*.[40] The legislature passed it.

Importantly for Cuomo, the budget was adopted April 1, 2015, the beginning of the new state fiscal year, meaning it was on time (technically, however, it was a couple of hours past the midnight deadline). Past years' state budgets had been adopted weeks or months late, even as late as August, a symbol of state government dysfunctionality and a symptom of the distrust between the leaders of the different branches under past governors, including George Pataki and David Paterson.[41] Passing an on-time budget became for Andrew Cuomo, a talking point, if not a point of pride; he reportedly handed out hockey pucks to celebrate when the legislature approved a budget deal by the deadline in a previous year.[42]

The issue of corruption stayed very much in the news, however, especially as Silver's monthlong trial was not to begin until late 2015. Silver's attorney claimed that the former speaker's alleged corruption amounted to business-as-usual for the legislature because it is a part-time institution and, due to the fact that many legislators hold outside jobs, merely created the appearances of conflicts of interest such as those facing his client. Those apparent conflicts, he claimed, were quite unexceptional and certainly not illegal.[43]

The jury disagreed. On November 30, 2015, capping heavy publicized proceedings, Silver was convicted of all charges; he automatically lost his seat in the assembly and was sentenced on May 3, 2016, to twelve years in prison for corruption schemes that generated more than $5 million in gains. "Silver's corruption cast a shadow over everything he has done," said Justice Valerie Caproni of the federal court in Manhattan, who also ordered Silver to make restitution of more than $5 million and pay a fine of $1.75 million. At the time of this writing, the former speaker was appealing his conviction.[44]

The story of Albany corruption retained its high public profile because of Bharara's concurrent prosecution of Senate Majority Leader

Dean Skelos, who was arrested along with his son, Adam Skelos, in May 2015, four months after Sheldon Silver's indictment. The father was alleged to have used his influence to help his son at the public's expense. According to the twenty-two-page indictment, "Dean Skelos attempted to secure and did secure hundreds of thousands of dollars for Adam Skelos, including . . . over $100,000 in payments and health benefits from a medical-malpractice insurer who provided Adam Skelos with a no-show job while actively lobbying Dean Skelos on legislative matters."[45] In the prosecutor's complaint, the malpractice insurance firm went unnamed but was identified in media reports as a politically connected company in Long Island's Nassau County, the home of Skelos's senate district.[46]

Skelos was also accused of trading the legislative needs of Glenwood Management to leverage additional benefits for his son. Glenwood senior vice president and general counsel Charles C. Dorego, who was also its point-person on lobbying and political contributions, was said to have arranged for Adam Skelos to receive a $20,000 commission from a title insurance company for work he did not perform. Dorego additionally arranged for the younger Skelos to receive a consulting job at the environmental firm AbTech Industries, which had connections to Glenwood Management. The firm paid Adam Skelos $200,000, and subsequently obtained a contract with Nassau County allegedly after Dean Skelos exerted his influence.[47]

The Skelos indictment and trial provided a rare insight into how the leaders of the New York legislature have viewed their power. Skelos was recorded on a wiretap as saying, "I'm going to be president of the senate, I'm going to be majority leader, I'm going to control everything, I'm going to control who gets on what committees, what legislation goes to the floor, what legislation comes through committees, the budget, everything."[48] The indictment also led some to speculate that Skelos's desire to limit renewals of rent regulation and New York City's 421-a housing construction tax-credit program to two years was intended to maximize his ability to exploit interested parties in the real estate industry, including Glenwood Management.[49]

Like Silver, Skelos tried briefly to cling to power in Albany, but was forced to resign from his leadership post, replaced by Long Island's John Flanagan, as members of the entire senate felt considerable pressure from their constituents, advocacy groups, and the media. His resignation as majority leader, when it did come, was more symptomatic of life in the legislature than it was anomalous: it actually took place just as another state leader—Senate Deputy Majority Leader Tom Libous of Binghamton—was facing criminal charges as well (and thus could not succeed Skelos).[50] Tom Libous was one of six senate leaders who was arrested within the prior ten years after holding a top-tier leadership position for a long or short duration (the others being Dean Skelos, Joe Bruno, Malcolm Smith, Pedro Espada Jr., and John Sampson, who had also served chair of the senate's Ethics Committee).

Libous was a long-serving state senator who had succeeded Binghamton's former senator, Warren Anderson, whom I especially admired for having served with a memorable sense of public purpose as the Republican Majority Leader during the 1970s New York City fiscal crisis and many years thereafter. Prosecutors alleged that Libous made false statements to the Federal Bureau of Investigation (FBI) about his role in getting his son, Matthew, a job with a politically connected Westchester County law firm. They alleged the senator arranged for an Albany lobbying firm to pay one-third of his son's $150,000 salary at the law firm. Senator Libous, according to prosecutors, promised that the law firm would have to "build a new wing" to handle all the new business he would send its way.[51] In July 2015, a jury found him guilty of lying to the FBI, which is a felony. Sick with cancer, he was sentenced to six months of electronically monitored home confinement rather than the six-month prison term possible for the charges. So tarnished, he died on May 3, 2016 (the day of Silver's sentencing).[52] Libous's son, meanwhile, served prison time for a related federal tax conviction.[53]

Dean and Adam Skelos were convicted of all charges on December 11, 2015, ending the senator's thirty-year career in the legislature.[54] The father drew a five-year prison sentence on May 12, 2016, and the son, six and a half years. The former majority leader also was ordered to pay $800,000 in restitution and fines.[55] As of this writing, the Skeloses were appealing their convictions. Their case reflected the potential for legislative leaders and other state lawmakers to misuse their offices to enrich themselves and their families at public expense—as when, for example, legislative earmarks to fund projects in a member's district end up benefitting the legislator's own family members. Several recent corruption cases also reflected the unsavory ties lawmakers may have with lobbyists, law firms, and companies seeking to obtain special advantage from the legislature with the help of individual legislators.

Clearly, the figurative Hall of Shame in Albany has really bulged of late, and the reason, in large measure, is the spadework of federal prosecutors, particularly U.S. Attorney Bharara, using the federal honest-services fraud statute where New York State corruption laws were inadequate. Bharara assiduously developed the cases against Silver and Skelos as well as others in the state capital, which proved a target-rich environment. Bharara effected a significant shift in the current state of politics as usual in Albany. President Barack Obama had appointed him in 2009,[56] and Bharara began the prominent job as federal prosecutor by investigating more than 100 finance and business executives and prosecuting insider trading in the wake of the 2007–2008 Wall Street meltdown.[57] He subsequently turned his attention to Albany and its culture of corruption, especially after Governor Cuomo shut down the Moreland Commission in March 2014.[58]

After announcing the indictment of Silver at the start of 2015, reporters asked Bharara if he was satisfied and finished with Albany. He answered the question ominously: "Stay tuned." His office was hardly finished investigating the state government. In fact, it was already investigating Skelos and putting the entrenched modus operandi of the legislature on notice. Only a day after Silver was indicted, the prosecutor delivered a speech at New York Law School in which he ridiculed the state's secretive, rigidly controlled manner of operating. I myself had depicted the legislature in a similarly undemocratic fashion in *Three Men in a Room*. I hoped it would act as a catalyst for reform as well as an analysis of the workings of the legislature. But a decade later Albany remains as insular and unrepresentative as it did when the book came out. Bharara, who quoted from the book during his speech, made clear that the lack of public accountability inherent in the three-men-in-a-room construct—with its last-minute negotiations privately conducted by the governor and the two top legislative leaders, and the marginalization of the other members of the legislature—might have helped bring about the kind of malfeasance his office was looking into.[59]

The secretive, authoritarian mode of the Capitol, the federal prosecutor continued in the address, discouraged average citizens from understanding the process or thinking that they could possibly have a meaningful effect on major issues before the legislature and government agencies.[60] He echoed this point when he subsequently accepted an invitation to speak before the Kentucky legislature, after securing the Silver and Skelos convictions. As he told the Bluegrass State's legislators, referring to Albany corruption: "People knew, and did nothing. This, perhaps, was the most unfortunate feature of the status quo in my home state—the deafening silence of many individuals who . . . saw something and said nothing."[61]

If Silver and Skelos lose their appeals and are incarcerated, then nine former New York State legislators will be in prison. The late Libous would have brought the number in federal custody to an even ten.

A waterfall of scandals can indeed erode the public's confidence in government and willingness to participate in politics and government, as well as voter turnout. Flagrant misuse of power in New York has become routine—a kind of cost of doing business in the legislature. The many instances of corruption of elected officials with whom I worked, and many others since, did not happen in a vacuum, but several deep-seated factors instead precipitated them. Among these are loosely designed, sometimes ambiguous and often poorly enforced legislative ethics rules; torrents of campaign cash and the loopholes and party committees through which they gush; platoons of lobbyists with relatively easy access to lawmakers that no average citizen enjoys; and the essential powerlessness of most legislators, who quickly learn they must go along to get along. For many legislators, the benefits of acquiescence outweigh the risks of using their power to speak out, so disagreement or debate with the nearly omnipotent legislative leaders is rare. For some lawmakers, whether or not they feel demoralized by their second- and third-class status, whether or not they have outside income, the opportunities to commit ethical breaches for self-gain have been too ample and easy to ignore. A sizable number, albeit a minority of the total, convince themselves that they are entitled to use their office to enrich themselves and have done so.

Consider, for example, just one telltale aspect of the perennially lax atmosphere, based on my legislative tenure: assembly members and senators did not need to submit any proof of their expenses when they submitted vouchers for food and lodging reimbursements for the days they spent working in Albany—it was all automatic. State lawmakers may request the maximum of $111 a day for lodging and $61 for food and other per-diem expenses, the tax-exempt limit currently allowed by the Internal Revenue Service (IRS).[62] They may also obtain reimbursement for actual travel expenses (for taxi, bus, train, or air, or tolls paid while driving), along with the IRS allowance for mileage driven. While they must provide receipts for travel costs and detail any mileage they have driven, reimbursement from the legislature for food and lodging remains based on the honor system. Many legislators can and do realize thousands of dollars in reimbursement payments each year—no receipts needed, no questions asked, and, until the reforms of 2015,[63] no requirement that the member actually be working in the Capital Region, just that he or she was present. The top recipient of reimbursements in the first half of 2015 was an upstate assemblyman who drew $19,500 for travel, food and lodging, all legal under the assembly's rules.[64] Like so many other arrangements in Albany, the reimbursement procedures are wide open for abuse.

There is, of course, no shortage of checkered, ethically compromised statehouses in the United States. But New York's image as not only corrupt, but also as one of the least deliberative and perhaps most lax and dysfunctional has only grown with each new scandal-stained year, especially given the unusually large volume of business that continuously flows through the Capitol. The Moreland Commission's preliminary—and only—report, studies by good-government groups and academics, and media reports, op-eds and editorials have all served to support the widespread view that the New York legislature needs wholesale structural reform. The guilty verdicts against the legislature's former top two leaders—two of the "three men in a room"—one after the other, have not only hardened public perceptions but, in some ways, caused the legislature to gird itself reactively against proposals for meaningful reform and examples of best practices from other statehouses.

While the federal prosecutions under the forceful Bharara have been exceedingly helpful in illuminating where corruption festers, they are not the ultimate answer to what ails the state polity. As the Moreland Commission wrote, "Public corruption is a New York problem that requires a New York solution."[65] I certainly agree.

Given the constitutionally enshrined autonomy of the senate and assembly chambers, a counterbalance to the powerful executive branch, bringing democracy and effectiveness to the legislature will require continuous pressure and quite possibly consideration of a constitutional convention, which the public has a right to vote for, or against, once every twenty years, next in November 2017.[66] In a 2015 data-driven survey of all the states, the respected Washington, D.C.–based Center for Public Integrity, gave only three states a grade higher than D– for their policies and procedures to combat secrecy, questionable ethics, and conflicts of interest. That New York merited a D– in the ranking[67] further shows that the force for change needs to come from sources largely *outside* the hidebound legislature itself. These include reform-minded legislators in each party, reform groups, citizen litigants, academic researchers, media outlets, and the power of social media to awaken new voices and calls for action. Whatever avenues by which structural reformation and democratizing may coalesce, voters will always retain the ultimate means of redress in a democracy—the ballot. They can elect new legislators, and, unlike in 1977 and 1997, when voters turned down a constitutional convention measure because they were concerned about highly emotional issues such as abortion, the death penalty, and aid to private and parochial schools, a convention can, in 2017, open this door to badly needed legislative reform and reduce corruption.

My motivation for updating *Three Men in a Room* is really based on a fundamental belief: Americans are entitled to a voice in their state politics and a clear window on its dealings. This is especially so in a world where quickly transmitted information is power, and secrecy—which is so antithetical to well-informed choices or allowing ideas and policies to be debated or debunked—runs rampant at all levels of government. Winston Churchill memorably called democracy the worst form of government except for all the other alternatives.[68] Democracy can be improved even if it cannot be perfected, and the American people have a right to a real democracy, rather than merely window dressing or photo opportunities and public relations, the parts that make up the current charade that calls itself democracy in Albany. Real democracy is what our soldiers are asked to fight for in foreign lands. For public participation to be short-circuited anywhere within the United States, as is exemplified every day in the Empire State, should be galling and unacceptable to us all. Tragically, only in presidential election years do more than 50 percent of voting-age individuals go to the polls. In nonpresidential years, when state legislators and governors are elected, turnout is approximately one-third of potential voters. In off-year special elections, the turnout is between 5 and 10 percent.

Still, New Yorkers are sensitive to the problem of corruption afflicting their state government. Recent polls reveal deep-seated disappointment in the conduct of state government. A Quinnipiac University survey of New York voters in mid-2015 found that 55 percent of those polled would favor, in theory, banishing the entire legislature, or cleaning house, with just 28 percent saying the current crop could be counted on to eradicate corruption.[69] There could hardly have been a more discouraging evocation of public perception than an April 2016 Siena Research Institute poll: Of 802 registered voters surveyed, 93 percent said they believed that corruption in their state government was a very serious or somewhat serious problem, and 65 percent said they thought the problem even extended to legislators from their own area.[70]

All of us should support the extremely important recommendation that we, as citizens, begin looking to our state governments for a restoration of both the idea and the practice of good government in our country. Advocates of reform will not be acting in a vacuum. In New York, they have laid down important markers since the early 2000s, but there almost certainly will be the need for a state constitutional convention to achieve reform. Allowing the cascade of ethical and legal improprieties to continue unimpeded in the coming months and years would be regrettable, to say the least. I would venture to call it unthinkable.

Look back to recent history and you can see that contemporary pressure building for reform did not begin with Bharara's important prosecutions and is not a flimsy reed. Rather, as anyone can see, the foundations for change run deeper.

Since at least early 2002, many newspapers across New York State have played a consistently strong role in the push for legislative reform, editorializing powerfully about the need for systemic changes of many aspects of New York State's government. Most editorial writers have aimed their quills at the processes and practices designed to perpetuate the iron grip on decision making held by three people: the governor, the assembly speaker, and the senate majority leader, regardless who they happened to be at any given time.[71]

The last ten to fifteen years of editorializing, then, have firmly established the rationale for change. The *New York Times* began a lengthy string of significant editorials in February 2002 decrying what the editors correctly termed a deadlocked and demoralizing situation in the state capital, given many built-in incumbent protections. The paper assumed an incumbent-wary stance in its candidate endorsements, determined to see the entrenched status quo shaken up or at least sent a message: make substantial changes or get out of the way.[72] Many more editorial boards and columnists around the state have exhorted readers to vote against the incumbent, whatever his or her history of securing funds for projects directed to the district or the degree of influence in the Albany hierarchy, and regardless of the caliber of his or her opponent.[73]

The frustration editorial boards expressed, whether they were conservative, liberal, or centrist, was highly understandable. Officeholders in Albany have no term limits and are rarely voted out of office because of the extraordinary powers of incumbency accorded to them in a self-serving system of rules and practices geared to the cultivation of campaign funds and "safe" districts. The districts are not created by a body independent from the legislature's leaders, as in some states, but by the majorities of each house in the New York legislature.

Not surprisingly, then, the *New York Times* returned to its nonendorsement posture vis-à-vis Albany incumbents during the 2014 election cycle. With the heavily favored and well-funded Andrew Cuomo running for reelection as governor, the newspaper refused to endorse him in the Democratic primary.[74] Governor Cuomo managed to persuade the Republican-led state senate to go along with assembly-supported bills legalizing same-sex marriage and tightening the state's gun control laws after horrific mass shootings in other states while reducing pension payouts for future public employees (a cause of many editorial boards, though the bane of public employee unions).[75] Despite his having gained timely approval of the yearly state budget throughout his first term, a feat that had eluded his predecessors, the incumbent governor had only partially made good on his campaign pledge to make cleaning up Albany his "Job Number 1."[76]

Nor was Cuomo successful in ending the gerrymandering of legislative districts, a longtime practice that had resulted in a truly shameless 98 percent reelection success rate for legislators.[77] Instead, the 2012 redistricting was conducted under the control of Assembly Speaker Silver and Senate Majority Leader Skelos,[78] and a constitutional amendment passed in 2014 promised only a bipartisan redistricting guided by some written standards and not the nonpartisan independent redistricting that government reform groups argued were needed to draw fair districts.[79] Cuomo was also unable to firm up the state's loophole-riddled campaign donor laws—at least during the first five years of his leadership.

In 2004, then–Nassau County Executive Tom Suozzi, a Democrat, launched a notable effort to highlight the severity of corruption in Albany called the "Fix Albany" campaign. Under his early banner, Suozzi successfully targeted for defeat a Long Island incumbent who he said was too close to the Democratic assembly speaker and would never challenge

Sheldon Silver's failure to address ballooning Medicaid expenses and inefficiencies, a problem putting pressure on suburban counties to raise property taxes. Tom Suozzi argued that his constituents on Long Island and around the state deserved a greater voice in Albany through their elected state representatives. The challenger whom Suozzi backed was someone he said would confront the problems in Albany with more vigor and independence than the longtime incumbent did. Although incumbents almost never lose an election in New York State, and especially those from Long Island, this time one actually did: Glen Cove city council member Charles Lavine defeated a well-liked, competent, six-term Democratic assemblyman in the Democratic primary. Lavine's victory sent a message to Speaker Silver that there were political consequences for avoiding the subject of legislative reform.[80] Suozzi also recruited a Democrat to challenge Majority Leader Skelos for his Nassau County senate seat, but this candidate was unsuccessful in the November general election. Suozzi later lost the Democratic nomination for governor in 2006 to then–Attorney General Eliot Spitzer and was defeated in his 2009 reelection bid for Nassau County Executive by Republican Edward Mangano.[81]

Additionally, Republican state senator Nancy Larraine Hoffman of Syracuse fell to an insurgent candidate who, like Lavine, bore a similar message about the need for reform to the senate majority leader position (then held by Joe Bruno, a Republican representing Rensselaer County and Saratoga Springs).[82] However, her successor has become a leader in the Independent Democratic Conference (IDC), which is rewarded for its support of the senate's Republican majority with chairs of important committees, all of which give their members an extra stipend.[83] Republican state senator Nick Spano of Westchester County survived a surprisingly strong challenge from Democratic Westchester County Legislator Andrea Stewart-Cousins and won by eighteen votes.[84] Stewart-Cousins rebounded in a rematch two years later in 2006, defeating Spano, who in 2012 would plead guilty to federal tax evasion charges and draw a prison sentence of a year and a day;[85] in contrast, Stewart-Cousins rose to Democratic Minority Leader and holds that position at the time of this writing.[86]

Even before Stewart-Cousins's victory in 2006, reinvigorating the legislature was unquestionably an issue for legislators to reckon with. Both Republican and Democratic incumbents who had never dared broach the issue now gave it, at the very least, a cursory endorsement, and some even made it the focus of their campaigns.

Some legislative reforms were passed in response to the public's deeply disenchanted mood during those years, particularly in light of the striking success of the Suozzi-backed assembly candidate in concert with the Clean-Up-Albany initiative the late New York City mayor Ed Koch in 2010 sponsored. Both those efforts, for all the attention they deservedly received, were short-lived and achieved only limited success. Suozzi's influence declined after he lost the Democratic nomination for governor in 2006. Koch's efforts led many legislative candidates to pledge to support the campaign finance and ethics reforms in the "Contract with New York" that he developed with government reform groups, only to abandon the promises after the election: they backed off after signing on to Koch's reforms. "They lied to me," Koch, who died in 2013, said.[87]

Reformers can indeed be "morning glories," to quote George Washington Plunkitt, the candid Tammany Hall politician who died a rich man in 1924 after a career dedicated to what he liked to call "honest graft." They "looked lovely in the mornin' and withered up in a short time—while the regular machines went on flourishin' forever, like fine old oaks."[88] It is also true that reformist zeal fluctuates constantly for all sorts of reasons. Some ethics measures resulted from the reformist energies of the first decade of the twenty-first century; unfortunately, these were limited, with some even qualifying as regressive. Given the legislature's tradition of intractability and habit of delaying in addressing important issues or kicking the can down the Thruway, some began to say that incremental reform was at least better than nothing and little more was possible.

Nothing in his hard-driving stint as New York State attorney general indicated that Eliot Spitzer would have agreed with that defeatist sentiment. He became known as the "Sheriff of Wall Street" before the 2007–2008 worldwide financial crash.[89] Independently wealthy from his family's real estate holdings, he proved to be a popular choice of the voters for governor in the Democratic primary against Suozzi and in the general election.[90] His team brought what came to be called a "steamroller" approach to managing the prickly legislative leaders, particularly Majority Leader Joe Bruno. Spitzer assumed an unusually confrontational posture when he openly campaigned for Democratic candidates for state senate.[91] Typically, sitting governors do not get involved in legislative contests. He also sought evidence linking Bruno to the use of a state helicopter for political fundraising trips, an alleged connection Bruno called false. A veteran of Albany, Bruno vocally complained he himself was the target of executive-branch skullduggery. Spitzer's aggressive style backfired when he was accused of improperly assigning state troopers to follow Bruno. Democrat Andrew Cuomo, then the state attorney general—Spitzer's successor and sometime rival—looked into the headline-making dispute. Cuomo's office issued a report favoring Bruno's side of the story.

Andrew Cuomo had worked closely as a confidante of his father, three-term Governor Mario Cuomo, and later served as U.S. Secretary of Housing and Urban Development under President Bill Clinton in the 1990s. He saw an opportunity to become the second "Governor Cuomo" after having campaigned unsuccessfully for the office in 2002. Elected as attorney general in 2006, Cuomo served effectively in that office, seeing it as the pathway to the governor's office.

With ethics reform positioned at or near the top of his 2010 campaign agenda, Andrew Cuomo repeated his vow on election night to set Albany's house in order, asserting he would end the "dysfunction and degradation" in the Capitol. Once in office, his campaign promises, a category his father once likened to poetry, turned inevitably to realpolitik pragmatism, or, in Mario's framing, prose, as he was faced with a $10 billion state budget deficit and legislative leaders who as usual wanted to prevent stronger ethic rules or disclosure requirements in their carefully guarded houses. The leaders had a history of viewing any such reform proposals as encroachments by the executive branch, and the legislature was not willing to allow such intrusions.

In Andrew Cuomo's second term, between the indictments of Silver and Skelos, the governor was able to force through some new ethics-related safeguards. Legislators are now required to disclose their outside sources of income and the monetary range for this income, although they can still avoid disclosing clients' names under some circumstances. The top earner was an assemblyman (Stephen Hawley, a Republican from Orleans County) who disclosed earning $455,000 to $570,000 as the owner of an insurance company. The income disclosure forms must be filed with the JCOPE. The average outside income of 2015 lawmakers elected before the previous year stood between $47,000 and $80,000, excluding capital gains, interest, and dividends.[92]

In the budget talks with Skelos and Heastie, Governor Cuomo also gained disclosure and certification requirements for member-item grants that lawmakers give out to community organizations based on varied allotments from their legislative leader, which have long exerted a corrupting influence on the legislature. Under the measure, nonprofit organizations that receive member-item grants must disclose any potential conflict of interest or existing financial relationship with the sponsoring legislators and their staff.

Such measures, while laudable, are not transformational. They fall short of the high expectations for reform that Cuomo set during his first gubernatorial campaign or that the arrest of the speaker of the assembly and the majority leader of the senate, as well as many other legislators of lesser rank, should have occasioned. In his January 2016 State of the State address, the governor returned to the issue of ethics reform, calling for limiting legislators' outside income to 15 percent of their base salary, or $11,925. Cuomo also called for enlarging the definition of "lobbyist" in order to require political consultants working with elected officials to register with the state's Ethics Commission, and he proposed sealing the so-called limited liability company (LLC) loophole, which allows all but unlimited contributions from wealthy individuals and businesses.[93]

It is encouraging that recent advocates for reforming the state legislature reflect the entire political spectrum. Some are liberals, some are centrists, and others are conservative. An example of the last is Assemblyman Jim Tedisco, a conservative Republican from Glenville, N.Y., in Schenectady County, who has been elected and reelected to the assembly since 1982. He has come to the view that postponing dramatic reform of Albany's legislative procedures would be nothing short of dangerous. "We have less of a representative democracy right now and more of a kingship," he said on the public-affairs television show "New York Now" in August 2016. "It's not three men in a room anymore—it's three men in a bunker now. They won't even tell you where they meet anymore."

Tedisco is the author of what he called the "Spirit of '76" bill, which requires that any piece of legislation supported by a majority of a chamber's members—76 in the case of the 150-member assembly—must proceed to the floor for debate and a vote. "What my colleagues need to understand is . . . you can't be a representative if you let a majority leader in the senate or a speaker in the assembly control every single bill that gets to the floor." His proposal makes common sense, yet Tedisco also recognizes it would be revolutionary, as it effectively calls on rank-and-file legislators to revolt against their leaders, something that has never occurred. Still, his measure would create a pathway to true democracy and transparency. "I believe a lot of these ethics and corruption reforms will get to the floor if rank and file members get an opportunity to bring those to the floor," the assemblyman said.[94]

Whether legislative leaders will respond to the proposals is still unknown. It does not seem likely, however, based on history or even in the wake of the embarrassing conviction of its two top leaders. Given the incomplete nature of contemporary reform measures that have been enacted—especially when compared to the magnitude of the legislature's corruptibility—New York, as well as most state governments, clearly requires stronger remedies. Legislative members require more sustained attention and pressure than they have received traditionally from governors, legislative leaders, the media, and the public. As I have stated, in no state should residents accept gross abrogation of America's democratic ideals, either in their state capitals or in Washington, D.C., where corporations, lobbyists, and special interests have turned Congress into a massive feeding trough for the richest and most connected and have contributed to a political polarization that debases our national government and democracy.

Greater attention to these problems can, and sometimes does, lead to progress. At the very least, continuous public pressure can become an important reminder of the great power of state legislatures over the lives of the citizens and can lead to an expansion of disclosure, ethics safeguards, and, critically, the decentralization and redistribution of much-coveted control by the leadership in the legislature.

2

Son of Immigrant Parents

My parents, Louis and Sarah, were born in Poland. My father had been a yeshiva (seminary) student until he lost his parents by age twenty-one and could no longer be a full-time student. After my parents were married, they left Poland to seek a better life in America, arriving at Ellis Island aboard the *S.S. Paris* in July 1922.[1] Before leaving her native land, my mother said goodbye to her recently widowed mother, not realizing that she would never see her again.

My father, a highly intelligent man, was the only person I ever knew who was fluent in six languages. He briefly owned a candy store, which closed during the Great Depression. He taught himself English and learned about America by reading Professor Allen C. Thomas's book *A History of the United States*, written in English with a parallel Yiddish translation,[2] and he became an American citizen as soon as he could do so. I discovered the book after he died while going through his papers and other books. My father worked very hard as a steam presser in a men's clothing factory. My mother was a homemaker and worked day and night to take care of her family. She was a thoughtful person, and many women came to her for advice regarding personal and family issues. My parents dedicated their lives to their children's well-being and always emphasized how important a good education was.

Many immigrant families have a story of hardship from which later generations can draw lessons and inspiration. Mine is no different. My parents lost siblings and relatives in the Holocaust and dreamed, like many American Jews, of perhaps moving to Israel in the future. At one point before World War II, my father bought an orange grove in what is now Tel Aviv, Israel, with what little savings he had, only to sell it prior to the war to help rescue a brother and his large family from the Nazis. Similarly, my mother had a sister who was able to escape to England.

One of my most vivid and earliest memories as a child was after World War II when my parents went to government and private agencies searching for information about the dozen brothers and sisters they had left in the old country. Not one sibling left in Poland survived the death camps of the Holocaust. My parents always came back from these meetings visibly depressed. Besides my uncle in Israel and my aunt in England, none were left. One nephew found refuge in Ecuador before the war, and only one other nephew and a few cousins had survived. My parents were disconsolate and, as my brother and I grew up, rarely spoke about what had happened to their family during World War II.

When I was born, my parents were in their mid-forties. Their oldest son, Izzy, had died when he was less than five from a burst appendix; a doctor misdiagnosed the disorder, told them to take the boy home, and give him an enema, which, before antibiotics, led to his death.

After the horrible loss of their first child, a second, my brother Leon, was born a year later. It took another five years before I showed up, giving my parents two boys to raise.

The death of their first son, however, challenged their spirit for the rest of their days. My parents would do anything that would benefit their children's lives. My father died when I was just twenty-two, and my mother died not long thereafter, before my wedding, living just long enough to meet Susan, the woman who would become my beloved wife.

The early loss of my parents will always remain with me as well as a deep, hard-to-describe feeling of obligation to my oldest brother, whom I knew only from framed black-and-white photographs and family remembrances. I felt an obligation to conduct my personal and public life to become the type of person he might have been if he had lived and the type of people my parents were during their lives. At the heart of that feeling was a desire to be religiously faithful with a good education, public-spirited, and mindful of and helpful to those in need. My goal was to be as ethical a person as humanly possible, emulating my forebears as much as I could.

After graduating from Brooklyn College, I taught social studies at Thomas Jefferson and Lafayette high schools in Brooklyn to children of immigrant and working-class families. A few years later I earned a doctorate from New York University and later taught at the CUNY. I was appointed to the New York City Board of Education at age thirty-five in the early days of school decentralization and eventually was elected by my peers to serve as the board's president.

I was drawn into the community battles over the direction of New York City's public school system, the nation's largest. I helped guide the central board through one of the school system's most volatile periods during the early and mid-1970s. The period came shortly after low-income, minority parents in neighborhoods such as Ocean Hill/Brownsville, Harlem, and the Lower East Side demanded and obtained a stronger voice in the operation of their children's troubled schools.

The 1954 Supreme Court decision in *Brown v. Board of Education of Topeka* had outlawed "separate but equal" schools,[3] stirring African American protests around the country, including in Brooklyn and Harlem, and demands for improved educational opportunities for their children. By the 1960s, black-white politics had overwhelmingly captivated all aspects of life in the United States. Sit-ins in the South to end segregation gave way to protests to integrate and make more equitable New York City's public schools, which were also segregated, not by legislative law (de jure segregation) but rather by residential patterns and practices (de facto segregation), including redlining, blockbusting, and school district gerrymandering. Middle-class New Yorkers, mainly whites of European ancestry, were leaving the city in droves for the booming suburbs. Zoning and racial steering were used to keep blacks and Hispanics out of suburbia. If anyone still doubted that a national movement toward equality was under way, Congress passed civil rights legislation between 1964 and 1968, championed by President Lyndon B. Johnson, including the Civil Rights Act of 1964, the Voting Rights Act of 1965, and the Fair Housing Act of 1968.[4] Additionally, for the first time in U.S. history, a bill allowing federal aid to education was passed.[5]

In New York, minority parents' demands for a voice in their children's education was galvanized in Albany when a historic law containing many grammatical and substantive mistakes was hurried through the state legislature. The law decentralized the New York City school system in 1969 into what became thirty-two and later thirty-three semiautonomous community school districts, each with its own elected school board. The voting process for school board elections under the legislation was badly flawed; the complex, difficult-to-comprehend "weighted" system for determining elections of community school board candidates allowed organized interests, such as professional and religious groups, to gain control of many local boards. The Board of Education retained, under the legislation, great powers over policies, purchasing, security, and school performance largely through its appointment of a school's chancellor. The chancellor, however, became a convenient political target of whoever happened to be mayor and, sometimes, of the most formidable education groups as well.

During the rocky transition from a single central board to a constellation of community school district boards, well before the advent of the current mayoral-controlled school system, I sought with some success to integrate the ranks of the central school administration. During the same period, the board also accorded civil liberties and due process for the first time to students including a student's right to appeal a suspension by the principal. That was among one of the most important achievements I helped bring about. Murray Polner, who was my associate at the Board of Education, played a major role in the rights and responsibilities initiative.

I can remember feeling guilty after my appointment to the Board of Education. I never realized there would be so many interminable late-night meetings, sometimes going beyond midnight into the early-morning hours. I never thought I would not be able to see my wife, Susan, our five-year-old son, Elliot, and our three-year-old daughter, Sharon, as much as I wanted. One evening, when I managed to reach home early for family dinner, Elliot said he had a question for me, and I immediately thought it would be a complaint about my late hours. It was not. He asked, "Daddy, why are you always on those boring news programs? I'd like to see you on a better show, like *Beat the Clock*." I grabbed and hugged them all, and we sat down for supper without any mention of the Board of Education or even *Beat the Clock*.

The results of this period of late nights and massive change were imperfect, but the inauguration of a democratically driven system cooled emotions and blunted the potential for violent disruption and further deterioration across a system of approximately 1 million mostly low-income students. Because the structural changes had stemmed in large measure from grassroots protests, all parties had given the school system a chance to prove itself.

Throughout my tenure at the Board of Education, I learned, sometimes the hard way, that we must listen to the voices of the public and that our decisions, whether mistaken or wise, were better reached not by mandate from a select few, but by public argument, intense discussions, and open and public hearings. Such are the trappings of a democratic society struggling to do the right thing. In much the same spirit, community-planning boards were introduced across New York City during John Lindsay's liberal mayoralty, and, beginning in the 1960s and 1970s, they too became an essential avenue of public involvement—a source of information, advice, and experimentation about community needs that had been overlooked; these boards exist to this day.

One of my victories as Board of Education president occurred in 1974 when I sued the Office of Education of the U.S. Department of Health, Education and Welfare (HEW) over a "polarizing, . . . inflammatory, and racist" questionnaire on racial attitudes sent out to school districts around the country. After my objections, the department eventually withdrew the survey not only for the New York City public schools, but also for schools nationwide. *Time* magazine concluded, "It was just as clear that HEW had been insensitive and once again the government had been unwisely prying into the private lives and personal attitudes of its citizens, particularly children."[6]

Beginning in 1988, New York City implemented several landmark election and government reforms. In the wake of several major city corruption scandals involving leading city politicians, New York's city council passed the landmark Campaign Finance Act, which required all candidates for city offices to disclose their fundraising and spending.[7] Also in 1988, following the recommendation of a Charter Revision Commission appointed by Mayor Ed Koch and chaired by Richard Ravitch, the people of New York City voted to approve a new system of public campaign financing for city elections.[8] This was a model program, albeit one the New York legislature has refused to adopt for state campaigns, which would have made elections for state office more competitive and less subject to the disproportionate influence of wealthy interests.

In 1989 the U.S. Supreme Court ruled that the existence and operations of another major city panel—the Board of Estimate, a smoke-filled back room at city hall where the mayor, city comptroller, city council president, and five borough presidents bartered and brokered huge land-use and budget decisions—violated the constitutional principle of one person, one vote.[9] The powerful body was scrapped in favor of a much larger and more representative fifty-one-member city council.

Adding to the democratization of the New York City government, in subsequent years voters backed the creation of the New York City Independent Budget Office, which remains a key oversight board independent of the mayor and the city council. The voters also passed a two-term limit for the mayor, the two other citywide officials (public advocate and city comptroller), the borough presidents (with their already-reduced powers), and all fifty-one council members. I should note that when each of these changes was taking place, incumbents and other critics said that the structural reforms would lead to paralysis and chaos in city government. But we live in a democratic society, and this improved democracy, while never neat and trim, brought in fresh ideas, new leadership, and other benefits, where before there had been a hidebound system stuck in some self-serving habits and, often enough, cronyism and corruption. In 2008 the mayor and city council speaker pushed through a one-time extension of terms limits, allowing a third term to officeholders who otherwise could not have sought reelection in 2009. The opposition and protests that followed hurt its supporters and ensured that such a measure will not be proposed again, at least in the near future.

After I left the Board of Education, I returned to CUNY, teaching political science and educational administration classes at both Baruch College and the CUNY Graduate Center, eventually becoming University Dean of CUNY. During that time, I started the National Collaborative of Public and Nonpublic Schools, the only such organization in the United States. It brought superintendents and other administrators from public and nonpublic schools in the twenty largest cities in the nation together for an annual three-day conference and facilitated follow-up year-round contact. Participants included all of New York City's public school chancellors and CUNY's chancellors as well as leading American education officials, such as Republican U.S. Secretary of Education Terrel Bell, Democratic U.S. Secretary of Education Richard W. Riley, governors, mayors, and members of Congress and state legislatures.[10] The collaborative brought people together who had never met with each other despite being major educational leaders in the same city. An example of this was the Superintendent of Schools of the Catholic Archdiocese of Atlanta, who thanked us for bringing her together with the public schools superintendent. It was the first time in ten years they had ever met and spoken to one another. This led to future collaborations that strengthened both school systems. When I left the national collaborative and CUNY to become a state senator, Michael Costelloe continued to do an excellent job of chairing the national collaborative for the next decade.

Despite having taught political science and education law at Baruch College, my knowledge of Albany's arcane workings was theoretical. Looking back much later at my career as a state senator, I realized that I had been naive. I had believed in the separation of powers, the implicit if not explicit authority of the voters, and the classical theory of the democratic arena, in which competing interests offset and blunted one another's reach, creating a rough equilibrium and quality of fairness. I was wrong. As a state senator, I discovered firsthand that the reality in Albany was quite different from the theory I had taught in the classroom.

3

A Can of Worms

I first ran for the New York State Legislature in February 1996 in a senate district covering parts of Brooklyn (and, after a 2002 redistricting, parts of Staten Island as well). After winning the backing of a wide array of Democrats, including reformist Assemblyman Frank Barbaro and Borough President Howard Golden, I was nominated by the powerful Democratic organization in Kings County after a raucous meeting of the Democratic County Committee members from the district, with some individuals passing around flyers that could be interpreted as anti-Semitic, racist, and anti–public schools. In the early morning hours, I received enough votes to constitute a majority over my opponents.[1] This culminated in my winning a special election in the district. That November, I ran successfully for the first of four full two-year terms.

After about a year in office I began to see the legislature for what it was and what it still is: a Potemkin village whose elaborate and impressive chambers and rhetoric hid its lack of integrity, democracy, and, all too often, substance.

As I was learning how things worked, I traveled more than three hours from my home in Brooklyn to spend many days and nights in Albany. The more I grew to know about the often-inscrutable operations carried on there—unknown to most outsiders—the more I grew determined to keep from becoming too compromised. I tried to protect my independence, sometimes at the price of giving up a chance to rise quickly in the ranks; at other times, admittedly, I participated in voting for things I did not in my heart or head support. In fact, most bills on which I voted passed unanimously or nearly unanimously in the Republican-controlled senate, yet were never even brought to a vote in the assembly.

Like anyone in the legislature, initially I did not want to do anything that could cause difficulty every two years when I came up for reelection.

I wanted to be accepted by my colleagues and amass some influence that might benefit my district and political aspirations. I was ambitious enough to dream of one day serving in Congress. However, the redistricting in New York State soon made it obvious that it would be very difficult. While other states' populations (that is, California, Texas, and eventually Florida) exceeded New York's, and the number of their congressional seats grew, New York's representation in Congress declined.

Within a short time of my arrival in the state senate, I was appointed to the senate's Finance Committee. I began to vote my own way on important issues of concern to me and to my constituents. Shortly thereafter a senior member of the Democratic conference said to me, "Listen, you can either support the Democratic leadership and rise to the very top, or be an independent who votes on principle and sink to the bottom."

I felt somewhat as Tom Suozzi's handpicked reform candidate, Charles Lavine, must have felt in 2004 when he was asked to cast an immediate vote for the reappointment of the speaker of the assembly. He did as requested, explaining later to a reporter that even though he had run on a platform of independence from the certain-to-win speaker, Silver, he determined that he would have no effectiveness from the very start of his tenure if he stood on principle and voted against the man at the pinnacle of a top-down organization.[2]

Something happened in 1999 that solidified my growing unease with the way the legislature worked. Silver, along with Senator Martin Connor, the Democratic minority leader in the Republican-led senate chamber, joined with Republican Senate Majority Leader Bruno to do away with the so-called New York City commuter tax—the tiny, fractional income tax on suburban commuters to the metropolis. The cost to individual taxpayers of this levy was minute, but collectively the tax produced between $400 million and $500 million annually at that time for New York City[3] (and perhaps as much as $1 billion today). As was well known, the commuter tax helped pay for the city-subsidized services and amenities that commuters depended on, benefited from, and enjoyed, from policing and firefighting to world-renowned museums, legendary parks, and nonprofit research hospitals of the highest quality.

Silver's and Connor's rationale in seeking to eliminate the commuter tax was to help a Democratic senate candidate with his uphill attempt to gain a seat representing a suburban district in Rockland County. He was not expected to win because the Republican frontrunner also benefitted from the repeal of the commuter tax. It was a political maneuver on their part, diametrically opposed to the interests of their own New York City constituents. I refused to back the bill, the decision being so obviously correct since virtually no constituent in my district was bound to disagree with my urban-protective stance.

Even so, many of my Democratic colleagues later told me I had been mistaken to resist the political might and will of the Democratic leadership; there had been no way to stop that particular juggernaut, so my vote was only symbolic, and could only be detrimental to me and my political aspirations. While I implored my Democratic colleagues in the assembly to save the commuter tax, most Democrats in that Democratic-led chamber, predictably, followed Speaker Silver's lead and voted to repeal this significant source of public revenue for New York City. Some who did not support the ban received special dispensation. Others, like me, broke the party line without such dispensation—hardly a brave feat, but unusual all the same in Albany.

At the time I asked Deputy Minority Leader David Paterson of Manhattan, who would become minority leader, lieutenant governor, and then governor in 2008 after Eliot Spitzer's implosion, why he had voted to kill the commuter tax. After all, the city had depended heavily on the levy at least since the fiscal-crisis years of the 1970s, and the tax was much smaller than many believed was needed to offset the devastating financial impact of the mass exodus of city residents to the suburbs in those years. (Suburban legislators made sure that it remained tiny, catering to an ever-growing suburban voting population at the expense of the urban center.) Paterson smiled. He leaned toward Connor, implying that he had to go along with the vote because the Democratic leadership of both houses demanded it.

Ironically, despite the repeal of the commuter tax by decisive margins in both houses, the Republican candidate in Rockland County won anyway, having garnered the support of Republican Majority Leader Joe Bruno, then–Deputy Leader Dean Skelos, and the Republican governor at the time, George Pataki. The senate Republicans benefited from the tax's repeal because they represented many of the suburbanites affected. The Democratic leadership in the senate and assembly went along with the Republican governor and senate majority because they thought that it could help them win both assembly and senate seats. However, the tax repeal did not attract Republican voters to the Democratic Party, yet it has cost New York City billions of lost revenue in the years since.

This fiasco, typical of Albany's blindingly self-serving ways, crystallized for me the reality that the legislature's leadership ran the government much like the stacked Presidium of the former Soviet regime. From early in my tenure, I witnessed legislative leaders changing the votes of an elected official right out in the open when they did not agree with his or her opinion, sometimes to the embarrassment of that senator. That was, they felt, their prerogative. I differed, yet I came to see that such a thing was not uncommon, even if it embarrassed key Republican senators in the process. It blatantly showed the overwhelming procedural power that the leadership wielded and its desire to exercise near-tyrannical pressures on all chamber members.

As a result of voting my conscience against repealing the commuter tax, I was seen as too autonomous of the senate Democratic leadership. I also realized that by voting my conscience, leadership would almost certainly prevent my rising to a position of rank and influence in the senate. After a few years in the senate, I was named deputy minority whip. The position, one of several conference "leadership" positions with few if any responsibilities and no real power, offered little insight into the motivations and strategies of the conference leadership and was more to support the pretense that power was shared and decisions were collaborative.

I do not view myself as a martyr and never have. I tried, rather, to work within the system, but in so doing, I too compromised some of my personal standards simply to be able to function with a reasonable degree of effectiveness for my district in the tightly controlled halls of power and with the hopes of being granted more responsibility. I also realize that many legislators felt as I now do but believed they could do nothing given the subservience the top level of the Albany hierarchy required. Some compromise on legislation by reasonably independent legislators is, of course, how a deliberative and functioning legislative body should work to achieve the will of the people. Nevertheless, Albany was, and remains, a kind of cosmic black hole in this regard, a place where most politicians, Republicans and Democrats alike, cannot be influential or even have a small role with regard to important decisions and tradeoffs for the state. We were forced to cede our autonomy—our free will—to our conference leaders in return for staff allowances, office space, committee assignments, leadership positions, member items for the district, and reelection assistance when needed. Play along or be a political pariah: that was the unwritten yet unmistakable message.

"If people understand what is going on in Albany today," explained the late governor Mario Cuomo in a 2005 interview with me, "they would say it is a can of worms."[4]

Or perhaps, based on the flood of indictments of the past decade, a can of snakes.

I have come to see that scandals involving New York legislators tend to fall into three broad categories: bribery and kickbacks; embezzlement from either the state (such as false expense reimbursements) or from nonprofit organizations funded by the legislator's discretionary earmarks; and malfeasance primarily related to the legislator's outside employment.

Consider these representative cases of contemporary scandals involving my former legislative colleagues:

- In 2003 Bronx Democratic Assemblywoman Gloria Davis resigned, was prosecuted by the Manhattan district attorney's office, and served a brief jail sentence after being caught accepting cash bribes. Davis also accepted free rides between Albany and the Bronx in vans owned by the Correctional Services Corporation, a business that received an extension of its state contract with her assistance.[5]

- Senior Assistant Majority Leader Guy Velella, longtime Bronx/Westchester state senator and prominent in the state's Republican Party, pleaded guilty in 2004 to one count of bribery and agreed to serve up to one year in jail (in the end he served six months).[6] Velella was alleged to have pocketed $137,000 in bribes to help steer public works contracts through state agencies. Despite the serious nature of the charges, then–Majority Leader Joe Bruno raised about $150,000 from the Republican senators' campaign funds to pay the legal bills of this besieged political insider.[7]

- Assemblyman Roger Green of Brooklyn resigned in June 2004 after pleading guilty in state court in Albany to petty larceny for billing the assembly $3,000 in false travel expenses. He was sentenced to three years' probation, a $2,000 fine, and restitution of the $3,000 he had improperly received. While he agreed to resign from his seat, as is sometimes a condition attached to a guilty plea, he ran for it three months later and easily won.[8]

The downward spiraling has not slowed. The New York State Senate was dysfunctional while I served my five terms in this chamber but the corruption continued to grow after I retired:

◆ Brooklyn District Attorney Charles J. Hynes prosecuted Brooklyn Assemblyman Clarence Norman Jr. multiple times for alleged corruption. Leader at the time of the Kings County Democratic Party organization and deputy speaker of the assembly, Norman was found guilty in September 2005 of soliciting and trying to conceal illegal campaign contributions. He was found guilty again in December 2005 of stealing $5,000 from his 2001 reelection campaign by depositing a check to his campaign committee from his club, the Thurgood Marshall Democratic Club, into his personal account. In March 2006 he was acquitted of stealing travel reimbursements for a vehicle the Kings County Democratic Party paid for. (Assembly rules allowed for reimbursement for use of non–state-owned vehicles regardless of whether the member owned them or paid their expenses.) Almost a year later, Norman was convicted of grand larceny and extortion for a scheme to force two judicial candidates to hire certain campaign consultants or lose county party support in the 2002 primary.[9] He was sentenced to three one- to three-year terms for all of his convictions, and beginning June 2007 he served less than eighteen months in prison before being sent to a work-release program; he was paroled in 2011.[10]

◆ Longtime Senate Majority Leader Joseph Bruno gave his son Kenneth, a former Albany lobbyist, his sympathetic attention on important matters facing the New York legislature despite the complex questions that this personal/professional relationship raised.[11] By way of some background, in 1995 there was a push to clear the way for Las Vegas–style casinos in New York's Catskill Mountains. Governor George Pataki introduced a bill authorizing five casinos there, each to be given to Native American tribes to settle their longstanding land claims against the state. The governor withdrew the bill, however, after it encountered opposition in the legislature and complicating court decisions. Pataki then offered a bill to allow one casino only, to settle a claim by the Akwesasne Mohawks. The assembly passed it, but the senate did not, saying it wanted to approve three casinos to generate more revenue and satisfy more tribes—including one represented by Bruno's son.[12] What is the average person to think about the motivations for that decision? Could it have been another case of favoritism, or mere coincidence? Whatever the truth, the results were of a type known to longtime observers of the New York legislature: inaction since the body did nothing. In 2006 Bruno's son gave up his lobbying job and started to work as an independent attorney.[13]

◆ After weathering criticism for assisting his son's career and upon outmaneuvering then–Governor Spitzer's accusation of using state-funded travel for campaigns, Bruno stepped down in June 2008. In early 2009 he was indicted and, late that year, convicted of charges related to alleged influence peddling connected to his outside consulting business and his position as senate majority leader[14]—only to be acquitted in 2014 in a second trial. Bruno's exoneration came after a U.S. Supreme Court ruling in 2010. The court held that the federal statute that makes it a crime "to deprive another of the intangible right of honest services" only applied where there was proof of a quid pro quo in the form of a bribe or a kickback, not just a showing of a concealed conflict of interest.[15] That, in fact, was the theory under which Bruno was initially convicted of honest-services fraud, when a jury found he had concealed hundreds of thousands of dollars in payments from a businessman who wanted help from the legislature. Bruno's departure from the senate in mid-2008— he had arrived in 1977—allowed Dean Skelos to become majority leader.[16]

◆ Former Senator Efrain González Jr. of the Bronx was indicted in 2006 for defrauding two nonprofit organizations in his borough. González directed member-item grants to Pathways for Youth, which in turn funneled those and other monies to another nonprofit, West Bronx Neighborhood Association, which González controlled and from which González took hundreds of thousands of dollars for his own personal use.[17] After being reelected in 2006, González lost the 2008 Democratic primary to Pedro Espada Jr. González pleaded guilty in federal district court in May 2009 and was sentenced to seven years in prison a year later after unsuccessfully attempting to withdraw his guilty plea.[18]

- Brooklyn Democratic Assemblywoman Diane Gordon was convicted in April 2008 on eight counts of bribery and misconduct related to an offer to help a contractor acquire a piece of city-owned land in return for building her a home for free. She lost her seat and was sentenced in January 2009 to two to six years in prison.[19]

- Brian McLaughlin, a Queens assemblyman who was also president of the New York City Central Labor Council, was arrested in October 2006 on forty-four federal corruption counts. He stood accused of stealing $2.2 million from the state, his union, his political club, his campaign, and a Queens Little League organization, and was formally charged with racketeering, embezzlement, money laundering, bank fraud, and bribery. In 2009 he was sentenced to ten years in federal prison. However, after he cooperated in another case—against Assemblyman Anthony Seminerio of Queens, and others—the sentence was reduced to six years.[20]

- Anthony Seminerio, a thirty-year state legislator, and at the time seventy-four years old, pleaded guilty in February 2010 to one count of fraud. Prosecutors claimed he took hundreds of thousands of dollars in payoffs from a hospital and local chamber of commerce through a shell company he created while serving in the assembly. He received a six-year prison sentence, telling reporters as he left the courthouse, "I've been through enough, please. Just be kind."[21] Seminerio, in failing health, died in prison while also under investigation for his involvement in another bribery scheme, this one involving the healthcare provider MediSys that led in 2011 to the unsuccessful prosecution of Brooklyn Democratic

Assemblyman William F. Boyland Jr. and the guilty plea of Brooklyn Democratic Senator Carl Kruger.[22]

◆ For years, Bronx Democratic Senator Pedro Espada Jr. leveraged his position to obtain funding for the health-care nonprofit that he founded, Soundview Health Center. At least three times during his senate career of four terms over three noncontinuous periods, he changed or threatened to change his allegiance to the Republican conference in order to increase his power in the senate.[23] In 2008 he won a seat in the state senate by defeating in the Democratic primary indicted incumbent Senator Efraín González Jr.[24] Long a thorn in the side of the Bronx County Democratic Party, Espada lost the 2010 Democratic Primary for renomination and was soon indicted in federal court for embezzling a half million dollars from Soundview. He was convicted in June 2013 and sentenced to five years in prison.[25]

◆ Queens Democratic Senator Hiram Monserrate was under a cloud from the time he took office. After initially holding back his support for the slender Democratic majority of the senate following his election in November 2008, along with Pedro Espada Jr., Bronx Senator Rubén Díaz Sr., and Brooklyn Senator Carl Kruger, he changed parties and joined the Democratic majority.[26] He was indicted in March 2009 on a charge of domestic violence for allegedly slashing his girlfriend's face with a broken drinking glass.[27] Pressure mounted not only on Monserrate to resign, but also on the fragile Democratic majority conference to discipline or expel Monserrate if he refused. Holding on, Monserrate joined Espada in supporting a Republican conference attempt to wrest effective control of the senate in June 2009, only to return subsequently to the Democratic conference.[28] After Monserrate was convicted of one count of misdemeanor assault in October 2009 in connection with his girlfriend's injury, Democratic Conference Leader John Sampson appointed a bipartisan committee led by then–Manhattan Senator Eric Schneiderman (who was elected as New York's attorney general in 2010) to decide Monserrate's political fate.[29] (Conviction of a felony means automatic expulsion from the legislature, while a misdemeanor conviction is left to the member's house to decide what, if any, punishment should be meted out.) The committee called for Senator Monserrate to resign or be ousted; the senate expelled him in February 2010.[30] His troubles were just beginning, however. In 2012 he pleaded guilty to having used approximately $109,000 in city council discretionary funds to pay members of a nonprofit he controlled to work on his unsuccessful 2006 state senate campaign and was sentenced to two years in prison.[31]

◆ Bronx Democratic Senator Larry Seabrook left the senate after an unsuccessful run for Congress in 2000. In 2001 he won a seat in the New York city council. In 2012 Seabrook was convicted in federal court of misappropriating funds that he had allocated to nonprofit organizations he controlled.[32] Seabrook received a sentence of five years in prison[33] and forfeited his pension to pay restitution for crimes.[34] (Unfortunately, most elected officials convicted of corruption retain their pensions despite efforts to pass pension forfeiture in recent years.)

◆ Queens Democratic Senator Malcolm Smith was the leader of the Democratic conference when it took the majority in the senate in 2009. He lost much of his power during the leadership crisis of June and July 2009 involving senators Democrats Hiram Monserrate's and Pedro Espada's voting with the Republicans to replace Smith with Skelos as the new senate majority leader.[35] After the 2012 general elections, Smith joined the breakaway IDC, which worked out a power-sharing coalition with the Republicans beginning in 2013.[36] Smith's membership in the IDC lasted only a few months as he was expelled from the conference after the FBI arrested him in April 2013 on charges related to his attempts to secure a position on the Republican primary ballot in that year's approaching New York City mayoral election.[37] Smith was convicted of bribery and extortion in early 2015.[38] He went to prison, upended, like Espada, by his unbounded pride and arrogance. These are characteristics the ancient Greeks called *hubris*. It is rarely far from the heart of New York's Romanesque Revival/Neo-Renaissance–style Capitol.

◆ Senator Carl Kruger, another unscrupulous person who knew how to circumvent difficulties, was from my home borough of Brooklyn. Nominally a Democrat, he was at various times rewarded by the Republicans for his assistance to them. Majority Leader Joe Bruno made Kruger the first minority-party member ever to chair a committee in the Republican-majority senate—the Committee on Social Services, Children, and Families—with a yearly stipend of $12,500 on top of his lawmaker salary. In 2011, though, the ethically challenged Kruger lost everything. He surrendered to authorities to face federal charges in a wide-ranging bribery case involving the medical services firm MediSys, and pleaded guilty near the end of that year. Kruger drew a sentence of seven years in federal prison, providing what a news reporter called "yet more evidence of the apparently unending wave of corruption in Albany."[39]

◆ Shirley Huntley of Queens defeated incumbent Senator Ada Smith in the 2006 Democratic primary after Smith had been found guilty of misdemeanor harassment earlier that year.[40] As it turned out, Huntley's conduct in office was far worse. She revealed at an unusual news conference in August 2012 that she expected to be arrested later that month. Two days later, the Democrat turned herself in to the Nassau County district attorney's office. In the state indictment that followed, the office of New York Attorney General Eric Schneiderman alleged that four people with ties to a social services and education nonprofit that Huntley had founded had conspired to help the senator's niece and an aide steal state funds from the group. In January 2013, Huntley pleaded guilty to mail fraud for embezzling $87,000. Shortly before her sentencing—she drew a year and a day in prison—it was revealed that she had recorded discussions from June 2012 to August 2012 with various elected officials and their consultants, donning a hidden wire in the unsuccessful hope of obtaining information to trade to prosecutors to go free or have the possibility of a lighter sentence.[41]

◆ One of the legislature's most long-lasting power brokers was Clarence Norman's successor as Kings County (Brooklyn)

Democratic leader, Assemblyman Vito Lopez. A longtime power broker whose assembly career dated back to 1985, Lopez ended up as the contemporary poster child for sexual harassment of legislative staff[42] and was forced to resign in May 2013, leaving the taxpayers to fund almost $600,000 in settlement payouts to his alleged victims.[43]

◆ Brooklyn Assemblyman William F. Boyland Jr. faced multiple charges. While he was acquitted in Manhattan federal court in November 2011 on charges that he received a no-show job in the MediSys bribery scandal that felled Kruger,[44] that trial led to more troubles. In 2013 state Comptroller Thomas DiNapoli ordered him to repay the state $67,497 after an audit showed that he had claimed travel and per-diem reimbursements more than 600 times for days that he was not in Albany, including days he was on trial in Manhattan.[45] In March 2014 he was convicted in Brooklyn federal court on twenty-one counts of bribery charges and extortion for promising to direct state grant money in exchange for more than $250,000 from a favor-seeking businessman who was actually an undercover federal agent. The sting took place during Boyland's Manhattan federal trial. Boyland's father, former Assemblyman William F. "Frank" Boyland Sr., an unindicted coconspirator in the son's case, was shown on videotape accepting a blank check from an FBI agent at the son's district office. Prosecutors quoted him as saying, "Let's step outside, and you and I'll take care of this"—and later, "All right, just legally, you know, you know this is against the law, right?"[46] In September 2015 a judge sentenced the younger Boyland to fourteen years in prison, with federal district court Judge Sandra Townes remarking that he "clearly had no respect for the law" and that she did not see "any redeeming characteristics of the defendant."[47]

Evidence of the legislature's malaise goes further:

◆ Former Senator Vincent Leibell, after twenty-eight years in the legislature, incurred a sentence in federal district court in White Plains in May 2011 of twenty-one months in prison and three years of supervised release after pleading guilty the previous year to obstruction of justice and tax evasion. The charges were related to an investigation into his alleged extortion of payments from both lawyers and a nonprofit doing business for Putnam County, which was part of his district. The nonprofit, established and partly controlled by Leibell, received millions of dollars in member-item grants he sponsored.[48]

◆ In April 2013 Bronx Assemblyman Eric Stevenson was indicted for bribery for a scheme involving the operators of adult day-care centers[49] after having been recorded by fellow Bronx Assemblyman Nelson Castro.[50] A jury convicted Stevenson in 2014, and a judge sentenced him to three years in federal prison.[51] Castro had been secretly cooperating with state and federal prosecutors since 2009 after authorities charged him with lying under oath to the New York City Board of Elections during his 2008 campaign.[52] In return for his cooperation, Castro was sentenced to probation and community service for federal charges of lying to public authorities while receiving a conditional discharge of the state perjury charges.[53]

◆ Queens Assemblyman William Scarborough pleaded guilty in May 2015 in a case involving the misuse of campaign funds and submitting false travel expenses for reimbursement. Scarborough admitted to falsifying requests for travel and per-diem payments adding up to $50,000 along with using $40,000 in campaign funds for personal expenses. While not excusing his actions, Scarborough attributed them partially to the low base salary for lawmakers, last increased in 1996.[54]

◆ Senator John Sampson of Brooklyn had risen to lead the senate Democratic conference after the leadership crisis of June and July 2009 forced Malcolm Smith to cede that position.[55] Sampson was found guilty in 2015 of trying to thwart a federal investigation into an embezzlement that Sampson carried out when he was serving as court-appointed referee for foreclosed properties in Brooklyn beginning in the late 1900s. Rather than returning surplus money from the real estate sales to the state Supreme Court, as he was supposed to do, Sampson, a lawyer, kept about $440,000, according to prosecutors. He set the funds aside for his own use, including his unsuccessful bid in 2005 for Brooklyn district attorney. Upon his arrest, Sampson was "excluded" from the senate Democratic conference. Very soon after the guilty verdict against then–Republican Deputy Majority Leader Libous, a jury in July 2015 found Sampson guilty of three charges, the most serious of which was obstruction of justice, but not guilty of the six remaining counts; Sampson automatically lost his senate seat.[56]

This is but a partial listing of the dozens of scandals that have plagued the legislature since 2000. For example, throughout this streak of unrelieved legislative corruption, few changes to ethical rules and safeguards were made. Outside critics and progressive legislators called for the closing of notorious LLC loophole the state Board of Elections created in 1996.[57] The loophole was, and at this writing remains, a major weakness. Under the law, LLCs—business entities with characteristics of both corporations and partnerships—are treated more liberally than either one with respect to campaign contributions in New York State. While corporations have strict $5,000 limits on aggregate campaign donations, and partnership contributions are attributed to each partner, each LLC is allowed to donate the maximum contribution allowed for an individual person and may do so without disclosing the LLC's owners. Wealthy interests, in control of multiple LLCs, can effectively direct the donation of many times the individual contribution limit to one or more candidates for state or local offices and to party committees during each election cycle. They may also give many times the $150,000 individual annual cumulative limit of contributions to all candidates,[58] effectively purchasing access to lawmakers and state executives. In the 2015 corruption cases that federal prosecutors brought against both former Assembly Speaker Sheldon Silver and former Senate Majority Leader Dean Skelos, LLCs were important aspects.

The loophole's existence is a real oddity that clearly should have been eliminated. It is based on a federal rule that has long since been changed. Democratic Board of Elections commissioners attempted to convince the board as a whole to revisit the ruling in April 2015, but Republican commissioners' opposition left the board gridlocked. In July, though, the chief law enforcement counsel to the board challenged the

LLC loophole in a civil lawsuit against an unsuccessful candidate in a Brooklyn special election for an assembly seat.[59] Professional legislative watchdogs were happily surprised to hear about the case. The candidate's campaign settled the action by agreeing to pay a $10,000 forfeiture for having accepted contributions from LLCs, funds that it knew or should have known had originated from a source other than the LLCs, in an attempt to evade individual campaign contribution limits.[60] Whether the case will prove important in the future is uncertain because it was a settlement, rather than an agency or court ruling. Still, the watchdogs at least perceived a precedent, of sorts, in the Board of Elections' challenge to business-as-usual. "Eureka!" commented the New York Public Interest Research Group's (NYPIRG) Blair Horner on hearing of the lawsuit, "Signs of independent enforcement on Planet Albany!"[61]

Most real estate LLCs are established for tax reasons as well as to insulate property owners from liability in connection with each of their properties, not to make campaign donations.[62] That an LLC need not readily disclose its owners, though, is clearly in opposition to the legislature's original intent, established in the 1970s during the era of the Watergate scandal, to insist on full disclosure of all donors to state election campaigns. Full disclosure allows voters and the media to know who is trying to influence legislation and appropriations as well as the existence of conflicts of interests.

Ultimately the LLC loophole for large contributions helps foster a "pay-to-play" culture so pervasive for many reasons in the legislature. Ordinary citizens and community groups have little chance of influencing the state's course compared to the big-money interests and deep pockets with their channels of access to the three men in a room, among others. One certainly cannot hope to depend on one's assembly member or senator to go up against his or her leader or have the authority to make a difference—or simply know who is influencing policy—in this kind of cash- and lobbyist-flush environment.

Money and its vehicles are so important in Albany because reelection is a legislator's paramount concern, a priority almost as soon as they are elected, driven by two-year terms. Incumbents look for every way to retain and boost their advantage. To do this they maintain the status quo and accept existing leadership-imposed arrangements. Their base pay often comes with committee-chairmanship stipends, or "lulus," ranging from $9,000 to $40,000, plus health insurance coverage and pension benefits.[63] Those committee assignments help them convince the voters back home that they have influence.

Rare is the lawmaker who advocates making the playing field for donors and candidates more fair, more competitive, and more open to scrutiny and inspection. However, in mid-2015 Manhattan Democratic Senator Liz Krueger joined with the Brennan Center for Justice at New York University School of Law and others in seeking a judgment in state Supreme Court in Albany County to eliminate the LLC loophole.[64] If the suit is successful, this will go a long way to loosening the stranglehold that often-furtive campaign contributions exert on our democratic process. Time will tell if the lawsuit or Governor Cuomo's subsequent call in early 2016 for eliminating the loophole that he himself benefited from as a candidate for office[65] will overcome the history of legislative resistance to campaign finance reform of any type.

In my last year in Albany, the stranglehold that the leaders exerted on their members, and its enervating effects, were very evident. I remember all too well. The three men in a room failed to agree on a budget, and, therefore, the legislature failed to pass its budget on time for the twentieth year in a row. It thus set a record for foundering, by not coming to agreement until August 11 and then, too, without the full support of then–Governor George Pataki. Pataki vetoed parts of the budget despite having issued a "message of necessity" to allow the budget bills to be voted on immediately without the required three-day "aging" period during which members of the legislature might have been able to read them. As a result of the tardiness, low-income teenagers did not immediately have the summer jobs they or their parents had counted on; low-wage workers did not get the tax rebates they were promised; and thousands of college students from struggling working-class families did not know how much tuition aid they might get come the fall semester.

There would be no plan that year, despite a federal mandate and warnings of a loss of $150 million in federal reimbursement, for upgrading the state's century-old voting machines—that, too, would have to wait. By January 2006, however, the legislature faced the threat of a lawsuit from the U.S. Department of Justice over these particular delays, more than five years after the 2000 Bush–Gore presidential election debacle in Florida prompted Congress to pass the Help America Vote Act (HAVA), which required every state to upgrade voting machines and systems. New York's modernization plan arrived too late for new equipment to be put in place for the November 2006 elections, including the gubernatorial contest. The Justice Department said New York State, which critics contended was influenced too much by voting-technology vendors, had the worst record in the country with regard to complying with the mandate. In March 2006 the Justice Department sued, making an example of the Empire State and forcing the state to move ahead with new voting machines.[66] Even after the lawsuit, the state Board of Elections struggled to comply with HAVA in advance of the 2008 presidential primary.[67]

New York also received scathing criticism in early 2006 from a federal district court judge over its clubhouse-controlled system for selecting jurists to run, usually uncontested, for their seats on the bench. The judge called the state's selection system one of the least fair in the country, ruling that a party's judicial candidates must be chosen instead by a nonpartisan blue-ribbon panel before being placed on the ballot.[68] Unfortunately, the U.S. Supreme Court unanimously reversed the lower court's ruling,[69] and the judicial selection process in New York State remains largely unchanged as of 2016.

Stalling is a time-honored negotiating tactic, but in New York State lack of effectiveness has damaged public confidence in the political process. For five years in a row the state's persistently low minimum wage of $5.15 an hour had not changed and, in 2004 (my last year) it appeared that things would be no different, thanks to a divided legislature and a politically timed gubernatorial veto of a bill to raise it. The assembly could not and the senate would not vote to override Republican Pataki's gubernatorial veto, with the Republican Party presidential convention coming to New York State that summer and the three-term governor hinting at presidential ambitions. After the senate overrode Governor Pataki's veto in a special session after the 2004 general election, the minimum wage was finally raised, though incrementally and without regard to issues of enforcement.[70]

More than a decade later, Governor Andrew Cuomo established a task force to look at fast-food workers' wages in New York amid widespread worker demonstrations against low industry pay, and later accepted the panel's recommendation to increase the fast-food minimum wage in New York from $8.75 to $15.00 an hour over the next few years. The measure required the approval of the state Labor Department, controlled by Cuomo, not the legislature, or it might never have come about.[71] Indeed, when Cuomo proposed an increase in the state's minimum wage to $11.50 in New York City and $10.50 elsewhere at the start of 2015, senate Republicans were indifferent to his proposal.[72] The five members of the breakaway IDC allied with the Republican senate majority did not have the power to convince or overrule their Republican leadership allies to generate a floor vote on a minimum wage increase, where some say it might well have passed.[73]

Based on my direct experience, the core of legislative dysfunction, the continuing sense of a halting governmental process heavily swayed by immediate election calculation and by wealthy individuals, labor unions, and corporate contributors and their lobbyists, resides in this fact: although 213 legislators serve in Albany, just three men hold virtually all the cards—the governor, the speaker, and the majority leader. In a few recent instances, the minority-party leaders of each chamber have appeared with the Big Three in state budget negotiations, but the process was neither participatory nor transparent in reality. Overall, it was, and is, the Big Three who dominate and determine the broad outlines and fine details of the budget, the third-largest in the nation, behind the federal government's and California's. The speaker and majority leader hire most of the key legislative staff members, including those who draft most bills. The leaders also dole out committee chair positions, set staff and office budgets, assign offices, dispense office supplies and furniture, and run all the services legislators rely on, from publications to payroll. Should a member of one of the two houses author a piece of legislation, it is the top leader, and he alone, who decides the committee or committees to which it is assigned, whether it is passed out of committee, and when or even if it should get a (predetermined) vote on the floor. Committee hearings on major issues, including executive oversight, or to discuss and possibly to amend proposed legislation—or bill markups—are not as common, to say the least, as they are in Congress and other state legislatures.

The leader of each Albany chamber can stop a bill from advancing at virtually any point in its journey toward becoming law. This power is accepted, and acceded to, by most legislators, who realize they can probably remain in office comfortably as long as they do not challenge this top-down arrangement. Senators do not even have to attend the meetings of the committees on which they sit because committee votes can be cast for them under a legally questionable proxy-voting system. While the senate changed the wording of its rules in 2006 to eliminate reference to a "proxy," the process is largely the same: committee members may vote by sending the committee chair a signed sheet with their intended votes on each bill on the agenda.[74] They need not be present.

Much to my chagrin, dozens of bills were in my time, and since, given to members to read with only hours or minutes left before the floor vote and with no time to consider them. Would it cause "chaos," as some contend, if assembly members and senators were given a reliable voice within the leadership and legislative-whip system during the process of debating and passing of bills and budgets on behalf of their state and their constituents? It would not. Yet, it is not allowed as befits the authoritarian control of the leadership.

When the situation on rare occasions brings on a revolt, those rebellions are quickly suppressed. Michael Bragman, an assemblyman from Onondaga County, tried in 2000 to oust Sheldon Silver from his speakership, arguing that drastic changes in the operation of the assembly were urgently needed. Some newspapers even called it a "coup attempt."[75] Perhaps he was motivated and inspired by Joe Bruno's 1994 ascension during a similar bruising struggle in the senate when Bruno defeated then–Majority Leader Ralph Marino, who refused to support George Pataki in his race for the Republican gubernatorial nomination.

The usually imperturbable Silver pounced. He stripped Bragman of his high-level position as majority leader in the assembly and demoted not only his coconspirators but also members who spoke publicly about the need for reform and openness while still professing support for Silver's leadership. Other assembly members were threatened with challengers in their next election if they did not support Silver's reappointment. Silver, though, did make minor changes after Bragman's failed bid to oust him. Nonetheless, he retained the post of speaker, with the vast majority of Democrats voting for him to avoid being ostracized. Bragman, for his part in this, went from being one of the most senior people in Albany's hierarchy to becoming an outcast.[76] He resigned from the assembly in December 2001,[77] having stuck his neck out in a legislature in which the leaders have no one within their houses to countervail their powers.

Since I left office at the end of 2004, there have been far less dramatic but still substantial efforts by sitting lawmakers to revive democratic processes in Albany. A key one was a pair of lawsuits brought by a Republican Assemblyman Thomas Kirwan from Newburgh and Manhattan Democratic Senator Liz Krueger. The first lawsuit challenged the ingenious ways the legislative leaders disempowered the minority parties in both houses (Democrats in the senate, Republicans in the assembly). They argued the leaders unfairly and unconstitutionally abrogated the constitutional right of one person, one vote as it applies to the minority-party legislators' constituents (some 14.5 million people of voting age).[78] In late 2005 a state Supreme Court judge ruled that the lawsuit, a push for a more transparent and fairly run legislature, could proceed on some of its main arguments,[79] but it did not result in the desired changes. On appeal the case was dismissed on the principle of separation of powers: the courts would not interfere with the rules and operations of the legislative branch of government. It is no coincidence, probably, that one of the sponsors of the suits, Krueger, had her newsletter to constituents censored by the leadership (an act of suppression that would become the subject of Kruger and Kirwan's second lawsuit targeting the actions of legislative leaders, filed in 2006),[80] just as some of my Democratic colleagues and I had at other times—a reminder, no doubt, of who was in charge.

This defeat did not deter Liz Krueger, and in recent years she was part of an attempt to forge a more progressive agenda by changing the senate through elections—which for her and a few like-minded Democrats in the senate meant trying to win enough seats to take away the majority rule of the Republicans in that body. These electoral efforts by Democrats, a seat at a time, fell short until the November 2008 elections, when the Democrats secured a majority in the then–sixty-two-seat senate, seemingly vindicating the electoral path to reform.[81]

Following the results of the election, the path proved to be illusory. Four Democrats who were part of the slender Democratic majority announced that they would not attend a meeting of the senate Democratic conference. These four turncoats, if you will, were Senator-elect Pedro Espada Jr. of the Bronx (who had defeated indicted incumbent Efrain González Jr. in the September primary to return to the senate after a six-year absence), Senator Carl Kruger of Brooklyn, Senator Ruben Diaz Sr. of the Bronx (who had defeated Espada six years earlier), and Senator-elect Hiram Monserrate of Queens. The group, dubbed the "Four Amigos" and the "Gang of Four," flatly refused to support Democratic leader Malcolm Smith of Queens for senate majority leader as they held out for greater power for themselves from the Democratic conference.[82] Quickly, under heavy pressure from his colleagues and constituents, Monserrate rejoined the Democratic conference, leaving Espada, Diaz, and Carl Kruger (now the "Three Amigos" or "Gang of Three") to negotiate between the Democrats and Republicans.[83] After concessions to them, the Three Amigos also rejoined the Democratic conference with the help of behind-the-scenes brokering by former Independence Party gubernatorial candidate Tom Golisano, who was pushing for reform of senate rules and procedures.[84] Malcolm Smith was chosen to be the senate majority leader and temporary president, positions generally held by the same individual.

Democratic control of the senate lasted but a few short months. In June 2009 two of the Democrats involved in all the negotiations over the future of the senate, Hiram Monserrate and Pedro Espada Jr., joined with the Republicans in a 32 to 30 vote to replace Democrat Malcolm Smith as majority leader with Republican Dean Skelos.[85] Democratic whip Jeffrey Klein tried to halt the vote by unilaterally moving to adjourn, while Malcolm Smith ordered the lights and internet shut off in the chamber in a further attempt to stop the voting.[86] Successful despite last-minute resistance, this "parliamentary coup" was purportedly instigated, at least in part, by Tom Golisano, who was disillusioned by lack of promised reform in the senate during this period.[87] The remaining Democrats in the senate said that the vote was out of order and refused to recognize Skelos as the majority leader. Still, Skelos himself declared victory. "Today will be remembered in state history as a day when real change and real reform began and dysfunction ended," he said.[88]

The dysfunctionality had only deepened, however, and all the hopes of structural reform through Democratic election victors fell short. In a near-chaotic environment, Republicans rewarded the nominally Democratic Espada with the position of temporary president of the senate and, therefore, was also the acting lieutenant governor. (The lieutenant governor position had been vacant since the former lieutenant governor, David Paterson, had ascended to the governorship after the 2007 resignation of former governor Spitzer).[89] Even more dysfunction ensued, with both conferences claiming control of the senate and attempting to hold sessions.[90] Both sides went to court.[91] Monserrate, in voting with the Democratic conference, left a 31 to 31 senate effectively deadlocked with no bona-fide lieutenant governor to break the tie.[92]

Eventually the extraordinary stalemate was broken after Governor Paterson appointed the highly respected Richard Ravitch as lieutenant governor, and Pedro Espada returned to the Democratic fold, where he emerged as senate majority leader in a power-sharing arrangement. Under that arrangement, Malcolm Smith retained the title of temporary president of the senate (which normally is held by the majority leader), and John Sampson, a Brooklyn Democrat, became the leader of the Democratic conference.[93] Ravitch later said that the most useless task in his life was being lieutenant governor of New York, a description that has also been applied to the U.S. vice presidency, though his appointment did at least help end the stalemate. He added, "The quality of people in elected office has deteriorated from when I worked for Governor Carey. It is not as it once was and it is not as it should be."[94]

Democrats' numerical majority in the senate lasted just until the end of the term, when Republicans retook the majority in the 2010 general election, and, critically, gave the Republican leaders control of the 2012 redistricting process based on the 2010 federal census.[95] The majority parties in each house use redistricting to bolster their hold on power each decade by maximizing the number of districts in which they have a majority or are at least able to remain competitive in elections. The two legislative leaders have an arrangement whereby each house controls its own redistricting. While the assembly has a fixed number of seats (150), the senate does not, its size being determined by convoluted and controversial methods based on population changes, and this has enabled Republicans to increase the total number of senate seats to their advantage when necessary.

After the 2012 general election, however, Democrats once again appeared to achieve a slender majority in the senate. Undaunted, the Republicans simply formed a new "power sharing" arrangement to control the senate, using a small group of frustrated, breakaway Democrats (the IDC), as well as adding Senator Simcha Felder of Brooklyn, who was elected in 2012 as a Democrat and subsequently joined the Republican conference.[96] The IDC, led by Senator Jeffrey Klein of the Bronx, originally organized in January 2011 after Klein could not become the senate minority leader or convince the Democratic conference in the senate to support some of his goals. It included, along with Klein, senators David Carlucci of Rockland County, David Valesky of Oneida County, and Diane Savino, who succeeded me in my Brooklyn and Staten Island seat.[97] Joined after the election by former Democratic Majority Leader Malcolm Smith of Brooklyn,[98] the IDC members received desirable senate posts for their cooperation with Republicans, as well as approval of some of their legislation. Klein served as comajority leader and cotemporary president of the senate for the two years in which the IDC was used to secure Republican Party control.[99]

Though this dance occurred just three and a half years after the 2009 parliamentary carnival featuring Pedro Espada Jr. and Hiram Monserrate, it drew far less public attention, despite the fact that the voters of New York State voted for a Democratic majority for the senate, yet found themselves with a Republican-controlled senate. The lack of public outcry in 2012–2013 might have resulted from the relatively quiet ways in which this power bloc had materialized, shorn of the carnival atmosphere of 2009. When, as a result the 2014 elections, the Republicans regained an outright majority of the senate, the unorthodox liaison became less relevant to Skelos, and Klein's title was diminished to "majority coalition leader."[100] So much for loyalty.

In mid-2015 Senator Liz Krueger conceded the "failure" of the reform efforts that she and some of her colleagues embarked on from within the legislature. Resistance by assembly and senate leaders frustrated reformers' successful efforts to win elections, she told host Ronnie Eldridge on the CUNY cable television show "Eldridge and Co." The leaders prefer to hoard all the power within their chamber, while keeping their decision-making criteria largely hidden, maneuvering to negotiate effectively with the more-powerful executive branch as well as with each other, and to keep their members in line, she explained.[101]

If the Democrats are ever able to gain and hold control of both chambers simultaneously through the popular vote, the Democrats ascending to leadership in both chambers would probably not move to dilute and disperse their own powers. Achieving this prerequisite to restoring democracy, vibrancy, and effectiveness and changing the poorly behaved, self-serving parliament on a durable basis, is simply unlikely—even impossible—regardless which party gains control. This has become extremely clear to me after years of legislative debacle and corruption scandals. The New York legislature is incapable of reforming itself, regardless which party is in charge of its two houses. Under the state constitution, it is empowered to sustain the status quo and invariably will do so. Only a constitutional convention, which would throw open the state's charter for amendment, can change the governing structure sufficiently to become more accountable, transparent, and truly representative. As the pressure on both parties must come from outside the legislature, I increasingly believe that a constitutional convention, while not without risks, is the most effective means to press for the desired reforms.

During my years in Albany, I experienced firsthand the legislature's dazzling dysfunction. I observed a statehouse where preordained decisions played out, session after session, with legislators acting as veritable puppets in a cynical show. Now, with the arrest and conviction of so many legislative leaders, New York's legislature has become known as perhaps the worst-performing in the nation. Neither half-hearted reform bills nor the hope of future election success can satisfy the conspicuous and pressing requirement for far-reaching changes designed to make the moribund body transparent, accessible to the public, and effective.

4

Like a Meeting of the Supreme Soviet

Senator Liz Krueger, chosen to represent the East Side of Manhattan's "silk stocking" district in a hard-fought special election in 2002, says she may never forget her first committee meeting, which served as an introduction to the peculiar habits of the Capitol. No one other than she and the panel's chair was present, she recalled. Most of the seats were still empty at future meetings that she, like her colleagues, had been elected to attend faithfully. She remembered wondering, "Where the heck was everyone else?"[1]

It was no different for me or for any of the other minority party members of either house of the legislature—the Democrats in the Republican-controlled senate, like Krueger, or the Republicans in the Democratic-controlled assembly. The curious thing about it was that their relatively powerless condition was not much different for majority members of both of Albany's houses as well. They were equally subservient to the leaders of their legislative branches.

Outside the irregular lines of the New York State legislator's election district, beyond the trappings of his or her elected office, or the formal gestures of respect he or she generally is accorded, the Albany legislator quickly learns his or her place in the required subservience that poses as democracy.

To be sure, as legislators we could attend as many committee meetings as we wanted to. For many of us, however, doing so was pointless. We were expected simply to give our party's ranking committee member our proxy to vote any way that the house leader advised, which ensured that the committee meetings had on paper enough attendance, or a legal quorum, for the committee's decisions about bills to count. As individuals, we knew we could not influence legislation or force our own bills to a vote, which members of Congress and other state legislatures permit.

Citizens were not likely to know of their representatives' submissiveness or many lawmakers' frequent absence from legislative committee meetings, because, unlike the Brooklyn elementary school of my youth, our attendance was not recorded. Our proxies, which Robert J. Freeman of the New York State Committee on Open Government, an oversight office, once publicly described as constitutionally dubious at best, misleadingly indicated our presence to anyone who bothered to check our voting records.[2]

We could show up for the sessions of the full house if we chose. Amazingly enough that was not required either because of a separate and equally objectionable procedure known as empty-seat voting, in which a senator's absence indicated an affirmative vote on whichever bill the leader favored as long as he or she briefly signed in before or during the day with the senate clerk. At the state level, just five other statehouses in the country use a system of empty-seat voting.[3] Public outrage and rule changes in 2005 limited (but did not end) empty-seat voting,[4] much to the distress of those legislators who unabashedly felt that they should not be required to attend debates in which their votes might be required. Nothing more has happened to reform this situation a decade later.

Another charade at which many legislators have long excelled is getting their names on as many unobjectionable, popular bills as possible—those that merely renamed a street in their legislative district, for example, or honored a recently deceased constituent. They regularly had their names appended to readily popular bills they knew would never pass the other house. The senate leadership placed my name on four or five such bills during my tenure, at least until the final two years, when I became known and was more outspoken as a dissenter with a reformer bent.

When elections rolled around, otherwise impotent legislators pointed to the many bills they had thus sponsored and, for members of the majority party in each house, had been passed in their house. But these "one-house" bills were crafted not to pass the other house and become law but to impress voters or wealthy individuals and interest groups that could be counted on to contribute large sums of money to their campaigns. "Sorry, voters," was the basic message; "though we tried to cut your income taxes, increase school aid, punish criminals, assist small businesses, or increase the pensions of union members, our vile opponents in the other party just would not go for it." The illusion of an active, relevant state legislature was thus sustained—and quite a mirage, at that. In connection with the 2001–2002 session, of 16,892 bills introduced, 4.1 percent were passed—the third lowest percentage of any statehouse in the nation.[5] In connection with 2015–2016 session, the numbers were similar: more than 15,000 bills introduced though January 2016 with only 589—less than 4 percent—passed by both houses.[6]

Still, the legislators who played along—it was all but impossible not to—could hope to garner prestige and lifetime job security in the marble corridors of the state Capitol. As a reward, they could receive a prestigious committee assignment with a large stipend or see their names appended to leadership bills destined to become actual law through negotiations among the senate majority leader, the assembly speaker, the governor, and their senior staffs.

Rarely did any of the committees on which I served at different times—including finance; transportation; education and higher education; aging; consumer protection; corporations, authorities, and commissions; and crime victims, crimes, and correction—hold public hearings on proposed legislation. What would be the point of hearing from constituents and experts on any given issue, one might reasonably ask, if the committee members themselves did not have the authority to discharge bills to a floor vote, like their contemporaries in the U.S. Congress or other state legislatures, where committees have autonomy and power?

Besides, any committee chair in Albany who followed his or her convictions was not likely to remain chair for very long, thereby forfeiting the attendant perquisites and influence. He or she might even face unexpected obstacles to being reelected to another Albany term. The chair's or ranking minority member's job was to follow the will of his or her party conference leader, who often issued directions after conferring with lobbyists, favored members, and senior staff. During the testimony given as a witness for prosecutors in their successful 2015 corruption trial of Dean and Adam Skelos, Queens Senator Tony Avella noted that after his 2011 election, when he joined the IDC—the small group of Democrats who caucused with the Republicans in a power-sharing agreement—he was named chair of the Ethics Committee. He soon learned, however, that despite this impressive-sounding role, all the talk of the need to pass ethics reform in Albany was vapor. "No bills had ever been referred to that committee, and no bills ever came out of [that] committee," he said on the stand.[7]

When Avella decided to hold a hearing on ethics reform issues, he was told that it needed to be rescheduled to make room for budget negotiations. He was never given another date, thereby effectively ending the possibility of a committee hearing.[8] U.S. Attorney Preet Bharara remarked after the Skelos trial ended that Avella's inability to consider ethics reform measures as the committee chairman "tells you everything you need to know about the enabling nature of all the people in the state Legislature who may not have been convicted of crimes but seem not to care that they're going on."[9] As of this writing, the senate's Ethics Committee has not considered a single bill on ethics reform since June 2009, when Senator John Sampson, convicted in 2015 of criminal charges, was its chairman (a position he held for two years). The assembly's Ethics and Guidance Committee was not much more useful than its counterpart in the senate was. The assembly committee does not deal with legislation either, but handles policy violations, such as complaints about sexual harassment and discrimination, "a service apparently in enough demand to require the panel to meet at least once every other month."[10]

As state legislators, we were known and even appreciated by many our constituents, but in Albany, we were required to go along in order to get along, get ahead, and of course—to mention the singular preoccupation of career Albany politicians—ease our way to reelection. It was really that simple, and I came to realize that as an elected participant in Albany's processes, it had corrosive effects on my sense of duty, character, and obligations, and on that of the entire government system and state. Based on his testimony, Senator Avella apparently felt much the same way.

To me, the undemocratic way in which the state has operated was shown by the penchant of the leaders of both houses to give bleary-eyed legislators an hour or two, in the wee hours of the morning or night, to digest phonebook-thick bills and budget amendments before having to vote on the items in a preordained way. The state constitution mandates three days for the legislature to consider legislation. The avoidance of that requirement often relied on the excessive use of the governor's so-called message of necessity—permitting immediate votes on bills in ostensibly urgent situations. Its abuse further underscored our powerlessness and hobbled the processes of collaboration, review, and public involvement and debate most Americans expect from their elected representatives at all levels.

We—and our constituents—made no meaningful difference to the final deal the Big Three and their staffs worked out. The governor happily contributed to this state of affairs. Our comments were barely tolerated. If any of us dissented too loudly or too often from the leadership position, we soon found it redounding to our political and financial detriment (as in committee assignments and stipends, and even district and election aid). In a sense we were treated throughout our tenure as freshmen lawmakers, or, as former Governor Al Smith wrote in his autobiography of his arrival in Albany in 1904 to serve his first term in the assembly, he and other freshmen legislators were permitted to observe but never to speak with the leaders. They had no greater status when the legislature was in session than the citizen-spectators in the gallery.[11]

After I was elected the first time in early 1996, and once I had gotten over my awe at how physically grand and impressive the Capitol was, I encountered a huge amount of rust that exists in the gears of the democratic process as it is practiced Albany. I came face-to-face with business as usual.

New York had once been a model for state legislators and legislation nationwide, but the legislature I found when I got to Albany really did not have much democracy left. Obscured by its elaborate chambers, flowery rhetoric, and arcane procedures, it ran a bit like a corrupt regime. Leadership collaboration with most legislators was rare. Powerful lobbyists and political consultants had disproportionate access to and influence on one or more of the Big Three. Ultimately, the voters were kept out of the loop. At the end of session, more lobbyists were present than senators.

Making matters worse during my time in the senate, Governor Pataki, Assembly Speaker Silver, and Senate Majority Leader Bruno barely got along with one another, though their parties in many ways operated symbiotically to ensure that none of them lost control of their respective houses on any given Election Day. Governors, too, preferred it that way: the better to have an opposite party, and one of the houses, to blame for their own inaction, ethical lapses, patronage, and boondoggles, or simply when their policies went awry.

Consider again the longtime Albany routine: the dispensing of so-called member items by lawmakers. These were the funds legislators were allowed to give to community organizations with an implicit understanding that in return the grateful recipients would work for their reelection.

While a minority Democrat in the Republican-led senate might have expected between $100,000 and $200,000 a year in member items to distribute for sometimes useful services such as free lunches for seniors, summer park concerts, children's sports, and veterans' assistance, the senate Republicans received ten times more. This was particularly true if they were entering a reelection campaign where some interparty competition was believed to exist. These programmatic legislative grants were just one of the ways that leaders, whether Silver or Bruno, helped smooth the way for incumbents seeking reelection.

At times, these grants did serve valid civic purposes. Nonprofit organizations relied on them to buy fire engines and ambulances for volunteer companies, replace broken playground equipment, and fund support groups serving the poor and elderly. I accepted them believing that they assisted the community and that rejecting them would harm local organizations. But the process was far too politicized. Many of the appropriations should have been funded through annual line items in the state budget, including an application process for community groups to the relevant state agency. In reality, member items were seldom evaluated in terms of the need these small pots of money would fill and the potential success of the grant. Some member items were quite unnecessary and even ludicrous, as good government groups and newspapers pointed out. More than once, the loosely vetted earmarks became conduits of corruption, going to community-based groups controlled by or closely linked to legislators, such as in the cases against Assemblyman Brian McLaughlin and Senators Pedro Espada Jr., Larry Seabrook, Vincent Leibell, Hiram Monserrate, and Shirley Huntley.[12]

The overriding political purpose of the member items guaranteed that the community organizations that depended on the grants and the legislators who got credit for delivering them remained beholden, ultimately, to the Albany legislative leaders. This process was an example of the old ward heeler system of Boss Tweed's Tammany Hall, the one memorable reformers such as former Mayor Fiorello La Guardia helped to vanquish. Pitch in to reelect your benefactor, and you just may be well rewarded in return. Go your own way, and you will get nothing. The late Governor Mario Cuomo was right when he told me that many member items were "awful" and constituted "a slush fund of hundreds of millions of dollars without any state evaluation."[13]

In a sign that member items were viewed as political capital, funds were sometimes cut off to worthy community recipients when their district's assembly member or senator informed his leadership that he or she intended to retire. Such notifications were typically made six or seven months before an election, and the member-item money was then transferred to election races in which the incumbent faced a potentially serious challenge in order to help the incumbent. The politicization of member-item money unconscionably left community groups in the retiring legislator's district without anticipated aid, and as a result, often forced to cut staff and services to the public. Leaders often kept a lawmaker's plans to leave office secret to better thwart any potential rivals to their handpicked replacement candidates and to ensure the successor would be beholden to them should he or she prevail on Election Day. But what happened to the member items?

In the years before I decided to leave Albany, I annually received about $140,000 to distribute to community groups. After I won reelection in 2002 in a reconfigured and more competitive district, I was given a one-time additional 2003 distribution to community groups. David Paterson, as the new minority leader of the senate, was responsible for setting legislators' member-item allocations. I had supported Paterson for minority leader the year before.

Paterson wanted me to give half of the allotment to a Brooklyn organization, and the rest to another one in Staten Island. I had different ideas, preferring to distribute funds to organizations that had requested a grant in the past but had not yet received one and other groups that received less than they requested. Paterson and I settled on four groups I had helped in the past, two in each borough—the Astella Development Corporation and Neighbors Helping Neighbors in Brooklyn, and Project Hospitality and the Alzheimer's Foundation in Staten Island.

When I told Paterson of my plans to retire, nearly a year before actually leaving, things changed dramatically. He redeployed my member-item funds to help an upstate legislator looking ahead to a strong Republican contender for his seat in 2004, and the groups in my district suddenly found themselves without a grant. I also felt bad that the groups I had originally hoped to fund—including a Catholic youth organization, a Jewish mental health group, a Latino community and cultural organization, an African American education project, and a community soup kitchen—

were also left without funds. Vital programs were hurt. Their clients suffered. When the more powerful local groups complained, $5,000, $10,000, or $15,000 was offered to placate them. Other complainers were ignored. One community leader was advised, he later told me, to "look to the future and forget the past." He got the message and renewed his organization's pitch to my successor, Senator Diane Savino, after the 2004 election.

Senator Paterson's decision to redirect the member items to competitive district races was indeed a symptom of the tendency of legislative leaders of both parties to use public funds for politics. Paterson's predecessor as minority leader, Senator Martin Connor, chose to carry over some member-item funds in anticipation of the 2004 election. Paterson, however, decided to distribute the funds as part of the 2003–2004 state budget to help certain Democrats facing competitive races ingratiate themselves with voters and organizations in their districts.

Member items are not inherently bad. I accepted them and gave them out, as did virtually all legislators. It makes sense to have small pots of money available for programs that otherwise would not qualify for funding directly by a state agency, either because the programs are new and innovative or because they are too small to be worth the paperwork.

The question remains, however: Who should decide which groups get member-item grants and how should the allocations receive oversight as to their impact and effectiveness? Currently, the larger, better-connected organizations have an advantage in jockeying for aid. Another problem is these grants have at times gone to community groups controlled by legislators. Lawmakers have the power to decide who gets the funding they receive from their party leaders, which allows them control over their communities and nonprofit groups in return for electoral support.

The member-item phenomenon began in the early 1980s, according to a 1984 article in the *New York Times,* which mentioned that member items had increased by 33 percent in just one year, costing $40 million within a then–$36 billion state budget.[14] In mid-2006, the paper editorialized that "slush funds" had reached $1 billion, including member items, in a state budget of $112 billion and demanded that the total be reduced.[15]

Even so, member items continued to be allotted based on leadership decisions made behind closed doors without public debate or evaluation. Even now, getting an accounting of member-item expenditures by the legislators and the governor's office is difficult and sometimes impossible. Former Manhattan Democratic Senator Franz Leichter, who spent many years hunting down and questioning the state budget's more obscure caches of funds,[16] told me that the grants are intentionally scattered throughout each year's state budget, with recipient legislators' names left unrecorded, further obscuring who gets what and why.

Democratic Assemblywoman Sandy Galef of Ossining, a reformer, was one of the few elected officials who, in her many years in the legislature, refused to accept any member items because they were such a murky part of the budget, were distributed to community entities in a nonequitable manner, and represented tax dollars spent without proper evaluation or public consent. An April 4, 2006, *New York Post* editorial rightly called this an example of "Albany's Pork." The *Post* went on: "Two hundred million bucks—that's the lump sum buried in New York State's fiscal 2007 budget for 'services and expenses, grants in aid, or for contracts.' In fact, it's for what Albany euphemistically refers to as 'member items.' "[17]

As a candidate for attorney general that year, Andrew Cuomo called the member-item system the "silent conspiracy of Albany."[18] Once in office as attorney general he promised to scrutinize member items, eventually reaching agreement with the legislative leaders to require that all earmarks be certified that they have a public purpose and that no conflict of interest exists between the member designating them and the organization receiving them.[19] After his 2010 election as governor, Cuomo was partially successful in eliminating some of the lump-sum allocations. "Member items" no longer exist as such, although there are still tens of millions of dollars of unitemized "reallocations" of unspent past budgetary earmarks, along with many times as much distributed at the discretion of the assembly speaker and the senate majority leader.[20] Cuomo has vetoed hundreds of "new" member items.[21] Nonetheless, the legislative majorities' leaders have continued to direct millions of dollars in public spending to favorite projects.[22] Furthermore, the governor and legislative leaders continue to have access to millions of dollars in discretionary funds.[23] Sheldon Silver's indictment and trial revealed the existence of Healthcare Reform Act (HCRA) Assembly Pool fund, which paid out almost $39 million between 1999 and 2006.[24] As the case revealed, Silver directed two HCRA Assembly Pool grants to Dr. Robert Taub's mesothelioma clinic at Columbia in 2004 and 2007. Does such opaque accounting, typical of Albany, work for the benefit of the rest of the legislators or the public at large? I very much doubt it.

Serious questions about discretionary funds and possible corrupt conflicts will continue to cause problems for Albany as long as special pools of funding are readily available for legislative leaders and governors to dip into freely and allocate in lump sums. The so-called State and Municipal (SAM) Facilities Program is one recent example, which got its first $385 million from one of the last additions to the 2013 state budget, showing up in the final print after Skelos, Silver, and Cuomo wrapped up their three-men-in-a-room discussions.[25] Although analysts from the state comptroller's office would note in 2014, "It is unclear how these funds will be allocated," or which agency was overseeing them, lawmakers tripled SAM's size in the ensuing years, reaching $1.16 billion by 2016. At least one use for the money generated controversy—a $25 million grant through the state's Dormitory Authority for private developers' proposed outlet mall near the St. George Ferry Terminal on Staten Island.[26] A $16.5 million subsidy from the Empire State Development Corporation (ESDC) for the project in January 2016 was also approved, with this financing coming from a $400-million "Transformative Investment Fund" created by former Senate Majority Leader Dean Skelos in the 2015 budget negotiations. Here again, the criteria for spending decisions and involvement with local and regional officials struck many good-government groups as lax, an invitation to corruption. "Given the situation in Albany," remarked NYPIRG Executive Director Blair Horner, "these are precisely the kinds of arrangements that raise eyebrows because they are connected to, maybe indirectly, some of the most gigantic scandals that have engulfed the state Capitol."[27]

One day in 2002, my office received a surprising message from the office of then–Senate Majority Leader Bruno that he wanted to meet with me. This was a very rare invitation for a Democratic member of the Republican senate to receive, unless he is the Minority Leader. I could not understand why he had requested this meeting.

Bruno was a robust, loquacious man with thick white hair. He raised and rode horses on his ranch in Rensselaer County. His party catered to business interests, mine to union and labor interests (although, in a striking development, the powerful health-care workers union was a happy beneficiary of the Republican Party as a result of its 2002 support of Pataki's reelection to a third term). Still, many who disagreed with Bruno on political issues respected him for his legislative legerdemain, longevity, and ideological consistency as a conservative member of his party.

This was the spring of a redistricting year, and our conversation quickly turned from pleasantries to his party's efforts to gain a senate seat in New York City during that year's November elections.

He explained that his staff was in the process of redrawing the boundaries of several city districts to put pressure on Democrats, under the legal gerrymandering that occurs every ten years in response to shifts in population tracked by the U.S. Census Bureau. The process is supposed to ensure that minorities' voting rights are not diminished by demographic changes. For Bruno, I felt, the goal was to strengthen the precarious Republican majority in the senate at any cost by redrawing districts to better suit that end.

Like so much else that passes for democratic governance, the reapportionment process is misused. In Brooklyn, Bruno sought to create a new Republican seat primarily because he understood that his party would probably not regain former Republican Senator Roy Goodman's seat in Manhattan, the one that Democrat Liz Krueger had filled in a February 2002 special election after Goodman's resignation to head the United Nations Development Corporation.[28]

Bruno quickly came to the substance that he wanted to discuss. "You're a reputable guy," he ventured, as he put on the table a copy of the tentative Brooklyn redistricting map, which the Republican conference was considering for enactment. It contained, from what I could see, a much more competitive and uncertain district than the one I represented at the time. But Bruno said that he could make my district safer for me by eliminating the parts that would be most difficult for me in an election. He then said that he knew that I was accustomed to receiving approximately $140,000 annually in member items from the senate Democratic minority leader for programs to aid community groups and constituents in my district. He asserted that an additional $2 million to $3 million in member items would come my way if I agreed to support him as majority leader (as a few other Democrats had done). The proposal left me uncharacteristically speechless.

Soon the secretary knocked on the door and told him that Governor Pataki was on the phone. I got up to leave in order to give the majority leader privacy. Bruno waved me back to my chair, to which I returned warily, wondering why he would want to have me present when the governor wanted to speak with him. After a couple of minutes of listening to their polite talk, I was shocked when Bruno told me that Governor Pataki now wanted to speak to me. Initially, I did not understand, but I soon realized the call was never meant for Bruno; it was meant for me. The governor told me that he would very much like to have me in the Republican Party, one way or the other. He said that I was the type of centrist Democrat with whom he could work, and considering this request would be beneficial for me. He then offered a few minutes of inconsequential chitchat and hung up.

I sat there, staring at the majority leader, feeling disconcerted. When I had recovered, I stood up to leave. "I have always been a Democrat and will continue to be a Democrat," I told Bruno. "Furthermore, if I were ever to reconsider my position regarding this, it would be based upon my conscience rather than money." Then I left.

When I did so, I found Senator Carl Kruger outside the door, waiting. He obviously had known about my meeting with Bruno and asked me what I had said to the offer. When I told him that there was no deal and I had rejected the offer, he immediately entered the majority leader's outer office and scheduled an appointment to see him.

Kruger, from Brooklyn, was concerned that he could lose a primary in his own ethnically diverse district as it had been tentatively redrawn, and he wanted Bruno to configure the boundaries in ways he felt he could reliably count on to help him in his upcoming reelection race. Obviously, in order to satisfy Kruger's request, Bruno most likely asked Kruger to do some things for the Republican Party in return.

Just a week later, I was astonished to learn that Kruger was doing something that had never been done before in the senate Democratic conference, in an effort, seemingly, to ingratiate himself with the majority leader. He publicly stated he would not support the Democratic incumbent in a neighboring Brooklyn district, Senator Vincent Gentile, for reelection. Gentile's district was redrawn with new, "made for a Republican" boundaries,[29] drawn to favor Republican Martin Golden, a city councilman running for Gentile's senate seat. Every other Democratic senator in the conference was flabbergasted that Kruger would even consider doing this, not only to a fellow Democrat, but also to one from his own borough.

For an incumbent senator like the popular Gentile to lose an election is, as I have said, unheard-of, especially for someone born and raised in a central portion of the district, the heavily Irish American, Italian American, and socially conservative Bay Ridge section. But the new district stitched together Bay Ridge as well as several distant, Republican-leaning neighborhoods. In light of this, Gentile, of Italian ancestry, was unable to secure the support of even the influential Federation of Italian-American Organizations, whose assistance he had enjoyed in past elections. Golden, an Irish American and, like Gentile, a Bay Ridge resident, could promise this federation about $2 million in government funds for the construction of a youth center, courtesy of Bruno and his influence over the state budget. Neither Gentile, as a Democrat, nor his minority leader in the senate, Martin Connor, could even come close to offering that kind of community-level funding in order to enhance Senator Gentile's prospects.

Many Brooklyn Democrats were also shocked by Kruger's publicly working very hard during the campaign to defeat Gentile in return for new district boundaries that all but ensured his own reelection for the next decade. Golden and Kruger were able to turn around enough votes to enable Golden to prevail on Election Day.[30] (In a subsequent special election, Gentile ran for Golden's former council seat and won by thirty-one votes.[31])

With a favorably drawn district,[32] Kruger was handily reelected. Five years later, in 2007, Bruno assigned him the chairmanship of the Committee on Social Services, Children, and Families, an unprecedented step for a minority party member. Bruno stepped down as majority leader the following year and resigned from the senate amid allegations that he misused his office for private gain and following the loss of several seats to the Democrats.[33] When the Democrats won a narrow majority of senate seats in 2008, Kruger initially withheld his support for Democratic conference leader Malcolm Smith (see the "Three Amigos" episode discussed in chapter 3) before finally agreeing to support Smith for majority leader. To ensure he not once again support the Republicans, leaders of the slender new Democratic Senate majority named him chairman of the Finance Committee, the most powerful chairmanship, with a stipend second only to that of the majority leader.[35] His pretzel-like political dexterity, however, brought him no good result. Caught up in a bribery scandal in 2011, he ended up in federal prison.[36]

What happened in my awkward meeting with Bruno and in that election year in my small portion of the state was interesting for what it said about the routine game playing that characterizes Albany. My white, black, Latino, Italian American, and Jewish Brooklyn base of voters, where I was a fairly popular figure due to years of constituent work with the help of my talented and hard-working staff, was redistricted into several parts by Bruno. Borough Park, one of the largest Jewish communities in the country, became part of four (and possibly five) senate districts instead of the one (the former Senate District 22) I had represented—a fragmentation that some feared would be a blow to its political clout. My district, renamed Senate District 23, now included Coney Island and parts of the Borough Park and Bensonhurst areas of Brooklyn along with an entirely new swath within the north and east shores of Staten Island, across the Verrazano Narrows Bridge. Part of Sunset Park was substituted for Windsor Terrace, and Brighton Beach was taken out of the district entirely.[37]

In redrawing the map and increasing the total number of senate seats from sixty-one to sixty-two statewide, the senate districts in Brooklyn saw their population sizes reduced as they made room for an entirely new, predominantly African American/Caribbean American, seat in central Brooklyn (Senate District 21, where Democrat Kevin Parker was elected).[38] That the remapping fragmented the Jewish community, long a formidable factor in many city and state races, was somewhat ironic: When he first ran for senator, Pataki cultivated unified support among Orthodox Jews in Peekskill, an ingredient in his victory and a steppingstone to power. Nevertheless, Republicans' ties to key leaders and legislators in the Brooklyn community all but ensured that they would suffer little political fallout from the Brooklyn redistricting or from the potential fragmentation of the Jewish community's electoral impact there.

If ever I had entertained the thought of not running for reelection— and in truth, by then I had because I was weary of such shenanigans, though I had told no one but my wife, Susan—the Bruno confrontation made me even more determined to run again and to win. I won in the new district over my Republican opponent, Al Curtis, a former commissioner in the administration of New York City Mayor Rudolph Giuliani, by nearly two-thirds of the vote, winning majorities in both the Brooklyn and the new Staten Island portions of the district.[39]

The 2002 election clearly were feats of Bruno's gerrymandering, as engineered by his chief adviser, Secretary of the Senate Steven Boggess, and other staff members. Bruno's handiwork succeeded in achieving one of his party's main goals: dislodging former Brooklyn–Staten Island Democratic Senator Vincent Gentile in favor of a Republican, Marty Golden. The power of political leaders to all but determine the outcome of legislative elections hit me with new force that election year. It is one thing to discuss the theory and history of a political body's democratic—small *d*—processes. It is quite another thing to be personally ensnared in this sordid reality. I knew then that this was about all the frustration I could take, and I would not run again.

Soon after my reelection, and given that my new district was cut into geographically and ethnically disparate areas, I approached the secretary of the senate, Bruno appointee Steven Boggess. As Bruno's point man, Boggess was himself a powerful and influential man in many areas, from redistricting to office space. I asked him about the possibility of opening a second constituent services office on Staten Island. (The first district office in the state was opened in 1963 by liberal Manhattan legislators and paid for entirely with their own private funds. Within a few years, state funds were used to pay for district constituent offices.)

Boggess told me flatly, not once but twice, that under the rules of the senate, no senator was allowed to receive public funding for more than one constituent office.

I was surprised, but I accepted his statement and paid what amounted to about $30,000 that year out of my campaign committee to retain my Brooklyn office, while the state paid for my new Staten Island office, an essential beachhead as I introduced myself to a new constituency and began to help resolve community and individual problems there. Constituent service, after all, is the core of what any hardworking state representative does because it is not nearly as dependent on the perks of being in the majority. A year and a half later, a member of my staff and a colleague in the senate shocked me. They said that at least a dozen Republican senators (more than one-third of that conference) from various districts in New York City, Long Island, and upstate, received funds for two offices, fully paid for by the state government, and one even had a third office, and some of those senators served districts that covered less terrain than mine.[40]

So much about Albany breeds distrust and cynicism, so much of it emits a foul odor—the closed-door meetings; lobbyists insisting on quid pro quo; and vast amounts of questionable spending obscured by secrecy, excessively complex and arcane legal wording, and deviousness.

I soon went to Paterson, the newly elected minority leader of the senate, and asked for his advice, telling him that I wanted to publicly expose the special arrangements and the misinformation. These were just another one of the innumerable ways in which Bruno rewarded loyalty with public funds. (A more common way was to give committee chairs special stipends of as much as $45,000 a year to those who did his bidding on committees and on the senate floor.)

Senator Paterson indicated he was surprised to discover that about a dozen Republicans were being allocated two offices—which were denied to me, a Democrat who was told that it was in violation of senate rules to have two distinct offices. But just as quickly he urged me not to talk to the media because it could have the unintended effect of reminding voters of the far deeper financial reserves that the state's senate Republicans enjoyed. He intimated that the episode, if publicized, could undermine Democratic senate incumbents and candidates, showing that Republican candidates could bring more resources to a senate district than a Democrat could (an argument a Republican running for my seat once made against me).

I reluctantly went along but wondered whether there might be other reasons for asking me to remain silent. Each majority is afraid to criticize the other because they have similar weaknesses themselves when it comes to ethics. Assembly Speaker Silver had many special arrangements of his own with Democratic legislators, and the newly appointed senate Democratic leader did not want to open up an embarrassing public skirmish with the Republicans on the subject. It all reminded me of the tacit understanding that existed between Bruno and Silver. *Leave us our majority in the assembly,* goes the unstated credo, *and we will not mess with you or yours in the senate.* This is Albany's status quo, fortified against serious change from within or without. After this unbelievable incident, I began to think about leaving the New York State senate.

Few New Yorkers who live far from the statehouse—other than the politicians, their staffs, and the legion of lawyers, lobbyists, and consultants who have business before the body—readily recognize that state government is essentially a renewable wellspring of virtual permanent employment and revenue for its beneficiaries—nor can they immediately appreciate how much is at stake in the way the place is run.

Yet the truth is that Albany has at least as much influence over people's everyday lives and communities as the federal government.

Before the 1960s, some U.S. Supreme Court rulings went unheeded in the name of protecting states' rights in many parts of the country. The perception that gradually arose, as Americans watched on their black-and-white television screens while National Guard and Army troops moved in to enforce desegregation orders, was that many statehouses were corrupt and backward cesspools run by networks of white men beholden to the status quo.

Twenty years later, Ronald Reagan is president, and the former California governor invested new faith in the value of the states to spend taxpayers' dollars more sensibly than Washington and take over federal responsibilities. The trend found further expression during the Clinton years, when, for example, the federal entitlement to welfare based on income was ended, and the states were permitted to fashion their own rules for giving out—or, as was often the case, withholding—welfare checks.

Even before the revived trend toward greater federalism, or dispersing powers of the national government (and very likely destabilizing and diminishing its ability to respond to national problems such as Hurricane Katrina in 2005), the states have long had clout over fundamental aspects in the lives of their citizens. While Washington and New York City's city hall may get more media attention, the governor and legislature have a major impact. The state apparatus influences or directs the extent to which Medicaid funds are used efficiently; where highways are built; the timing and running of infrastructure repairs; how high the bridge and highway tolls and mass-transit fares and assorted public fees may be raised; the condition of the state's parks, forests, and beaches; and the availability of prekindergarten classes; income and sales taxes; university tuition and the quality of colleges' physical plants; civil servant pensions and experience requirements; industry licensing; private employee pensions and wage floors; economic development subsidies; hospital and housing construction; grants to small and large businesses; and the quality of the air we breathe and the water we drink. The list of how much the state affects the lives of the citizenry goes on.

To consider Albany's influence and the $142 billion state budget for 2015–2016,[41] and implicitly to think about the enormous influence of its troika, is to gasp with awe. To appreciate how much of the decision making concerning so many activities touching on the public interest takes place behind closed doors by three men in a room is astonishing. "Albany," wrote Eric Lane in the conservative *City Journal* in the spring of 1997 in an article whose main precepts are still true and relevant, "is anything but democratic."[42]

Lane's piece was an early red flag in the journey toward the day when, I hope, wholesale reform will come to Albany. "Yes," he wrote, "New Yorkers cast their votes for State Assembly and Senate, but when the vast majority of their representatives arrive at the Capitol, they don't legislate; they meekly follow the instructions of their legislative leaders."[43]

A Hofstra University School of Law dean and professor, Lane was counsel to the minority Democrats in the state senate from 1981 to 1986. He participated in the "undemocratic leadership culture and supported it." But after that experience, which spurred him to read extensively on the principles of good lawmaking, as it did with me, he realized he had been on the wrong path, and the Legislature's practices flouted nearly every rule in the book of sound democratic governance—"an embarrass-ing throwback to the days of bossism and party machines." In the article, now nearly two decades old, he went through a litany of problems that characterized the legislature even then.[44]

How many citizens know that during the legislative session, the workweek of the now 213 legislators in the Capitol usually extends only to Wednesday, giving them time to beat the weekend rush out of Albany? This is true for January, February, March, April, and May. In January they typically have only two days of session each week. June is usually a four-day session week. Legislators show up an average of sixty-seven days in session in Albany, for which many say they receive the equivalent of full-time pay (plus special stipends paid for each day in Albany). The rest of the time, 40 percent work at other jobs as, among other things, attorneys, real estate brokers, and insurance executives.

What goes on in the legislative chambers when they are there is so carefully regulated by the ultimate paymasters—the leaders of both houses—that their presence is merely a formality.

"In Congress, ..." notes Lane, "members often engage in robust debate off the floor, especially on controversial measures. Members of both parties freely offer and adopt amendments, and it is difficult at times to predict how a bill will fare in a final vote, despite the best efforts of party leaders to ensure a certain outcome. . . . By comparison, the New York State legislature looks like a meeting of the Supreme Soviet."[45]

When a leader sends a bill to the floor, legislators understand it is their job to pass it as is, without amendment or comment, and not a single bill goes down to defeat on the floor unless guided by the leader's unmistakable hand. Lane went on to describe the process by which the legislature passed the budget during 1996, my first year in Albany. On July 11, weeks after session was scheduled to be over the legislature printed a 541-page, $18 billion bill covering Medicaid, mental health, and prisons—and passed it the next day. It printed a 463-page, $12 billion bill covering education and labor matters and passed it on the same day. It printed Governor Pataki's 53–page, $1.75 billion Environmental Bond Act on July 12 and passed it on July 13.[46]

As one might expect, party conferences are also tightly controlled. The weekly conferences are where legislators of the same political party supposedly are able to make their voices heard on bills, to weigh in on their potential impact, and to discuss legislation from every vantage point. It is a time where, in theory, legislative leaders listen to the arguments of their members, lest they find themselves one day voted out of their leadership posts by these same members, just as Ralph Marino was ousted as senate majority leader after the 1994 election and replaced by Bruno. Governor-elect Pataki, a state senator who resented the fact that Senator Marino had opposed his receiving the Republican gubernatorial nomination, however, engineered that ousting.[47]

When one compares the Democratic conference meetings of one-time Democratic Senate Minority Leader Martin Connor with those run by his successor, David Paterson, one notices differences as well as similarities that can be instructive even now. For example, Connor managed practically every facet of the conference when he knew what he wanted, which was most of the time. Even his second in command, Paterson, seldom had an opportunity to influence Connor on major issues. Paterson's subsequent rise to take Connor's place in the senate arose partly from Democratic senators' feelings of being excluded from the decision-making process. Under Connor, there was little or no collaboration within the party on many important issues.

After seizing Connor's leadership position from him in 2002, Paterson developed a different style. He allowed the three or four top senate Democratic leaders to develop positions on issues with him before anything was taken to a Democratic policy conference meeting. Paterson often agreed to meet one-on-one with Democratic senators, unlike Connor, but almost invariably after he and his top associates had already decided their position. He did not even attend some conference meetings (though he went more than Connor did), where, supposedly, stands on major issues were thrashed out. Under him, the conference leadership of three or four senators spoke in one voice. On occasion, differences did emerge, but rarely if ever on substantive matters. In 2006 the Democratic gubernatorial candidate, Spitzer, tapped Minority Leader Paterson to be his running mate for lieutenant governor in the statewide election of that year, and he rose to governor when Spitzer resigned less than eighteen months later.[48]

Albany's problems were already deeply engrained when the Brennan Center for Justice at New York University School of Law, named for William J. Brennan Jr., the late U.S. Supreme Court justice, published a devastating critique in 2004, minutely comparing the New York legislature to statehouses in the rest of the country.[49] The media highlighted a catchphrase in a press release accompanying the report that characterized Albany as "the most dysfunctional legislature in the country,"[50] although the report itself did not go quite that far. Moreover, when the Brennan Center for Justice returned to the subject of Albany dysfunction in 2006 and again in 2008,[51] it found that little had changed. "Still Broken: New York State Legislative Reform" was the title of the second update, which noted that the legislative leadership had "largely dismissed" the findings of the original report.[52]

"Of the changes that the legislature did adopt, some, quite cynically, codified the status quo in new ways," according to the second follow-up study. "The continued presence of these rules stifles rigorous deliberation and debate and hobbles the sincere efforts of a number of rank-and-file legislators to represent the best interests of their constituents and the state as a whole." It further noted that in 2006 and 2007 standing committees met seldom if at all; there were virtually no hearings on major legislation. In addition, the leaders orchestrated which bills reached the floor for debate, and in any case, every bill that made it to the floor in either chamber was passed, the leaders always in control.[53]

There was as much concentration of leadership control during my tenure as ever in the senate's and assembly's history. It was fueled by the

leaders' staffs, by their unyielding grip on the powerful Rules committees (which control the flow of legislation to the floor of each house),
by committee assignments, connections to certain lobbyists, by largely
unaccountable reserves of political party funds, and by influence over
government hiring decisions. After I left the senate, efforts to reform the
system never succeeded in altering this fundamental imbalance or lowering the barriers to change.

In 1978 former Assemblyman Peter Berle, who also served as Governor Carey's commissioner of the Department of Environmental Conservation, wrote the book *Does the Citizen Stand a Chance? Politics of a
State Legislature—New York*.[54] Though it mentions some problems and
issues in the state legislature, it shows that at the time, forty years ago,
the problems pale in comparison to what has developed through the years
and are far more pervasive today.

"They—the Big Three—have almost complete power," commented
Manfred Ohrenstein, a former minority leader for Democrats in the
state senate. He recalled a brief moment of cooperation during the 1975
New York City fiscal crisis, when Republican Majority Leader Warren
Anderson worked hand-in-hand with him as minority leader to pass an
emergency rescue package for the beleaguered city and to free upstate
Republicans to vote against the package in keeping with their own constituencies' aversion to helping the Big Apple.[55] Ohrenstein, a Reform
Democrat, represented the Upper West Side from 1961 to 1994. Looking
back, that moment of intraparty cooperation within the senate looks like
a rare exception, born of the inescapable logic of the city's financial crisis.

The original Brennan Center for Justice report found that less than
one-half of 1 percent of the major bills the assembly passed and seven-
tenths of 1 percent of the major bills the senate passed—between 1997
and 2001—were given a public hearing.[56] This is unacceptable by any
standard, except that of authoritarian systems of governance.

The study also found that only 1.1 percent of the major bills the
assembly passed and none of those the senate adopted during that same
1997–2001 period were the subject of committee reports, which are used
in most legislative bodies to provide perspective, expertise, and analysis
prior to a vote. This is stunning. The New York senate had more standing committees—thirty-two of them—than all but one other state chamber (the Mississippi state senate, with thirty-five). The Brennan Center
for Justice comment that "the overall inactivity of committees in New

York . . . renders this problem less acute than it would otherwise be" is not reassuring, nor should it be.[57] The study aptly underlined the point that an anemic and centrally controlled committee system prevented the legislature from developing bills in a manner that allows for construction collaboration, expertise, hearings, and committee reports on the strengths and weaknesses of a proposal.[58]

Legislators need not even show up for committee votes, the report emphasized. Under the policy of proxy or empty-seat voting, it also emphasized, their absence was rigged to indicate preference for the leadership's position. Who loses in this system? I did. So did some of my elected colleagues. So did the public. Who wins? The three men in a room—the senate majority leader, assembly speaker, and governor—who jostle, feud, and work out deals among themselves, offering them to the public at the last minute. When the leaders are not getting along, or cannot come to full agreement, which of course is common, the result is deferral and delay.

Some of the Brennan Center for Justice's other findings were further cause for alarm.

"Even when a bill has the support of a majority of legislators within a chamber," the first report noted, "New York's Legislature makes it more difficult than any other legislature in the country to discharge a bill from a committee for the full chamber to consider."[59]

The senate majority leader and the assembly speaker held "complete control" over the legislative calendars to determine when and whether a bill reported out of a committee will be considered by the full senate or assembly. The senate majority leader can suspend action on any bill listed on the senate calendar by placing a star next to its listing. No action can be taken until one day after he removes the star. Does any other legislative chamber in the country give the majority leader such complete authority over legislation? My research revealed that they do not.

New York legislators, in fact, introduce more bills than those in any other statehouse in the nation, but the vast majority were just never really meant to be voted on. In 2002, when 16,892 bills were introduced in New York State, Illinois, the next closest, had 8,717, and Massachusetts, 7,924. Very little New York legislation goes anywhere except into press releases and publicly funded brochures sent to constituents.[60] Additionally, those that made it to the floor of either chamber were in every instance approved overwhelmingly, with no exceptions, reflecting, it would seem, the near-absolute control of the leadership. Individual legislators, and thus

their constituents, had virtually no direct way of obtaining votes on legislation they considered important without the approval of either of the
house leaders. Most of the bills that did pass were one-house bills that
had no possibility of passage in the other house because they either lacked
a counterpart there or were carried by a member of the minority whose
bills never come to the floor for debate and a vote. Where similar bills
were passed in both houses, the two leaders never convened conference
committees. For legislation to reach the governor's desk, a deal had to be
in place to pass it between the two leaders, with the language decided by
those two and their staff, not negotiated by the legislators.[61]

In the 2015 legislative session, while the senators and assembly members proposed more bills than just about any other state legislature in the
country—almost twice as many as New Jersey, in second place, according
to an independent analysis by the Bill Track 50 website—the New York
legislature also *passed* a smaller percentage of bills than anywhere else. A
mere two-tenths of 1 percent of all the bills that were proposed during
the 2015 legislative session actually passed both houses. "This is clearly a
sign of play-acting," wrote *Crain's New York Business* reporter Greg David
on his blog, which featured the analysis.[62]

The late Warren Anderson, who represented Binghamton in the
senate from 1966 to 1992 and was for many years the body's majority
leader, told me late in his life that for much of his tenure legislators had
more power through the committee system that existed at the time than
in recent years. "The average member has lost his independence," he said.
"The power no longer resides in the chairman of the committee or the
members of the legislature. The power resides in the hands of the top
leaders and their immediate staffs."[63]

He added that Albany's focus had shifted by the early 1990s to political survival. Thus it has remained, with the pressure to defeat the opposition and deprive it of any political success only intensifying with each
decade. "People only thought of survival, only thought of reelection, and
only thought of safe seats," he said. "There were no real programs created
in health or mental health or education or the arts originating with the
members of the legislature."[64]

Anderson noted that the senate majority leader often had to at least
consider, and would sometimes negotiate, the potential political impact
a bill could have on legislators from disparate parts of the state—those
from industrial cities such as Buffalo, rural areas of the Adirondacks, or

the suburbs of Long Island. But, he added, the speaker of the assembly was less challenged to negotiate with his members. This was because no single delegation group within the much larger assembly, such as the Black and Latino Caucus, had enough votes to overturn the speaker. "Bruno actually negotiates with his members, though he has procedurally taken their power away," said Anderson, who died in 2007.[65]

Opponents of the sweeping changes reformers sought contend that Albany has always been a battleground among conflicting interests and always will be, and that some of what is criticized is the healthy, adversarial politics of the two-party system, particularly in a state that has a strong, powerful governorship. Everyone recognizes that the competition for government contracts, regulatory favors, and laws has grown sharper, thanks to a growing array of enormously well-funded and sophisticated lobbyists, consultants, party organizations, and political action committees (PACs)—that is, special interests. It will forever be so, they insist, regardless what happens. So, the argument goes, there is a democratic arena, despite the Big Three's powers.

That view is a formula for continuing the status quo. The public must know not only which legislators are using their influence to ensure their objectives are met, but also power in the legislature must be diffused in a manner more consistent with the workings of the U.S. Congress. The Albany leaders have to be divested of their virtually absolute power, something that can be forced to happen only through public outrage and a constitutional convention. The three Brennan Center for Justice reports also call for the leaders to change their own rules, yet the result was largely cosmetic; the power dynamic remained intact despite the reports' scathing findings. The same, I believe, would be the case under a new governor from either party, regardless which party controlled either or both of the legislative houses.

In the early summer of 2005, the *New York Times* reported that a bill popular among consumer groups to make leasing a car easier in New York had been killed through the efforts of Assembly Speaker Silver. Put aside the fact that trial lawyers, a powerful lobby in the state capital, had long opposed the change and that Silver himself was a trial lawyer. The key point is that a bill that looked as though it might pass in the assembly's Transportation Committee in the summer of 2005 was not even permitted to come up for a vote. The committee chair, naturally a Silver appointee, suddenly took it off the agenda.[66]

One member of that panel, a freshman legislator who had said he was leaning toward supporting the measure, explained that he reconsidered, telling *New York Times* reporter Al Baker that he could see good points on both sides. A longtime Long Island legislator who had cosponsored the bill was reassigned from the committee after Silver offered him a seat on a more desirable panel.[67]

The legislators departed Albany, leaving unaltered an unpopular law that makes renting or leasing a car in New York relatively difficult. The U.S. Congress later passed federal legislation making it easier for motorists in all states, including New York, to rent or lease vehicles. The federal law effectively superseded Silver's resistance to change.[68]

Silver's efforts, which some contended were favoring a special interest, were hardly an isolated example. Baker, from the *New York Times*'s Albany bureau, reported that at about the same time another popular bill suffered a similar roadblock at the behest of Senate Majority Leader Bruno, a measure pushed by lawmakers in the upper house for about a year to remove a loophole that environmentalists contended had left numerous small, far-flung wetlands susceptible to development. This measure had the backing of both assembly Democrats and the Republican governor. Bruno repeatedly blocked it, however, calling it a needless burden on businesses and the sluggish upstate economy.[69]

Whether the Democratic assembly or the Republican senate, the will of the lawmakers and, in effect, their constituents are always secondary to the electoral concerns of their top leaders—a situation that irked a principled, liberal assemblyman, Frank Barbaro, who won his assembly seat in 1972 after running in Brooklyn as a staunch opponent of the Vietnam War. The onetime dockworker's willingness to challenge the status quo kept him from rising too high in the legislature, and finally saw him removed as chairman of the assembly Labor Committee by then–Speaker Saul Weprin in 1994. Barbaro left the body in 1996 for a Democratic Party-controlled judgeship on the state Supreme Court, where he served for six years.[70]

When legislators can influence legislation, it is almost invariably through indirect means and outside the normal boundaries of carefully planned conduct—and even then, nothing can become law without the leader's permission.

Senator Paterson first introduced hate crime legislation more than a decade before it became law in 2000. The shocking killing of Matthew

Shepard in Wyoming eighteen months earlier had led other jurisdictions to pass bias crimes legislation and increased pressure on New York to join them. A hate crimes bill finally passed with the help of Senator Tom Duane and others including me. As passed, after a long fight, it stiffened the penalties for crimes motivated by prejudice against a victim's race, religion, gender, or sexual orientation. Bruno's opposition inordinately delayed the legislature's adopting the bill despite there having been a version of the bill, which Manhattan Republican Roy Goodman sponsored, now more than forty years since the victories of the civil rights era.

During the struggle to get the bill passed, the senate minority conference established a task force on hate crimes legislation, and at one point we wanted to have a public hearing about the issue on Long Island to put pressure on Bruno and his Republican conference to allow the Goodman-sponsored version of the bill get a floor vote. It had been marooned in committee for years. My staff and I wanted to hold hearings in areas, represented by Republicans, where public support existed for the bill—in Westchester County, on the Upper East Side of Manhattan (home of Goodman), and parts of Long Island. Nassau County was where we wanted to hold our first hearing in April 2000, but again this proved difficult. Nassau and Suffolk counties were Republican territory as far as the senate leadership was concerned, and Democratic leaders on Long Island were not eager to provide a venue in their districts for the task force hearing for fear of antagonizing Bruno.

A search for a public venue lasted for weeks, but Democrats in Long Beach, led by me (I have a summer home in that oceanfront city), were finally able to secure a meeting room at the city hall of Long Beach, then one of two Nassau County Democratic cities (the other one being Glen Cove). Then, just before the scheduled event, the Long Beach city government reversed its position and withdrew their invitation to the Democratic senate conference. Such was the power on Long Island of Senate Majority Leader Bruno and Deputy Majority Leader Skelos, whose district included Long Beach. All nine state senators from Long Island, then and at this writing, were Republicans, and Bruno and Skelos could make life difficult for them—and difficult for Long Island Democrats in the assembly as well, who needed cooperation across the aisle to get their bills passed as well as to obtain funding for local programs. Skelos requested the then–Long Beach Democratic assemblyman, Harvey Weisenberg, to see that the invitation to city hall was withdrawn. The assemblyman was concerned that his bills and programs would not be passed without the support of the then-Deputy and later Majority Leader Skelos. Weisenberg demanded that our approval be revoked, and even protested to the Long Beach city council and city manager. Permission to meet at city hall was indeed revoked.

Still, the task force scrambled to hold the public hearing in an alternative location in Long Beach. Happily, the hearing, which I cochaired and which was cosponsored by the Anti-Defamation League, secured a meeting room at a local temple. Held before a standing-room-only audience, the hearing had the intended effect, drawing attention, including *Newsday* and other media outlets, to Bruno's opposition to hate crime penalties many groups of voters favored—African Americans; Latinos; Jews; women; the lesbian, gay, bisexual, and transgender community; liberals; crime victims' advocates; and all manner of civil rights organizations—including many constituents of Long Island Republican senators.[71]

Not surprisingly, the Democratic conference's hate crimes hearing angered Skelos, which he told me when we saw each other at an Albany reception later that year. He warned me, "Don't you ever dare come into my district again."

Nothing else happened with regard to hate crimes legislation until human rights groups handed out thousands of flyers at Long Island Rail Road stations. The media viewed the legislation favorably as the November 2000 elections approached. Editorial pages, the Anti-Defamation League, and many other community groups called for passage of a hate crimes law.[72]

The Republicans eventually came to support the bill, seeing little advantage in continuing Bruno's opposition to making bias crimes a special category under the penal code. Suddenly, the bill had new Republican champions in the senate; they agreed to support a Goodman-sponsored hate crimes bill with Bruno's approval. Despite the years of work by Senators David Paterson, Tom Duane, and me, no Democrats appeared as sponsors of the bill that was finally passed.[73] That was fine with me; this is how law making is done in Albany. The bill's success was in the end made possible by the leaders for all the usual reasons—the pursuit and protection of legislative seats rather than because of any passion for justice for crime victims or prevention of harm to any one group.

As "punishment" for our putting public pressure on the Republicans to allow a vote on the bill, which had support in both parties, several rules were changed to put the Democratic minority in the senate at a further disadvantage. There were no longer to be any recorded floor votes on proposed amendments to any future bills. Instead, the presiding officer—typically not the majority leader but rather a member of the majority sitting in the top seat in the chamber as "acting president of the senate"—would "canvass" members and determine whether there was sufficient support—or not—for a debate and vote. In addition, a rule was implemented to limit the number of times our conference could make motions to discharge from committee to the floor bills that the majority leader had refused to advance. This was the consequence for appealing for public support and forcing Senator Bruno and his Republican majority to consider a piece of legislation against their wishes.

I faced similar institutional resistance when I pushed for an education tax credit bill I had been working on since 1997, a bill designed to encourage donations to public or private educational institutions. In 2001, though, it looked as if it had a decent chance of passing, but with different sponsors and in modified form. Even then, it stalled and finally faded, even though public schools would gain more than private schools because the education employee unions saw it as a way to support the conservative cause of tuition vouchers or stipends for those avoiding public schools and choosing instead private schools.

And so it also went with a bill to require insurance companies, a Republican constituency, to cover infertility drugs. Democrats supported the measure, as they had in the past. I was a cosponsor; infertility medical practitioners, the National Infertility Association, and the Orthodox Jewish organization Agudath Israel of America all strongly supported the bill. The bill was also potentially beneficial to countless couples turning in record numbers to expensive infertility doctors in order to have children. The senate, gauging the cost to the big insurance companies and mindful of concerns of the Roman Catholic Church, consistently balked despite backing from other normally Republican constituencies—fertility doctors and the pharmaceutical companies that had developed fertility drugs—both of which would benefit from insurance coverage of the treatments. It was not until an election year, 2002, that Republicans addressed it, working out a compromise with the assembly[74] because they feared that their opposition to the measure could hurt them in some districts.

Instead of amending and passing my bill, however, the infertility coverage was inserted into one of the state budget bills passed in May 2002, allowing Governor Pataki, Majority Leader Bruno, and Speaker Silver to take credit for its passage.

Earlier that year, the senate, in characteristic fashion, had tried to pass a version the leadership knew would not survive in the assembly. It included clauses that would curb the cost and effectiveness of the insurance coverage provisions. The Republicans, it seemed, merely wanted to be able to issue a press release stating that they did something, when in fact their one-house bill would have done nothing. Indeed, nothing had happened for five more years, when additional negotiation and lobbying finally led to the passage of a bill that both houses' leaders could accept.

By the time I left office on December 31, 2004, some of my colleagues did not know what to think about someone who had insisted on considering the merits of an issue in addition to its immediate political consequences. But fighting the powers-that-be was the only way to influence the leaders. For instance, in 2005, when the state government passed its first on-time budget in two decades,[75] this timely result probably happened only because of the widespread criticism in newspapers across the state excoriating the legislature's paralysis and ineptitude following the previous year's record late budget. In addition, it occurred only after an election in which the politicians finally recognized that more and more voters were weary of the antics in Albany. But in no way did the first on-time enactment of the invariably baroque, politically charged spending-and-revenue blueprint open the door to serious changes in how the Capitol works. Then–Attorney General Spitzer called it a budget that managed to be on time only by dint of legislative leaders deferring "many, if not most, of the difficult issues that are confronting state government," such as "initiatives on the environment, aid to the needy, and college construction."[76] Former Governor Mario Cuomo commented that "it's not a real budget if . . . [the legislature knows] there are a billion and more dollars they have to add to it to meet their important needs."[77]

Nor did on-time passage of the budget compensate for the legislature's customary failure, yet again, to address many important issues of governance, such as a ruling from the state's highest court to increase state aid to New York City public schools by billions of dollars to ensure a "sound, basic education," a requirement found in the state constitution.[78] Pataki shrugged off the court's ruling, evoking, for me, the widespread resistance of southern states during the 1950s and 1960s to court-ordered school desegregation. Pataki just wanted the whole thing to go away until he departed from office, and it did.

5

In a Lofty Place

Clashes between big personalities, divergent upstate and downstate interests, organized economic forces, and competing political parties all have been a constant in the history of New York State government. Governors have often loathed legislative leaders and vice versa. Rivalries have been unforgiving at times. Greed and corruption, with more than a pinch of ambition for wealth and power on a national scale, produced catalyzing scandals. On occasion, it generated lasting consequences and even reforms. In New York's storied political history, secretive deals in smoke-filled rooms, framed by consideration of whatever collection of moneyed interests the top elected officials chose to serve, have been common. Cash has been the critical lubricant: receiving and dispensing it (in sealed brown envelopes or through legal, albeit loosely supervised, campaign channels) has been the abiding preoccupation, which is to say the prevailing concern is political survival and aggrandizement rather than principle. From its beginnings, Albany, for all its lofty rhetoric and even loftier architecture, has never been a magnet for piety, propriety, or good works.

Nevertheless, out of the cauldron of expedient conduct and sometimes craven behavior has come some of the most progressive and humane legislation passed by any state at any time. Unfortunately, one usually has to look back decades to find it.

The history of New York is endowed with many strong—even legendary—personalities who have occupied the governor's mansion. In all, eighteen former New York governors went on serve as U.S. president or vice president or ran unsuccessfully for the White House. Those who went on to become president include Martin Van Buren, Grover Cleveland, Theodore Roosevelt, and Franklin D. Roosevelt. Those who went on to be vice president were George Clinton, Daniel Tompkins, Van Buren, Levi P. Morton, Theodore Roosevelt, and Nelson Rockefeller. Two New York governors were also chief justices of the United States: John Jay and Charles Evans Hughes (following the latter's unsuccessful 1916 race for president and an earlier stint as associate justice of the high court). In light of this, expectations were high that whoever was elected governor of New York would go on to influence the course of U.S. affairs, and to a large extent this has remained so, increasing the intensity of their relationship with the state legislature and the levels of political and ideological conflict. New York's preeminence as the nation's financial and media capital, as well as its status, up to the 1960s, as the most populous state, has heightened the importance, potency, and volatility of politics in Albany.

In more recent times, Hugh Carey risked his political future, which included suggestions in the national press that he could be president, by helping pull New York City back from the brink of financial disaster, a political feat that prevented state, national, and possibly international economic repercussions. His successor, Mario Cuomo, liberal lion of his generation, succeeded in imposing some of the first significant ethical standards on the legislative and executive branches since World War II (while later coming very close to making a bid for president). Notwithstanding their aspirations, Carey and Cuomo stood fast against legislators and a majority of voters who were demanding the death penalty. George Pataki defeated the three-term Cuomo in 1994, in part on a platform embracing capital punishment, though no one on death row received a lethal injection during Pataki's dozen years in office.

Forceful governors, in any case, have been a feature of New York State government for generations. The witty Hugh Carey said that his larger-than-life, wealthy predecessor, Nelson Rockefeller, had owned one branch of the legislature and leased the other.[1] But the popular gang-busting Manhattan district attorney turned governor, Thomas E. Dewey, who nearly beat Harry Truman for president, broached little or no disloyalty from either the upper or lower house of the legislature as he professionalized the state government, including its financial essence, the budget division. He happily put the longstanding three-men-in-a-room system to use in the service of managerial efficiency.[2] Even with the ethical rectitude he projected, Dewey was not above using patronage or withholding important jobs to coerce legislative leaders or send a message to his fellow Republicans, who bridled against his expansive use of his executive and veto powers, both of which created a lot of sourness toward him from leading members of his own party.[3] Pushing the powers of the executive branch to their outer limit was, and remains, an occupational hazard for strong governors. But many of them have felt compelled to do so. The legislature, wrote Dewey biographer Richard Norton Smith, "was not a team, not a stellar gathering of keen minds and disinterested opinion, but a slightly shabby peerage of job-hungry provincials, given to gabbling and squabbles, respectful of no authority but local political machines."[4]

During the latter half of the twentieth century and into the present day, modern life and state politics have become increasingly complex, with increasingly diverse and varied interests—consumer groups, professional organizations, labor unions, and industries—invariably employing an unprecedented legion of lobbyists with unparalleled amounts of campaign cash to gain access, legislation, regulatory relief, and funding. There are also grassroots activists, citizens groups, and nonprofit organizations of all types. Their common goal is to educate and shape public opinion, but more important, ultimately, they wish to apply effective pressure on or woo the leaders of the contemporary legislature and executive branch. Not unlike kings, the two legislative leaders and the governor have assessed the pressures weighing on them from within and without and cut their political deals behind closed doors. The legislature, meanwhile, has remained at its core what it has always been known as: a self-perpetuating institution, offering virtually lifetime jobs for those legislators willing to play by the leaders' exacting rules. The government has long been a generator of patronage for the party faithful, to such a degree that imagining the struggling upstate New York economy being able to survive on its own without the public trough is difficult to imagine. This may be the state bureaucracy's biggest virtue, a hedge against the vicissitudes of the market economy for thousands and thousands of New Yorkers, their families, and their towns.

Given that it is such an enormous money machine, there have been few serious, open debates in the legislature about public policies affecting the citizenry at large in recent decades. Absent an activist governor and an aroused and informed public, the "Albany game"—"going along to get along" and not creating too many difficulties or problems for the leadership as it satisfies its major constituencies and desires to remain in power—simply rolls on. Carey, in a conversation with me in his later years, described his frustration with the "dark alliances" of most legislators, their fealty toward anyone who agrees to help them get reelected.[5] He clashed with them in his second term especially, partly because of the dim view he held and partly as a result of his consistent overestimating of the state's projected revenues (thereby depriving the legislators of the discretionary funds they had come to expect). When higher-than-anticipated revenues materialized, the shrewd Carey used the money in the state budget to lower the state's tax rates.[6] At one point the governor dismissed the whole lot of legislators as "small boys," which no doubt made negotiating with their leaders even tougher. Consequently, making policy on the merits, or on principle, became next to impossible in his second and final term. In any case, it was never really part of the Albany character.

Since being named the state capital in 1782, Albany has proved conveniently removed from the prying eyes of the nation's media capital, which even then was Manhattan. Situated within relatively easy reach of New York City, Montreal, and Boston, and with a population of 42,700, Albany was the sixth-largest city in post-Revolutionary America. Its national importance as the capital of the "Empire State" was established firmly in 1825 with the opening of the Erie Canal, the epic public works feat championed by Governor DeWitt Clinton that turned Albany into a significant inland seaport and New York City into an international crossroads of trade and commerce.[7]

The great Clinton, first elected in 1817, changed the state and the nation in a huge and dramatic fashion. Interestingly, he clashed with the legislature and faced opposition from politicians and their conservative business supporters, who believed his relentless support of the Erie Canal project, which they derided as "Clinton's ditch," was nothing more than a politician's boondoggle.

The canal was built, however, and finally in October 1825 Clinton arrived triumphantly in Manhattan to celebrate the grand opening. Beyond its economic implications, the waterway made New York City a political and cultural force for the nation and triggered the westward movement of American settlers. The epic migration opened up vast tracts of rich farmland in the Northwest Territories, which would in time become Illinois, Indiana, Michigan, and Ohio, all of which had been all but inaccessible to the large-scale movement of settlers and traders. No subsequent governor has ever approached DeWitt Clinton for believing in and carrying out a transcendent vision that has transformed the state and nation.[8]

Some New York governors became president, and due in part to this legacy, the massive Albany statehouse remains coveted by contemporaries as a precursor to the White House. Grover Cleveland, who started public life as an attorney in Buffalo and became the city's mayor, was a self-proclaimed reforming governor during 1883 and 1884. A Democrat, he was burdened by a very conservative and at times obstructionist legislature, and in the end his brief gubernatorial record was less than memorable. He was, however, a smart enough politician to develop a working relationship with an energetic, reform-minded Republican assemblyman from Manhattan named Theodore Roosevelt.

Roosevelt, age twenty-three when elected and the legislature's youngest member, was a man of great ambition and urgency. Within forty-eight hours of the start of his first legislative session in 1882, he introduced, as a member of the Committee on Cities, four bills: water purification, aldermanic election reform, finance reform for New York City, and judicial reform.[9] Although a much-changed version of the aldermanic legislation was the only one to meet with any success, the initiatives gained him popular attention as well as the leadership of an unofficial group of Republicans who strove to be independent of machine politics. Benjamin Harrison, after his own election as president in 1889, appointed Roosevelt to the U.S. Civil Service Commission. He held the post until 1895, when he became a commissioner of the New York City Police Department, styling himself a reformer and combating rapacious police corruption. In 1897 he joined President William McKinley's administration as assistant secretary of the Navy, zealously preparing for the war in Cuba. When the Spanish-American War erupted in 1898, he left and became lieutenant colonel of a regiment of volunteer cavalry he had organized from hunters and cowboys from the West as well as with fellow sons of wealth and influence in Manhattan, winning fame as leader of these "Rough Riders" in a charge up San Juan Hill against Spanish troops. He forever after reveled in the public's adulation of his masculine, warrior image. Roosevelt struck a responsive chord in those who believed the invasion was "a splendid little war," in Secretary of State John Hay's indelicate description.

"The charge itself was great fun," Roosevelt wrote his family from Cuba.

The press showed pictures of Roosevelt on horseback, striking a heroic pose, leading his foot soldiers up the hill. With Roosevelt's ego expanding by the day, the American satirist Finley Peter Dunne had Mr.

Dooley, the fictional Irish immigrant barkeep of a new widely read news-paper column, saying of Roosevelt's breathless memoir of the war, "If I was him, I'd call the book 'Alone in Cuba.' "[10] William Graham Sumner, the Yale University sociologist and social Darwinist, was an anti-imperialist who despised Roosevelt. He dismissed the widespread spirit of triumpha-lism and flag-waving, saying, "My patriotism is of the kind which is out-raged by the notion that the United States never was a great nation until in a petty three-months' campaign it knocked to pieces a poor, decrepit, bankrupt old state like Spain."[11]

Rarely deterred by criticism, Roosevelt campaigned for New York governor in 1898 as a war hero, evoking the supposed glories of San Juan Hill and extolling the nation's new imperialism in the Caribbean. He was elected by a small margin—"New York cares little for the war," Roosevelt lamented—and served as governor from 1899 to 1900. He found Albany somewhat too provincial for his agenda.

Still, he quickly saw in Albany that while conservative politicians were in agreement with his nationalistic appeals, they did not like it when he spoke loudly about reforming the corruption-riddled state government so that it might become more responsive to the citizenry. They were espe-cially unhappy about his unpredictability and independence of mind, which led Senator Thomas Platt, the statewide Republican Party boss, to want him pushed out of the capital at the earliest possible moment.

Ohio's Republican boss Mark Hanna was apoplectic when he heard the news that Roosevelt might be chosen to be William McKinley's vice president. "Don't any of you realize," he warned his fellow Republican convention delegates, "that there's only one life between this madman and the White House?"[12] Theodore Roosevelt did push through environmental protections and streamlined and strengthened civil service requirements, neither of which most conservative legislators held much sympathy for. When, after his single two-year term, he departed to become President McKinley's second vice president, he unselfconsciously trumpeted, "I think I have been the best governor within my time, better than either [Grover] Cleveland or [Samuel J.] Tilden"—a remark historian Henry F. Pringle years later termed "a shade overenthusiastic." Then, in uncanny fulfillment of Hanna's fears, Roosevelt assumed the presidency after McKinley, who had survived the Civil War as a former Union Army private, was assas-sinated in Buffalo in 1901.

Two quickly forgettable politicians succeeded the swashbuckling Roosevelt, before Charles Evans Hughes, an ambitious reformist politician, was voted in as New York's governor in 1906, defeating William Randolph Hearst. Hughes, a corporate attorney, was elected in large measure because of his role as chief counsel in the previous year's life insurance investigation. Hughes fought hard for, and won, a state public service commission, as well as rates-related reforms of the politically connected gas and insurance industries, which were widely viewed as being predisposed to swindle the public. The Moreland Act was passed in 1907 under Hughes's leadership, giving governors the power to appoint commissions of one or more people to investigate matters related to executive agencies and functions.[13] Sympathetic to Theodore Roosevelt and the progressive wing of the party, he considered direct primaries the best way to free the political process from the oppression of big businessmen and corporate interests. "Those interests," he declared, "are ever at work stealthily and persistently endeavoring to pervert the government to the service of their own ends."[14] Even before Hughes's election, a few other states had already approved direct primaries, notably Wisconsin, where Robert M. La Follette had been calling for them for years in order "to emancipate the legislature from all subserviency to the corporations," as he put it. When Hughes left office near the end of his second term, his direct-primary measure faced probable defeat; it had angered bosses of his party who had long controlled the nominating process, and they had set out to try to defeat him. He won his second term by a narrow margin, and could not kick-start his direct primaries bill.[15] No doubt having his fill of Albany boss-controlled politics, Hughes gladly accepted Taft's nomination to the U.S. Supreme Court in October 1910. However, he had started something important: direct primaries were approved by the state legislature in 1913 for all statewide offices. Clearly Hughes's advocacy played a big role in its approval, just three years after he left for Washington.

Six years later Hughes ran for the presidency. On Election Day, he retired for the night after the polls closed in the East, believing he had beaten Woodrow Wilson. He awoke to learn that he had lost because, while he had slept, California had gone for Wilson. After later serving as Secretary of State under Warren G. Harding and Calvin Coolidge, Hughes returned to his private law practice until President Herbert Hoover reappointed him to the Supreme Court and made him, at sixty-seven, chief justice, though progressives in both parties opposed the appointment and confirmation, believing Hughes had become too friendly to big business. He remains the only person in U.S. history ever to have served as both governor and chief justice.[16]

Second in influence to the governors were the leaders of the assembly and senate. The legislative branches presided in exalted and elegant chambers. The interior of the senate, for example, was a luxuriant mix of ornate Greek and Roman styles. The overpowering sense of permanency and grandness found in both chambers symbolized a legal power and authority over everyone living in the state. Some have said that the New York State chamber looks even more impressive than the U.S. senate chamber.

Legislative leaders have had enormous powers in modern times and are often seen as the one who make changes in their distinct chambers. Historically, they have served as allies, rivals, or patsies to their governors. The near-absolute authority of the leaders has been the modern norm, as counterweight to an ever-stronger executive branch.

"Some pundits call the legislative leadership position 'the hardest job in Albany to get, and the easiest to keep,'" wrote Robert B. Ward in *New York State Government*.[17] Writing in 2006, Ward also commented on a basic rule of Albany politics: "If the leadership in a given house wants a bill to pass, it will." The crucial question, he noted, is "how to get the Senate Majority Leader and the Assembly Speaker to want a bill to pass."[18]

Throughout the state's history, the legislature's leaders have been called on to satisfy their loyal fellow party members by offering ever-enticing perks, ranging from largely unaccountable member items to patronage jobs for their friends and bigger Albany offices for members and their staffs. That is for the majority party of a respective house. The minority gets the leavings.

Despite infrequent successes at reform over the course of state history, wrote then–Queens assemblyman and future city and state comptroller Alan Hevesi in 1975, "even advocates of legislative reform often come out in favor of the kind of centralization of power and responsibility in the hands of party leaders." (Hevesi, as noted, was forced to resign as state comptroller for using a state chauffeur for personal and family use and later pleaded guilty to accepting kickbacks in connection with his powers as sole trustee of the state Common Retirement Fund.[19]) The central question rarely goes beyond an immediate, strategic determination of how far the leaders will choose to cooperate with the governor and whether they will rule their respective houses with a tough and aggressive style or in a rarer collaborative style.

Al Smith, one of New York's greatest governors, arrived in Albany in 1903 as an assemblyman during a period of enormous social change. By the twentieth century, more people lived in cities than on farms, where independent yeomen were being displaced by larger-scale commercial agriculture. Millionaires and gigantic trusts had emerged in the wake of the rapid industrialization of the late nineteenth century. Immigrants were still arriving by the millions from an impoverished Europe, many flocking to Smith's Lower East Side neighborhood.

Smith was born in 1873 in a South Street tenement beneath the under-construction Brooklyn Bridge, the son of a German/Italian American truck driver and Civil War veteran father (born Alfred Emanuele Ferraro, "Ferraro" being Italian for "blacksmith," he later took the surname "Smith") and Irish American mother, Catherine Mulvihill.[20] He grew to be fascinated by the political life. Smith was a consummate New York City ethnic politician, a self-appointed "man of the people." He was a liberal, his rasping voice that of a street-smart wisenheimer. He had a conquering, swaggering, proud-to-be-a-*New-Yawkah* stance.

Smith's autobiography, *Up to Now,* may be among the most interesting ever written by a politician, "a plain story of a plain ordinary man written from memory," as he put it. The book recalled with nostalgia and reverence his Fourth Ward's party rallies and clubhouse speakers on lower Manhattan's crowded street corners. Gifts and favors were handed out to immigrant newcomers by local ward heelers, as was the practice at the time. Tammany boss Charles Francis "Silent Charlie" Murphy, a judicious and galvanizing force in the all-powerful organization, sponsored Smith's rise, as well as that of Senator Jimmy Walker, who became the highly effective Senate Democratic Minority Leader under Governor Smith and the indulgent Jazz Age mayor of New York City. A young Smith loved the political life, the rousing Election Day celebrations, the good talk and fellowship in local saloons and Tammany clubhouses, and all the advantages public office could offer.[21]

Al Smith was thirty-years-old when this product of the Tammany Hall first gained a seat in the assembly. Despite his political heritage, no one ever accused Smith of taking a dime that was not his own. He worked hard as an assemblyman, and while others were out cavorting in Albany's fleshpots—flourishing houses of gambling and prostitution—he went home to read the bills and laws that few cared to digest. The knowledge and legislative sophistication he garnered led his Democratic colleagues to select him as majority leader and chair of the Ways and Means Committee in 1911, where he was able to determine which proposed spending and revenue bills could be considered by legislators. His biographer Robert Slayton notes that his Tammany bosses saw to it that he became assembly minority leader in 1912, speaker in 1913, minority leader again in 1914–1915. He became sheriff of New York County in 1915, a highly lucrative post, and president of the Board of Aldermen in 1916, before being elected governor in 1918.[22]

At first, Smith was disappointed with the capital, less because of the seamy political environment, which probably reminded him of Tammany Hall, than because of the depressing physical condition of the city itself. He preferred to commute from Manhattan so that he could be with his mother, his wife, his children, and even his cherished pets, whose intelligence he would later compare favorably to that of certain legislators who were opposing him. Many of those colleagues continued partying in the brothels and casinos, but Smith, ever the traditional Roman Catholic and exemplary family man, would have none of it.

As a budding humanitarian, Smith read some of the literature of the Progressive Era then sweeping the nation. More than likely he became familiar with its crusading journalistic accounts of injustices in field and factory, farms and cities, and developed an affinity for workers struggling against corporate behemoths.

The Triangle Shirtwaist Factory fire on March 25, 1911, which killed 146 workers, mainly girls and women, changed him as well as his ally on the senate side, Robert Wagner. Wagner, the State Senate Majority Leader (later a prominent and influential U.S. senator and New Dealer) and another loyal Tammany man with genuine reform impulses, was chosen as chair of the legislature's Factory Investigating Commission in 1911. Smith, as majority leader of the assembly, was its vice chairman.

Shepherded by Frances Perkins, the commission's main investigator, the two men discovered that aisles had been blocked and exits locked inside the factory. Meanwhile, the press published photos of terrified employees jumping to their death in an effort to escape the smoke and flames. There was an enormous outpouring of public outrage at the atrocious, Dickensian commercial firetraps proliferating throughout the city and state. The moment was Smith's (and Wagner's) epiphany, altering their view of what elected officials could do to relieve the burdens of the working poor. So-called social legislation was practically unheard of at the time. "In brief," wrote Smith, "it was the aim of the commission to devote itself to a consideration of measures that had for their purpose the conservation of life."[23]

He learned to his horror that the state and the legislature had done virtually nothing about any of the conditions that contributed to all of this. Inspections of workplaces were rare and announced in an advance. Children and pregnant women labored in firetraps. At one of the committee meetings in the assembly, he heard that a well-connected cannery was employing women and young children to work for up to sixteen hours daily. Soon after, he successfully urged the assembly to enact a law granting one rest day per week for all workers. The cannery firm and its legislative allies fought it, but Smith is remembered for having risen from his chair and intoned, " 'Remember the Sabbath Day, to keep it holy,' but I am unable to find any language in it that says 'except in the canneries.' "[24]

Smith became so possessed with changing things that he schooled his Tammany mentor, Charles Francis Murphy, a latter-day convert to economic and political reform as he looked to maintain Tammany's strength in the long term. Perhaps the shrewdest and most nimble boss Tammany ever had, Murphy knew enough to understand that the machine could not stand in the way of serious change. Not that he signaled his intentions to anyone except his most loyal subordinates, Smith and Wagner. When asked why Mr. Murphy—he was always "Mr. Murphy" to his minion— had failed to sing the national anthem when it was played, a Tammany member wisecracked, "Perhaps he doesn't want to commit himself." Yet with his legendary caution and monumental reserve, Murphy protected Smith and Wagner from scandal and encouraged them as they helped enact progressive laws such as the Workmen's Compensation Act, seeing the need for Tammany to keep in line with liberal segments of the voting population. There were many other reforms designed to ease the burdens of working people—the common goal for Smith, who never forgot the poverty he experienced growing up, as well as the German-born Wagner—and Murphy supported, as well, their desire to overhaul the state's arcane and limited administrative machinery.

Whatever the Tammany gang's role in dirty politics, and good or bad corruption (as George Washington Plunkitt drew the distinction)—and it was a starring role to be sure—Murphy's blessings provided Smith and Wagner with full Democratic Party support when Smith became governor. This set in motion the progressive humanitarian laws that, in spite of continual and ferocious skirmishes with rural upstate and conservative politicians inside the legislature as well as economic interests outside of it, would eventually became the hallmark of President Franklin D. Roosevelt's New Deal.

Along with the rising demands and economic power of the recent waves of immigrants in the Smith years, especially Irish, Italians, and Eastern European Jews, came increasing communist and socialist demands and mass protests, as well as organized labor's insistence on the legal right to unionize. One can only compare Smith's legislative achievements in furthering unionism and the rights of economically oppressed masses with those of the famed Progressive Party's Robert La Follette in Wisconsin. "The supreme issue, involving all the others," La Follette wrote in *La Follette's Autobiography* in 1913, "is the enrichment of the powerful few upon the rights of the many," a faith shared in the wake of the Progressive Era by governors in Iowa, Kansas, Nebraska, Indiana, Oregon, and by Charles Evans Hughes. In New York, Al Smith absorbed that faith and was its prime mover.

Defeated for reelection as governor in 1920 by Republican lawyer and fervid Prohibition supporter Nathan L. Miller, Smith sought election anew and was victorious in 1922, going on to serve three additional (two-year) terms. Although scarcely educated, he became a virtually self-taught master of Albany's legalistic legislative language and arcane procedures.

In his masterful biography of Smith's protégé Robert Moses, *The Power Broker*, Robert A. Caro writes of the Bureau of Municipal Research's 768-page report, issued in 1915.[25] Smith and everyone else could read in that detailed accounting of state government of the existence of 169 distinct agencies, departments, commissions, committees, and departments with swirling, complex strands of accountability and authority, some leading to the governor and some to the legislative bosses. (The state constitution currently limits the number of executive "departments" to twenty, although those departments have countless subdivisions and agencies within them, and innumerable public benefit corporations, public authorities, and commissions.)[26]

"The governor possessed little authority," Caro explained. "Not he, but the chairmen of the various committees of the reactionary and corrupt Legislature controlled the state's purse." Because power was essentially vested in the legislature, reformers from 1915 on understood that "more than any other single fact, [it] explained the utter failure of twenty years of effort by a succession of liberal governors such as [Theodore] Roosevelt and [Charles Evans] Hughes to increase the involvement of the state with the new needs of the people."[27]

Smith carried through the thoroughgoing reorganization of hundreds of largely unaccountable state departments and their agencies, which had acted as they wished without any control from Albany. The goal was to wrest power from what he deemed an obstructionist legislature singularly focused on patronage. Adapting the proposals of earlier reformers and the Bureau of Municipal Research study, he centralized the agencies, and allowed them to make only recommendations to the governor, who had the option of forwarding those recommendations with his budget to the legislature. In addition, the governor's term would be increased to four years. By winning elections and through constitutional amendments, Smith established eighteen state departments in all. "It was," Warren Moscow, who covered Albany for the *New York Times* for many years, wrote in his 1948 book *Politics in the Empire State*, "the most thorough renovation of a state government the nation had ever seen until then."[28]

Smith continued battling for and winning better conditions for working people, including restrictions on child labor and workmen's compensation for those suffering injuries on the job—he helped pass the state's first workmen's compensation law of its kind in 1914 and fourteen years later appointed a commission under the Moreland Act to investigate the law's administration. This son of the immigrant-packed Lower East Side ("The Brooklyn Bridge and I grew up together," he once recalled, as the epic span was being constructed practically right over his home while he was a boy[29]) was also an ardent conservationist. He also helped establish some of the first low-cost housing projects in the country, the Amalgamated Clothing Workers Union project in the Bronx and another in the vicinity of his childhood home. He secured legislative approval for equal pay for female public school teachers and persuaded the public to support bond issues on behalf of state hospitals and mental institutions. He even assigned the young Robert Moses to carry out a rehabilitation program for young prisoners. Smith did not attain his achievements easily from the largely conservative legislature. By threatening to veto all Republican appropriations bills, however, he was able to gain many of the measures he deemed vital to the progress of the state and his own political future.

True to his Progressivism, Smith was also a remarkably courageous defender of civil liberties, not merely during tranquil years but also during the post–World War I era marred by the infamous Palmer Raids and Red Scare. When socialist politicians in Albany were threatened with expulsion as "enemies of the government" in 1919 by the legislature's Lusk Committee, Smith excoriated the "false atmosphere" of vigilante justice and denounced the committee's action as "undemocratic" and "un-American." Unlike the vast majority of politicians of the time, he challenged the expulsions. And when the Lusk Committee also chose to require loyalty oaths from public school teachers, he confronted supporters of the bill, calling them "hysterical and interested in the control of liberal thought," and he promptly vetoed it. "The bill confers upon the Commissioner of Education a power of interference with freedom of opinion which strikes at the foundations of democratic education," he said.[30]

As Smith looked to leave Albany at the end of 1928, the great event in New York's political life was when the Democrats chose him to run for president against Republican Herbert Hoover that year. Franklin D. Roosevelt, not yet governor of New York, delivered the nominating speech for the Democrats, an electrifying speech. It was the first time a major political party had nominated a Catholic, much less a Catholic from New York. The shock of his campaign was not his defeat but rather the vicious anti-Catholic sentiment that surfaced among so many voters across the nation, especially in the South and the Midwest. His appearances in the American heartland were marred by cross-burnings and rallies by a resurgent Ku Klux Klan, which in the 1920s was as anti-Catholic (and anti-immigrant) as it was antiblack.

Smith died on October 4, 1944. At his funeral in New York City's St. Patrick's Cathedral, Frances Perkins remembered her old friend and colleague as "the man responsible for the first drift in the United States toward the conception that political responsibility involved a duty to improve the life of the people."[31]

In the wake of Smith's transformational reign, the governor's office grew in power to match the stature and sweep it had derived in part from Smith's gale-force energy, charisma, and willfulness. In 1927, voters passed a constitutional amendment conferring on the executive the power and obligation to introduce the budget and placed great restrictions on the legislature's ability to amend it. If there really is a moment when the stultifying "three-men-in-a-room" arrangement took root—and therefore I, as a state senator, could routinely receive the annual budget bill, hundreds of pages long, and asked to digest and vote on it with two or three hours to spare, its approval preordained—this was the moment. Legislative leaders after Smith's governorship sought at many junctures over the years to consolidate their control to offset the authority of the executive branch. Warren Anderson, whose tenure as a member of the senate overlapped the Rockefeller, Carey, and Mario Cuomo eras, stretching from the end of the 1950s to the late 1980s, said he and the assembly speaker never met alone with Rockefeller; rather, both legislative leaders brought along the chairman of the committee whose issues were on the governor's discussion agenda. "I didn't deal with only two people, and I would never deal with just the Governor alone," Anderson said in an interview for *Three Men in a Room*.[32]

Starting in the 1970s, procedures appeared that increasingly institutionalized the power of the assembly and senate leaders over their members—procedures that emphasized emergency action over slow deliberation in the wake of the disastrous New York City fiscal crisis of that decade. The crisis required emergency state legislation on an unusually fast track to keep the city from defaulting on its obligations and filing for bankruptcy protection.

In ensuing years, the legislative leaders also took greater control of the workings of their political parties, deciding which legislators would face a primaries and which ones would have an easy path to reelection or receive prestigious committee assignments, see his or her name attached to important bills, or receive generous district aid as well as campaign funds in election years. Such decisions were no longer the work of party bosses such as Charles Francis Murphy as they once had been.

The decades of drift toward centralization had still other roots. Sheldon Silver, for example, enjoyed a huge, unprecedented and unbreakable Democratic majority in the assembly throughout his two decades as assembly speaker, a ratio of two Democrats for every Republican; Joe Bruno's Republican majority in the senate was perilously puny by comparison, and Dean Skelos's was especially small. Both ample and narrow majorities have militated against democratization, as the long-serving Silver went largely unchallenged, and Bruno and later Skelos somewhat or very nervously held to the Republican Party control, as does the latest senate majority leader, John Flanagan of Suffolk County on Long Island.

In addition, the tendencies of the sitting governors have also played a role in the way that laws are enacted. When Thomas E. Dewey was governor (1942–1954), both houses were ruled by Republicans; he would call the two legislative leaders to his living room at times, where they would discuss his agenda. Mario Cuomo, for other reasons, tried to exert his influence by reaching a consensus with the two top legislative leaders, one of them a Republican and the other a Democrat. It was easier than trying to appeal to the varied and conflicting voting segments within the assembly and senate. Thus evolved over the course of a couple of generations the escalating means of control over state government held by the governor and the assembly and senate leaders.

Franklin D. Roosevelt was asked to run for governor following Al Smith's fourth and final term. He won the election by just 25,000 votes out of 2.2 million cast. Starting with his first year in power in 1929, Roosevelt battled the legislature with his pioneering use of radio talks, which would become a national phenomenon during his years in the White House. Sam Rosenman, his ever-present friend and adviser and sometime speechwriter, described how his boss proposed, in a personal appearance before the Republican-dominated legislature during the bleakest days of the Great Depression in 1931, that new taxes be enacted "to provide [poor and jobless people] with food against starvation and with clothing and shelter against suffering." His proposal infuriated conservative lawmakers and business interests. "The very foundation of the state is in danger from this message of avarice, usurpation and presumption," shouted a Republican assemblyman about Roosevelt's proposals.[33]

In time, the measures were passed because of Roosevelt's political wiles, as well as the devastating toll and social turmoil the Great Depression was exacting throughout the state. Still, legislators fought back ferociously. Vetoes and failed attempts to override followed regularly. Exasperated and furious at being denied the bills he wanted by the legislature, Roosevelt told the press that, in spite of Smith's modernization of state machinery, nothing much had changed since the time he had been in the state senate before World War I.

When Roosevelt departed Albany for Washington in 1933, the New Deal programs he would push through were built, in part, on Smith's successes and philosophy. Indeed, Roosevelt named Perkins, Smith's close adviser, as his secretary of labor, the nation's first female cabinet member. Moreover, Roosevelt once said that the goal of his administration was "to make a country in which no one is left out,"[34] a sentiment, one could argue, that was straight out of Smith, Wagner, and Perkins.

Roosevelt's successor in Albany was an extremely dedicated and popular liberal, Herbert Lehman. The historian Allan Nevins described working as a reporter for the *New York World* in Albany in those years in the preface to his book, *Herbert H. Lehman and His Era*. "Each house was usually controlled by a small group of iron-fisted leaders who kept what was euphemistically called debate under tight control," Nevins wrote, looking back in 1963. Many of the members owed their seats to lobbies and special interests. "Altogether," he concluded, "legislative Albany had its seamy aspect."[35]

Like Smith and Roosevelt, Lehman had no problem confronting a Republican-dominated legislature because it could be handily blamed for the state's problems. As a result, Lehman's relationship with the legislature was, wrote Nevins, "one of the most turbulent in the annals of the state."[36] In the 1935 session, for example, Democratic Assembly Speaker Irwin Steingut had to call in state troopers so that his loud and raucous members would not quit the assembly or cause a riot. The *New York Herald Tribune*, Republican and conservative in its editorial bent, gloated, "Legislature Ends in Row after 28½ Hour Tumult," and editorialized, "Nothing to Be Proud Of."[37] Yet as Nevins, Lehman's sympathetic biographer, noted, a long list of badly needed social legislation was enacted under Lehman's leadership, such as unemployment insurance, free milk for impoverished children, and raising the age at which children were permitted to drop out of school to sixteen; here, he followed in the footsteps of Smith at least as much as Roosevelt's New Deal response to the Great Depression. Despite opposition from the legislature, Lehman won the right to have the state join thirty-three others that had chosen to join the nascent federal Social Security Act. As governor he also forced the legislature to enact a minimum wage for female employees, added some muscle to worker's compensation laws, and, shortly before leaving Albany, helped make public housing an accepted principle by forging a bipartisan agreement, allowing the state to assume responsibility for low-income families in housing.

Though Lehman was too often deemed a plodder and poor public speaker, his legislative successes and the intense and lasting voter loyalty he inspired belied these perceived shortcomings. At the Democratic convention nominating Roosevelt for the presidency in 1932, Lehman raised the delegates to an emotional frenzy in defending Roosevelt and the hopes of containing and overcoming the Great Depression.

Thomas E. Dewey, Lehman's Republican successor, had been the crusading New York County district attorney, one of New York's most outstanding public officials and a national figure of enormous popularity and stature. He prosecuted infamous criminals such as Waxey Gordon, Lucky Luciano, Louis "Lepke" Buchalter, and the entrenched Prohibition-era district leader Jimmy Hines, ending the domination by the most notorious racketeers, murderers, and thieves who ever preyed on New Yorkers with impunity and steered the all-powerful Tammany Hall machine, the judges, district attorneys, police, and city departments. He arrived in Albany in 1943 a political moderate with libertarian sentiments and placed his political faith in state and local government and much less in the federal government. New York, he critically reasoned, had too great a reliance on the central government, a development magnified by the economic disaster of the 1930s and the coming of war.

"Life is more than unemployment, sickness and old age," Governor Dewey said. "Life is alive and vital, to be lived and enjoyed," by which he meant less power for the national government in Washington, fewer taxes, less waste in state government, and more reliance on a "vigorous and productive economic system."[38]

During his tenure, the onetime small-town boy from Owosso, Michigan, established the foundations of an effective state university system (which would eventually lead to Nelson Rockefeller's creation of a sterling network of state-supported community colleges, four-year colleges, and four major university centers), began a state thruway (since named after him). He helped pass one of the first civil rights bills in the nation, the Ives-Quinn Act, which effectively rendered racial discrimination in hiring illegal. As a result, one of the bill's supporters, Alvin Johnson, the first president of the New School for Social Research, called Dewey "a liberal without blinkers."[39] Obviously pleased, Dewey applauded Johnson as a realistic visionary "willing to wait until Monday morning if the millennium can be sure of arriving and be a little better when it comes."[40]

Overstaffing and party patronage in Albany's agencies and departments were then commonplace. According to his biographer Richard Norton Smith, Dewey learned it took twenty-nine office workers to order seventy cents' worth of glue. State employees in no-show jobs were fired. Resisting farm lobbyists, he shut down the Milk Publicity Board, "a $300,000-a-year nest of patronage jobs."[41] And possibly because of his experience as a district attorney confronting organized crime, he had a tendency to act swiftly without seeking anyone's approval (especially the legislature's) where obvious injustices were affecting the most vulnerable. Without waiting for lengthy commission hearings and copious studies, he reacted immediately when he heard from Republican state senator Seymour Halpern about dangerous conditions in Creedmoor State Hospital, a psychiatric institution housing 4,500 wards in his Queens district. Dewey followed up with a very brief inquiry, concluding that Creedmoor was a "Bastille of despair," and ordered firings and the state Mental Hygiene Department roundly censured.[42] The decision would be echoed years later in Governor Hugh Carey's legal settlement to close another long-troubled state institution, Willowbrook, on Staten Island, in recognition that it was neglecting its defenseless mentally disabled charges.[43]

Dewey turned down almost one-third of the bills passed in the legislature, reflecting a level of contentious—if not contempt—unequaled by his successors. During the last day of the legislative session in March 1944, he was appalled by the passage of an innocuous bill dealing with teachers in the New York City schools. Applying every bit of pressure he could muster, Dewey forced the assembly and senate to decisively put an end to it. Outraged, Senate Majority Leader John J. Dunnigan denounced Dewey's legislative allies in both parties. Dunnigan berated his beaten and frazzled colleagues huddled in their seats: "Who runs this legislature anyway, us or the Governor?" Victorious, Dewey smilingly called them "my Legislature."[44]

Rockefeller, Carey, and Mario Cuomo at times felt much the same way, with Carey vetoing bill after bill that arose from the legislature, sometimes just to put legislators in their place but other times for good reason, such as when the bills coming to his desk from the legislature struck him as too expensive or self-serving. Rockefeller, in particular, had little trouble keeping the assembly and senate under control. Carey's repeated conservatively low estimate of the state's projected revenues during budget talks caused so much friction with legislative leaders that they began making independent revenue estimates, creating a legacy of distrust and delays that caused the budget to be late on enactment then and in future administrations.

Dewey's successor, W. Averell Harriman, was the son of railroad tycoon Edward Henry Harriman. In 1954 Harriman chose to go to the state level after a career in national and international politics. He had been with Franklin D. Roosevelt and Winston Churchill when they drew up the Atlantic Charter in August 1941, and he later served as U.S. ambassador to the Soviet Union and Great Britain and as Harry Truman's secretary of commerce. A Democrat, he beat Thomas E. Dewey's ally, U.S. Senator Irving M. Ives in the race to run New York State. Among Harriman's worthwhile contributions as governor was trying to reform state policy concerning the mentally ill. His administration sought, with some success, to have local governments establish community-managed treatment sites with the state paying half the cost.

Harriman, like the up-and-coming Nelson Rockefeller, was born to affluence, and the parallels went further. Each man unsuccessfully sought his party's nomination for president, for example. In 1957, speaking informally to reporters covering the Albany beat, Governor Harriman told them, "There is a young man who sits among you tonight that would make the best Republican nominee for Governor: Nelson Rockefeller." He said this "jokingly," according to Robert H. Connery and Gerald Benjamin in their 1979 book, *Rockefeller of New York: Executive Power in the Statehouse.*[45] Not long after, the rising Rockefeller defeated him in the gubernatorial election, making Harriman a one-term governor. Yet Harriman may have had the last laugh, though not in the arena of state politics. After Albany, he returned to Washington and worked for John F. Kennedy and Lyndon B. Johnson in high-level posts. Rockefeller assumed the governorship in 1959, a somewhat liberal Republican in the days before Richard Nixon and Ronald Reagan and the party's sharp shift to the right. In 1966 Rockefeller decided to seek legislation against illegal drug use with a reasonably modest plan including treatment rather than automatic incarceration for addicts. Nevertheless, by 1973 contemplating a run for national office in the new landscape amid heightened voter concern about crime, Rockefeller's policy changed. He now proposed cruel, mandatory, lengthy prison sentences without parole for drug-related offenses, surprising even key members of his staff: up to fifteen years to life for those found guilty of peddling or owning more than a few ounces of a drug, usually cocaine or heroin. The sentences applied even when the perpetrators had no previous prison records or had not been convicted of a violent crime.

One lasting result was a jobs-creation program for depressed small towns in upstate New York where prisons were located and additional population for those towns, albeit as nonvoters (which Republicans could nonetheless use to create new districts in order to reassert their majority hold on the state senate, which they retained without interruption through 2008). Widely popular among a large, crime-panicked segment of the public but generally opposed by liberals, the senate supported the Rockefeller drug laws 41 to 14, and the assembly voted for them 80 to 65. The bills were signed on May 8, 1973.[46] Even with these laws in place, the drug scourge continued unabated, even worsened, and they were no match for the crack cocaine epidemic that swept urban areas of the state in the latter half of the 1980s. All the while, tens of thousands of poor, often minority, men and women were removed from their communities and incarcerated upstate, harshly and extensively, with scarce opportunities for rehabilitation.

Joseph Persico, who served for eleven years as Rockefeller's chief speechwriter—while he was governor and later when he was the nation's vice president under President Gerald Ford—said the passage of the drug laws revealed Rockefeller's dismissive attitude toward just about everyone: His "are-you-with-me-or-against-me test of loyalty," Persico called it. How, asked Persico in his biography of Rockefeller, did well-informed staff members "who knew better" remain silent and permit this "congenitally deformed scheme"—a reversal of Rockefeller's previous interest in methadone and drug treatment policies—to become law?[47]

He answered his own question in his book about his former boss. After reading what Irving Janis, a psychologist, had written about "groupthink," Persico concluded, "I never fully understood the psychological milieu in which the chain of errors in Vietnam was forged until I became involved in the Rockefeller drug proposal."[48] It was what happens when there is no one in a policymaker's inner circle willing to dissent or at least raise objections to a powerful and persuasive chief executive.

At times when Rockefeller also stumbled and failed—as during the 1971 riot at the Attica Correctional Facility, when many inmates and prison employees were killed during a prison revolt—far too many Democrats in the legislature simply looked the other way. They capitulated again when Rockefeller easily won laws favoring banking, insurance, and finance businesses. Sometimes, using power in an arrogant manner, Rockefeller managed to outmaneuver his critics in the state. New York voters elected and reelected him from 1959 to 1973, until he departed to prepare for a possible 1976 presidential bid that never came to fruition. Instead, he accepted appointment as vice president following Richard Nixon's resignation and Vice President Gerald Ford's succession to the office of president.[49] The presidency eluded him when right-wing opponents decided that he was still too liberal for the party.

His accomplishments as governor were nonetheless extensive. Small state colleges were absorbed into the prestigious State University of New York system, with excellent public universities in Albany, Binghamton, Buffalo, and Stony Brook. Smaller colleges at Brockport, Cortland, Oneonta, Plattsburgh, Purchase, and elsewhere were transformed into models of liberal arts and specialty schools. Community colleges were opened throughout the state.[50] In Albany, Rockefeller's pet project, the South Mall, later named after him, loomed forty-four stories high with four twenty-three–story towers behind it, including the Department of Motor Vehicles building, an iconic, other-worldly development, "as if Buck Rogers were creating a seat of government," one architectural critic wrote.[51]

Rockefeller also managed to revolutionize the malfunctioning Long Island Rail Road, the largest commuter railway in the nation, by pouring in money and working deals with the unions, almost overnight changing a troubled line into one of the country's finest. The Metropolitan Transportation Authority (MTA), the Urban Development Corporation, the Council on the Arts, and an extraordinary number of public authorities (many unaccountable to the legislature and extremely expensive) were some of his creations. With virtually no significant legislative opposition and widespread public backing, what Rockefeller wanted, Rockefeller got.[52]

Near the close of 1973, he departed Albany before the end of his fourth term, and the relatively little-known but knowledgeable and long-serving lieutenant governor, Malcolm Wilson, assumed the governorship in his stead on December 18, 1973. He started in the assembly in 1938, was tapped to serve as Rockefeller's lieutenant governor in 1959, and knew more than anyone about the internecine conflicts of the Capitol. He lost the 1974 election to a Brooklyn Democratic congressman, Hugh Carey, and was hardly in office long enough to make a mark. The economic problems of New York City amid a brutal national recession in the coming year became Carey's and the legislature's preoccupation, as the city's fiscal woes threatened to cause a domino effect of public-sector default.

Carey, a World War II infantry major and recipient of a Bronze Star, Croix de Guerre, and Combat Infantry Award, had served in Congress from 1961 to 1974, including service on the Ways and Means Committee, when he resigned to make his long-shot but successful bid for the Democratic nomination. He will certainly be remembered as governor for outmaneuvering his former congressional colleague President Ford and a largely anti–New York Congress in 1975 in organizing state, federal, and international support for New York City's rescue. Carey recruited competent people from the private sector, such as Felix Rohatyn, Richard Ravitch, and Peter Goldmark, to help resolve the problems of overspending, overwhelming debt, fiscal gimmickry—and the refusal of the nation's largest banks to continue making loans to the recession-battered, over-leveraged city government.[53]

Carey also recruited the eloquent and gifted Queens lawyer Mario Cuomo to state service, and pushed him to run as lieutenant governor on his ticket in his successful reelection effort in 1978. When Carey chose not to run for a third term, Cuomo ran and succeeded him as governor as of 1983. In 1987, after the start of his second of three terms, Cuomo formed a Moreland Act commission on government integrity, taking aim at what was then, as now, described as Albany's culture of corruption. The legislature's leaders, of course, resisted, contending that Cuomo's choice for the Moreland panel chairman, Joseph Califano, a prominent Democratic who had been a top deputy to President Lyndon B. Johnson and a member of President Jimmy Carter's cabinet, would focus the inquiry on the legislature, not the executive branch. Balking, too, at appropriating $5 million for the inquiry, senate and assembly leaders presented the governor with an alternative funding bill barring out-of-state residents from serving on the commission (Califano lived in Washington, D.C.).[54] It was all reminiscent of a protest that a complacent Brooklyn district attorney long ago had uttered when Mayor Fiorello La Guardia named a commission to look into Brooklyn's law enforcement apparatus, and the findings of gross malfeasance prompted Governor Lehman to name a special prosecutor, John Harlen Amen, to investigate the gangster-plagued borough: "Why pick on Brooklyn?"[55]

Cuomo acceded to the legislature's demand to rescind his support of Califano's appointment and replaced him with Fordham Law School dean and Citizens Union Foundation president, John Feerick. He struck back by vetoing a senate and assembly ethics bill with more loopholes than safeguards. A determined Cuomo, whom legislators cynically dubbed "Saint Mario," eventually forced the leaders to succumb to stronger ethics rules, and to exacerbate the situation, he added a provision for regular audits of all state agencies. The Feerick Commission operated for more than three years and put out some twenty reports. Given the absence of a sustained public outcry or interest, however, its investigative findings and insights generated little change in the Albany culture.

"In its final report to Governor Cuomo, dated September 1990, the Commission made a number of overall findings, two of which were that the laws of New York State fall woefully short in guarding against political abuses in an alarming number of areas; and that New York has not yet demonstrated a real commitment to government ethics reforms," Feerick wrote, shortly after the commission wrapped up its work. "The report concluded with the Commission urging the leaders of the State to act before the emergence of new scandals and to give ethics reforms the emphasis which they deserve."[56]

Legislative ethics battles aside, "Bring back the death penalty" was the campaign issue many politicians running for office in the Carey and Cuomo years used; both men refused, on principle, to budge. Both Carey and Cuomo were tough enough and stubborn enough to fend off the overwhelming degree of public and political opinion that favored capital punishment. Some Democrats stood by them and voted against the death penalty, as did some Republicans—Staten Island Senator John Marchi, a member of the Republican leadership, voted against the death penalty whether the governor was a Democrat or a Republican. Senator Marchi told me in one of our conversations that this was primarily due to religious convictions against taking a person's life. A similar set of beliefs animated both Carey and Cuomo.

After Cuomo was defeated for a fourth term, his law-and-order Republican successor George Pataki signed the bill reinstating capital punishment, which had been part of his campaign platform. But in 2005, a court ruling criticized the legal language of the state legislation enabling the death penalty, and the assembly—spurred mainly by black and Hispanic Democrats from New York City—blocked the restoration of alternate language the state senate championed. As a result, the death penalty disappeared from the books. Pataki's singular achievement, as he often described it, was eliminated and was never used to take a prisoner's life during his three terms of office.

Before becoming governor, George Pataki had been a relatively little-known, three-term assemblyman and one-term state senator from Peekskill, New York. He was "discovered" and groomed by Republican powerhouse and U.S. Senator Alfonse D'Amato to defeat Mario Cuomo, then running for his fourth term. The underdog Pataki won, and thus became the first Republican governor of the state in twenty years. He rode an initial wave of popularity among those voters who shared his enthusiasm for tax-cutting and longer prison sentences. He was, for many, a reassuring presence on September 11, 2001, and thereafter, though his authority as the leader of the state was eclipsed—as governors often are, at least in the media capital that is Manhattan—by the hard-charging mayor of New York City, Rudy Giuliani.

The Pataki administration successfully fought back the assembly's efforts to encroach on the executive branch's leverage over budget negotiations, with the conflict going all the way to the state's Court of Appeals. Perhaps Pataki's most enduring contribution, though, was as a guardian of the environment. However, the "three-men-in-a-room" syndrome flourished during his tenure and continued through Pataki's two successors— Eliot Spitzer and David Paterson—who were succeeded by the current governor, Andrew Cuomo, previously the secretary of the Department of Housing and Urban Development under President Bill Clinton and New York State attorney general. Andrew Cuomo is the first son of a former governor to be elected governor of New York. Unlike many other governors, Andrew Cuomo arrived in Albany as a reformer but was also schooled in the ways of the state capital and its atmosphere of intrigue and secrecy, having served as his father's most trusted confidante. Giving the eulogy at the Church of St. Ignatius Loyola in January 2015, the younger Governor Cuomo said movingly of his father, "He was humbled to be in public service and had disdain for those who demeaned it, with scandals or corruption, or cheap public relation stunts. It was a position of trust and deserved to be honored."[57]

6

The Great Gerrymander

During the past half-century, New York's governorship has changed hands eight times as a result of an election or an incumbent's resignation, with both Republicans and Democrats making the executive mansion their temporary home. At the same time, Democrats and Republicans have served as U.S. senators and representatives, state attorneys general and comptrollers, and seats in the House of Representatives have swung between both parties—all evidence that New Yorkers are at least capable of looking beyond a candidate's party label when they choose the representatives to whom they entrust the people's business. Orderly transitions from one political party to another are a hallmark of a healthy democratic system, one that is capable of shifting course to respond to new trends and challenges.

Over the same fifty years, however, New York's legislature has seen little party change at all. With little interruption over the decades, entrenched party majorities have dominated the Republican-controlled state senate and the Democratic-controlled state assembly. So it was that when *Three Men in a Room* was published in 2006, Republicans' ruling majority in the senate consisted of thirty-five seats to the Democrats' twenty-seven; that majority has fluctuated since, with Democrats controlling the senate for two unusually tumultuous years from 2009 to 2010. As of this writing, Republicans hold the barest of senate majorities with the help of a Democrat, Simcha Felder of Brooklyn, who caucuses with the Republicans. The slender Republican Party majority has further been strengthened by a coalition with the five IDC members led by Jeffrey Klein of the Bronx and including Diane Savino of Brooklyn and Staten Island, David Carlucci of Rockland County, David Valesky of Oneida County, and since he joined the IDC in early 2014, Tony Avella of Queens.[1] The coalition previously included former minority leader Senator Malcolm

Smith of Queens, until he was indicted for corruption in April 2013 and expelled from the IDC.[2] In the assembly, Democrats held a substantial margin, giving assembly Democrats a supermajority and the ability to override a governor's veto without Republican votes. In 2015 the supermajority edged upward, to sixty-one seats.[3]

Like the ebb and flow of ocean tides, the rise and fall in political party fortunes are typically thought to be natural phenomena. If so, there is something unnatural about the parties' almost uninterrupted dominance of their respective legislative chambers for decades, and that something is the way New York carries out its legislative redistricting mandate every ten years.

New York, like every other state (except Colorado and Texas, where Republican state legislative leaders have forced an additional mid-decade redistricting for blatantly partisan purposes), redraws its legislative districts following the outcome of the decennial federal census.[4] In doing so, it must comply with the requirements of the federal Voting Rights Act of 1965 and the decisions of the U.S. Supreme Court upholding the principle of "one person, one vote." Americans have always been a people on the move, and if electoral district lines were to remain fixed and unchanging while people moved in and out of electoral districts, we would soon find that some elected officials would represent more people in their district, and other officials fewer people. The result would be that voters in more populous districts of, for example, 1 million people would find their votes worth less, compared to voters who live in a less populated district comprising, say, 500,000 people. Such was the case in many legislative bodies including the New York State Senate prior to the 1964 U.S. Supreme Court case *Reynolds v. Sims*,[5] which mandated that state legislative districts must be roughly equal in population.

To make sure that every voter receives fair and equal representation in Albany, within two years of the national census each house in the New York legislature appoints a task force to determine which senate and assembly districts have gained and which have lost population. After analyzing the numbers, the task force is then supposed to recommend how district lines should be modified so that the new boundaries produce roughly an equal number of voters in each district.

That is the theory, and given the power of today's computers, entering the state's voting population data into a program and generating numerous suggested plans for districts that are contiguous and compact with similar population size should be relatively easy. In practice, however, redistricting is far more complicated, primarily because of the arrangement between the two houses of the legislature, which allows each house—and, in practice, the majority party in that house—to redistrict itself. Thus, the party in power in each chamber of the legislature can ensure that new district lines are drawn so that as many of its members as possible are likely to win reelection—and, if possible, that their majority is increased by a few members of the opposing party being defeated and replaced with one of their own members.

Allowing the ruling party in each chamber of the legislature to have the power to set district lines, however, is akin to self-dealing, and recalls the origin of the word "gerrymander." In 1811 the Democratic governor of Massachusetts, Elbridge Gerry, signed into law a bill that redrew a congressional district in his state with the intention of carving out a Democratic majority in an area long loyal to the Federalist Party. The lines of the new district were said to resemble a salamander, and a newspaper editorial cartoonist named this unusual district a "gerrymander," after the governor. This has since become a national appellation. Governor Gerry was rewarded by soon-to-be-president James Monroe by Monroe's making him the vice presidential candidate on his victorious ticket in 1816.[6] Gerry went on to serve less than two years as vice president before he died in office.

In our time, several other states, Iowa prominent among them, have handed the task of redrawing district lines to independent, non-partisan commissions. To draw both congressional and state legislative district lines, California and other western states have created independent commissions that include, in California's case, five Democrats, five Republicans, and four belonging to neither party, with panel of a state auditor selecting members from a pool of sixty nominees. To approve a redistricting plan, nine of California's fourteen members must vote for it, and the public may overturn the map, at which point the California Supreme Court must appoint a new group to draw a new map. The panel is insulated from, but not fully independent of, the politics of the state legislature. Whether independent partially or more fully, as in Iowa, the commissions and their staffs analyze factors such as census data about population shifts, Voting Rights Act requirements (to ensure minority representation), and other demographic information before recommending objective district lines. To varying degrees, the approaches are a non-partisan way to avoid conflicts of interest and self-interest in a critically important political process of the sort that characterizes New York's traditional redistricting process.[7] To my way of thinking, the more insulation from partisan manipulation, the better.

The 2000 federal census showed that some parts of New York State had gained population and other parts had lost population, making reconfiguring district lines necessary for the senate and the assembly. In 2002, using a complicated formula to set the number of state senate seats that comes from the 1894 state constitution,[8] one that is still in effect and available when it suits partisan purposes, the Republican senate majority determined that an additional seat was warranted, increasing the number of senate seats to sixty-two statewide.[9] The Republican senate majority under Joe Bruno added a majority African American Democratic seat in Brooklyn, the new Senate District 21, which Democrat Kevin Parker went on to win. This principally enabled the Republicans to reconfigure, dramatically, other district lines in Brooklyn and pave the way for then–Republican city council member Martin Golden to defeat a Democratic incumbent Vincent Gentile in a newly redrawn, more white, and Republican-friendly Senate District 22, enhancing the Republican Party's majority in the senate. My reconfigured district, formerly Senate District 22 and now Senate District 23, was pushed for the first time into Staten Island, among other changes, but it also included parts of former Senate District 22.[10] I was gratified that despite the manipulation, I was able to defeat my Republican challenger throughout the new district and even on Republican Staten Island.

A decade later, in 2012, long after I had retired from the senate, Republicans refashioned the district lines yet again to their advantage. They created a new senate seat for a Republican assemblyman in the Hudson Valley while also reconfiguring Brooklyn districts to create a safe seat for Democrat Simcha Felder, a former New York City council member, to win, knowing he had already committed to join the Republican conference in the senate and thereby improve the party's control of the body.[11] The assembly Democratic leadership acted in roughly the same manner in order to increase their total number in the chamber and ensure a veto-proof majority in their house. Might Democrats and Republicans possibly eliminate gerrymandering in either the senate or assembly on their own? Clearly the answer is no. The best possibility of eliminating this undemocratic process, I believe, is a constitutional convention, which could create an independent redistricting process and make it a part of the state's legal charter.

Up to that point, small towns in upstate New York were already the home of a large state prison population that cannot vote but that was nonetheless included in the population for the purpose of the federal census and for state redistricting. The state's 1990s prison boom—the so-called prison-industrial complex—benefits Republican upstate districts while weakening the legislative power and presence of heavily Democratic and densely populated New York City, where the majority of inmates formerly lived. About one-third of population growth upstate in the 1990s was due to the boom in prison construction. This shameless use of the prison population for politically charged redistricting purposes prompted Roland Nicholson Jr., chairman of the Fortune Society, to comment on "the resemblance between this system and early America under slavery, when a slave counted as three-fifths of a person for census purposes but had no rights whatsoever."[12] The law changed in 2010, and beginning in 2012 prisoners were counted at their last address of residence rather than at the prison address, which meant that an estimated 34,000 of the state's 60,000 prisoners were counted as residents of New York City, Long Island, Westchester County, or Rockland County rather than as upstate residents.[13]

If New York had in place a redistricting system such as Iowa's nonpartisan Legislative Services Agency, then voters in the district in which I was initially elected in 1996 might have been spared the calculated disruption that senate Republicans created, which happened soon after the decision was made to give the senate an additional seat following the 2000 federal population census.

Twenty-one states have some kind nonpartisan or bipartisan redistricting commissions, but Iowa is perhaps the most insulated from political pressures. It dates back to 1980. A nonpartisan legislative staff develops maps for Iowa's house and senate, as well as the U.S. House of Representatives districts, without any political or election data. A five-person advisory panel is also formed. The draft plan is submitted for public comment to three open meetings held around the state. A final redistricting plan is presented to the legislature for a straight "up" or "down" vote. If voted down, the process starts anew. If it fails three times, the state Supreme

Court steps in—something that has never happened, which is indicative of the system's workability.[14]

Iowa's process well appears to stand on solid constitutional ground, as the U.S. Supreme Court in 2015 upheld Arizona's bipartisan redistricting process for congressional districts, which, like Iowa's, operated outside direct legislative control or ratification. After voters approved it in 2000, members of the Arizona legislature sued to rescind it, but were unsuccessful in the nation's highest court.[15]

When drawing up districts, the Iowa process follows four principles, ranked in order of importance: equality of population in each district; contiguity; avoiding, insofar as possible, splitting city and county boundary lines while keeping its state's house districts within the state's senate districts and the state's senate districts within congressional districts; and, finally, attempting to make new districts as compact as possible. Most significantly, the Iowa statute that created this approach seeks to ensure that decisions will not be swayed by partisan interests. It forbids, for example, using voter enrollment data about party affiliation or results from previous elections when making its redistricting proposals.[16]

Conversely, in New York the legislature has drawn both congressional and state legislative district boundaries. In the absence of a nonpartisan redistricting commission such as Iowa's, the task of proposing new state senate and assembly districts in New York is the purview of the New York State Legislative Task Force on Demographic Research and Reapportionment (LATFOR). Created in 1978 following a number of court challenges that found previous redistricting plans had violated the one person, one vote guarantee of the U.S. Constitution,[17] LATFOR's structure appears to be nonpartisan. It is, however, bipartisan, and given the fact that each chamber of the New York legislature is controlled by a different political party, in this instance "bipartisan" means that each party lets the other one do as it wishes in the chamber it dominates. The primary goal of each party in redistricting, then, is to maintain and, if at all possible, increase its majority in the chamber it controls.

During my public service, using the 2000 federal census numbers, LATFOR made a pretense of seeking the public's advice before divulging its proposal about how the new sixty-two-member state senate districts should be reconfigured. Between May 2001 and March 2002, LATFOR held hearings in major cities upstate (Buffalo, Rochester, Syracuse, Albany, and Binghamton), in each of New York City's five boroughs, and in suburban Westchester and Suffolk counties. From the start, however, the outcome all but certain, and any doubt I may have had that partisan political advantage was *the* driving force behind the new lines vanished when LATFOR unveiled the senate's final redistricting plan in April 2002.

The heart of the senate district to which I was first elected in 1996 had been centered in Borough Park, Bensonhurst, Brighton Beach, Windsor Terrace, and Coney Island in Brooklyn. However, when the new senate plan was unveiled, it was patently clear that those basic, objective principles of redistricting, such as creating and maintaining compact and contiguous districts, had been completely abandoned. Borough Park was parceled among five disparate districts. Now, instead of having to deal with only one or two state senators in order to have their neighborhood's interests represented in Albany, Borough Park residents found themselves "diluted" among five state senators. Having fewer Borough Park residents in each of the new districts of roughly equal size meant, in effect, that Borough Park's voice in each district became fainter and easier to discount when its residents needed to call Albany's attention to a problem.

Not only was the Borough Park neighborhood greatly reduced as part of my district in the new plan, but the boundaries of my senate seat were also redrawn in an oddly puzzling way. Iowa requires that its state legislative districts be compact and avoid crossing county lines irrationally. My new district, however, instead of being entirely within the borough of Brooklyn, was now attached to Staten Island by a thin, four-mile-long corridor running along a highway.

Clearly, Republican members of LATFOR were primarily interested in keeping or extending their party's control of the senate. They proceeded on the basis that if compactness mattered to anyone in the new district, they simply had to file a lawsuit challenging the new lines, with the understanding that by the time the suit was heard and appealed in state and federal courts, the results of the 2002 election would be final.

No voters in Brooklyn or Staten Island sued to challenge the underlying partisan motives of LATFOR's redistricting plan. Some civic-minded citizens in Long Island's Nassau County, which had a similar problem, however, did sue, and a pretrial discovery motion exposed the blatantly political goals behind the new senate lines. At issue in the Nassau suit was the claim on the part of civil rights advocates that, under provisions of the federal Voting Rights Act, Long Island had a sufficiently compact minority population to mandate that New York State create a district in which minority voters would have an opportunity to decide the outcome of a senate election. Given that population changes throughout the state required that one or more new senate seats had to be added, thus requiring all senate district boundaries to be redrawn, this request would have been easy to accommodate.[18]

This request was not what the Republican members and staff of LATFOR intended, however. A key player in LATFOR's decisions was Mark Burgeson, an assistant to Senator Dean Skelos, who in turn owed his appointment as LATFOR's co-chairman to then–Majority Leader Joe Bruno. Skelos, first elected to the senate in 1985, was deputy majority leader, a loyal partisan, and very influential in his party. In a memo sent to Skelos in June 2001, almost a year before the new district lines were announced, Burgeson discussed the possibility that sixty-three senate seats could be created, not the sixty-two that were eventually announced. And, Burgeson noted, one option for a sixty-third senate district was to locate it on Long Island to accommodate black and Latino voters in Nassau and Suffolk counties. After having raised the prospect, Burgeson then countered: "The *only* reason to go to sixty-three," he told Skelos, "is to strengthen the Long Island delegation by combining politically undesirable areas in the extra district."[19]

When a three-judge panel of the U.S. District Court for the Southern District of New York finally issued its decision about the suit in March 2004—a year and a half after the state's 2002 elections were held—the court noted that blatantly partisan calculations had driven Burgeson's recommendation. "Plainly," the court wrote, "the political majority [that is, the Republican Party, which controls the senate] would have been strengthened in existing districts by removing voters not of that party [that is, Democrats] from current districts and placing them in a new district. However, Burgeson concluded that adding another district would have resulted in the loss of a Republican incumbent depending on how it was done, and it probably would not have provided an extra Republican seat."[20]

Nonetheless, the court, led by Chief Circuit Judge John Mercer Walker Jr., a Republican appointed to the bench by his uncle, former President George H. W. Bush, ruled against the suit, letting stand a redistricting plan that it recognized as having been distorted to serve partisan political ends. Even a coalition of clergy and community leaders who met with Senator Skelos to protest the redistricting were told that he was instructed to make no changes and make certain that a new Republican senator be elected from Brooklyn (Martin Golden) and that Democratic senator Carl Kruger, who was supporting Republicans, be given a permanently safe seat. Ten years later, Republicans did create an additional seat in the senate because they wanted to draw a district in the mid-Hudson Valley in which a sitting Republican assemblyman could win to increase Republican numbers in the senate.[21]

After serving for almost a decade in the New York Senate, and standing for and winning election five times—the last despite the attempt by the senate's Republican junta to redistrict me into defeat—it is clear to me that obsessions over party self-preservation clearly trump any and every consideration whenever decisions are made in either the senate or the assembly. Since the mandatory process of redistricting, a matter of protecting the right of voters to ensure their votes count equally, was left to a body of political appointees such as LATFOR, New Yorkers enjoyed only a pretense of democratic rights and liberties: an all-too typical Albany scenario.

Certainly LATFOR is an attempt to hide what is essentially a corrupt bargain between party bosses to let their respective legislators remain occupying powers in each chamber of the legislature. The Republicans have been in power almost continuously in the senate since 1939, and the Democrats have controlled the assembly continuously since 1974.[22] Deadlock in Albany will be broken only when redistricting is taken completely out of the hands of those who have a self-interest in the outcome—meaning partisan elected politicians and their staffs—and given to an independent, nonpartisan commission that operates with the public's interests uppermost in its mind.

The latest attempt to reform the redistricting process—as approved in a voter referendum in 2014—is slated to take effect in the redistricting after the 2020 census. It is an improvement over the previous model in that it increases the influence of the minority-party leader of each chamber and thus, in theory, dilutes the control traditionally exerted by the assembly speaker and senate majority leader in the process. However, the new approach leaves intact and institutionalizes the partisan role of the legislature—and in a top-down system, that of the assembly speaker and the senate majority leader. It also allows the legislature to substitute its own lines for those drawn by a new ten-member (as opposed to the former six-member) redistricting commission.[23]

Granted, as proponents such as the League of Women Voters of New York State noted, the legislature may only decide on the commission's plans by a simple yes or no vote, and the legislature must reject two separate sets of redistricting plans before it will be able to amend the broadened redistricting commission's proposals. Also, all districts will be required "to preserve minority rights, be equally populated, and consist of compact and contiguous territory," while state law will require that districts "not be drawn to discourage competition or to favor/disfavor candidates or parties."[24]

While all of that is laudable, envisioning that the fierce instincts for partisan advantage and political self-preservation will yield to such noble intents, given the recent history of blatant manipulation that I experienced, is all but impossible, at least to me.

My hope is New York will one day follow Iowa's lead, or at least take the significant steps toward fair, nonpartisan redistricting that California established in 2008. Because New York's leaders never voluntarily loosen their control, this important measure of progress could well require a constitutional amendment ratified by the voters of the state after being recommended by a constitutional convention or passed in consecutive legislative sessions. Both are difficult to accomplish. The most promising path to change—given the legislature's intransigence—is a state constitutional convention, which would propose constitutional amendments to go before the voters without the legislature's approval. Anything less than the creation of a truly independent, nonpartisan redistricting process will leave the citizenry where it stands today—deprived of competitive elections for their state representatives, and their democracy relegated to the decisions of the few.

7

Lobbyists and Legislators Gone Wild

Many New York legislators I came to know were decent and conscientious. They suffered unfairly from the low esteem in which the public generally holds politicians due to the actions of a minority of them. While a sizable collection of New York State legislators and their top staff people have been neither ethical nor conscientious (since the early 2000s more than one in seven who have left office were thought possibly to be involved in something illegal or criminal), judging all legislators by the actions of a few is hardly fair. The public and press, however, often treated us as guilty until proven innocent. It was true then and remains true today for those who brave the arena of politics and public service.

It is not human foible but rather the way the system works that chiefly offends my sensibilities. On and on, year after year, Albany's processes and practices have continued in ways that obscure how money is spent and how patronage jobs are handed out, short-circuit debate and public input, and allow a very few influential people to make the decisions.

The peculiar mechanisms of Albany, not readily obvious to constituents back home, first struck me in my freshman year as senator when one day I began a conversation with two state Capitol security guards. The gray-haired gentlemen were retired state troopers stationed in the massive building. Both stood ramrod straight in a stone hallway under the towering, vastly impressive ceiling. At the end of our chat, just to be friendly and respectful, I asked them for their names.

"I'm Jack, and he's John, Senator," one said.

"Since you identified yourselves by your first names, please call me Seymour, not Senator."

"Yes, Senator," they replied, almost in unison.

The following day, one of my colleagues, who overheard part of the conversation, told me that if the pair had called me Seymour, as I preferred, rather than Senator, and if that their supervisor discovered this, it could have jeopardized their jobs.

Not even a legislative staff member, I subsequently learned, was permitted, under senate tradition, to call a senator by his or her first name or even last name. When my staff assistants and I wanted to have a confidential talk in Albany, we had to close the door to be able to call one another by our first names (needless to say, we trusted one another implicitly, and there were certainly no worries about anyone secretly wearing a wire). If we met on the senate floor, however, amid the rows of plush leather chairs, my assistants referred to me, formally and stiffly, as Senator Lachman.

Still, one initial member of my staff, whom I considered a friend, turned to me on the floor of the senate without much thought and said, "Hey, Seymour, *whaddaya* think of this?" Hearing the outburst, one of my colleagues in the senate, a Democrat who was known for berating personal staff and requiring them to run personal errands, demanded to know the staff member's name—and to receive an apology. I did not oblige her.

As this anecdote shows, New York senators are made to feel they are very powerful. Some accept this, which can sometimes transmute into arrogance and misuse of power. Initially, I also went along with this, but the forced pretense of importance is actually just one of the ways house leaders use to manage all of their members. Legislators enjoy the perquisites, and the all-important illusion of power. All sorts of inane rules of conduct protect their place in the hierarchy.

The reality, though, is that most individual state senators and assembly members have little power. They must invariably bend to the whims of their chamber's leaders in order to preserve or enhance their member items, office supplies, staff allocation, official automobiles, and committee assignments. They are expected to do their part as agreed and, as part of that agreement, to be addressed only by their formal title, whether privately or in the presence of others.

There has long been a high degree of institutional adherence in Albany to this sort of artifice, and, as it sometimes follows, corruption bred of arrogance. That is more damaging to the character of legislators, even the well-intentioned, and to the state as a whole than many voters may realize.

The root problem in the Capitol, though, begins and ends with money to a greater degree than one might suspect even in this especially corrupt and cynical era in the history of state and national government ("A Wealthy Few Lead in Giving to Campaigns," read an August 2, 2015, *New York Times* front-page headline, referring to the presidential primaries).[1] To see the problem in the context of state politics, one must consider the question of fundraising, the primary preoccupation of politicians who wish to remain on the public payroll.

One winter's night in February 2005, the Republicans who run the state senate and the Democrats who preside over the assembly convened separate fundraisers in the very same Albany hotel. The fundraisers were in adjoining ballrooms.

This was just perfect for the lobbyists and their clients who exist because of the system in Albany, since many could cross the invisible partisan divide without having to get in their cars. Indeed, to show their love for the legislators of both political parties, they just walked their checkbooks from the New York State Senate Republican Committee fete hosted by then–Majority Leader Joe Bruno to the adjoining event hosted by Assembly Speaker Sheldon Silver. A statehouse-based reporter, Michael Cooper, who covered the accidentally—yet conveniently—conjoined events in an article for the *New York Times*, wrote, "The fact that it was Valentine's Day did not keep many big names away from the two parties."[2]

Alexander "Pete" Grannis, estimable former Manhattan Democratic assemblyman, was just as sardonic on the topic of lobbyist access. He had long been critical of Albany's tradition of holding hundreds of fundraisers a year and typically convening them while the legislature was in session—an ethically slippery slope that twenty-seven states, but not New York, had banned or limited by the time I was serving in Albany. Grannis whimsically suggested there be more joint fundraisers and that they be held in the basement complex of the Capitol building itself, already the site of annual trade fairs. "Each member would have a booth," he told Cooper. "It would be easier for the lobbyist, easier for the member, better for the waistline."[3]

The legislature started its session that year—2005, shortly after I gave up my seat—by passing a few minor reforms. One of them required, for the first time, that the lobbying of state agencies be public instead of secret, as had been the case for as long as I was in Albany and for as long as anyone there could remember. Obviously, this relatively minor reform was long overdue. New York State had more registered lobbyists per legislator—a ratio of 18 to 1—than any other state in the country, according to a Center for Public Integrity report that year.[4] I am sure, ten and eleven years later, that this dubious distinction lives on. Gifts and honorariums that lobbyists gave to lawmakers were barely restricted until early 2006, when the lobbyists had to make sure that any single gift was under $75, though that could mean a $74.99 breakfast, $74.99 lunch, and $74.99 dinner, all in the same day. Like this measure, the state requirement that lobbyists registered with the state was merely a tentative first step; it failed to interrupt the galloping influence of the special interests, which use lobbyists, campaign cash, campaign finance loopholes, and personal access to the Big Three who make the big-money decisions for their industries and businesses. When necessary, many can, and do, hire former aides to the legislative leaders to smooth access to them. Sheldon Silver's former top aide, Patricia Lynch, became a highly successful lobbyist, as did former Democratic Speaker Mel Miller, former state Republican Party chairman Bill Powers, and Bruno's son, Kenneth—though he eventually gave up working as a lobbyist for a more gainful job.[5] Working in a lucrative field, they and other former aides and officeholders were able to be helpful to those with a financial stake in the outcome of public policy, enriching their clients as well as themselves through their experiences, contacts, and close ties to the highest levels of the government.

In the decade I spent in the state capital, the number of lobbyists working the halls and parties more than doubled to approximately 4,000 individuals. The amount of money that New York State lobbyists were paid more than quadrupled in that period to more than $150 million annually, which was one of the highest statehouse lobbying windfalls in the nation. Consider the pharmaceutical industry alone. It was just one of many sectors whose companies poured millions into lobbying and contributions to legislators anticipating the time their help was needed to promote, stall, or defeat measures of special interest to them. The industry's ability to sway the legislature through lobbying and campaign largesse may help to explain why Medicaid costs in New York, with a population of approximately 19 million, far exceeded those of every other state, including California's, with a population of approximately 35 million. Fraud and waste were also excessive in New York, abetted by lack of political will to oversee Medicaid spending.

Proposals to open casinos or allow hydraulic fracturing also open the way for thousands of dollars of campaign contributions and increased lobbying by labor unions and private companies, as do periodic debates over rent regulations, real estate industry tax breaks, benefits of public schools versus charter schools, and transportation issues.

At the same time, more and more lobbying firms have attempted to influence the Democratic assembly and the Republican senate by becoming bipartisan, hiring former leaders of both parties. For me, reporter Greg B. Smith's July 23, 2005, *New York Daily News* article reflects their continued critical importance. The article describes a development team that included a former aide to Governor Pataki and a major donor to his campaigns and its push to build luxury condos in Brooklyn. The team included Thomas Murphy, former head of the state Dormitory Authority, and the insurance company AIG, which had donated $100,000 to Pataki in the past three years, according to the story.[6]

Along with developer Robert Levine, the group planned to build 450 condos at 360 Furman Street on the Brooklyn waterfront, inside a park eventually to replace state-owned piers and warehouses. "The state says the condos will help pay for the new park, but neighbors are baffled by the lightning-quick pace of development of a taxpayer-backed park they say will serve as landscaping for affluent condo owners," wrote Smith.[7]

Said one Brooklyn Heights resident quoted in the piece, "This is everything we fought against, this whole idea of getting housing." And a member of the Cobble Hill Neighborhood Association said that the net effect of the state's plan was to replace recreational areas that would serve the general public with landscaping "meant to sell apartments."[8]

It was the Pataki-controlled Economic State Development Corporation, or ESDC, the agency building the project, that had first proposed legislation in April 2005 that made the condominium plan part of the agency's planned Brooklyn Bridge Park, according to Smith's account. "The agency said it believed the bill was necessary because the area is zoned for commercial use only," he wrote, adding that the development team hired Murphy to lobby for the legislation. Murphy worked for the lobbying firm run by Bill Powers, the former head of the state Republican Party who had been instrumental in Pataki's first gubernatorial victory in 1994.[9]

The assembly in April 2005 passed the bill, making 360 Furman Street part of a state park. The state senate added its approval that June. Heightening the sense of a community not involved in the process, reporter Smith noted that the development property was owned by New York–based AIG in partnership with developer Levine. AIG donated $40,000 to Friends of Pataki on March 29, 2004, days before the state revealed it was in talks with Levine about the Brooklyn condo plan.[10]

It was all legal, of course. In Albany, it is how business is conducted.

Ten years later, a May 9, 2015, article by the same reporter opened this way: "To understand the connection between Albany corruption and the New York City real estate industry, take a look at Hampton Court, a new luxury condo building on East 102nd Street in Manhattan."[11]

This 230-unit building would have incurred $2.74 million in property taxes for 2014, but a property tax break under the 421-a program, the major tax abatement program created in the recession-battered 1970s to spur affordable, multiunit housing development, allowed its owner to owe just $91,567 in property taxes. This fortunate owner was Glenwood Management, the real estate developer that had been in the middle of the cases that took down Sheldon Silver and Dean Skelos.[12] Pointing to the long-established 421-a tax break, U.S. Attorney Preet Bharara said in the complaint against Skelos that Glenwood's "business model depends in substantial part on favorable tax abatements and rent regulations that must be periodically renewed" in Albany. Press reports had identified the firm, listed in the Skelos complaint as "Developer 1," as Glenwood Management.[13]

The watchdog group Reinvent Albany commented in Smith's article that the 421-a program, which the legislature renewed along with rent-increase limits in 2015 budget negotiations after the controversial shutdown of Governor Cuomo's Moreland Commission, had become a catalyst for political corruption. Susan Lerner of Common Cause New York described the longtime tax-break program as an example of "the state Legislature giving away city taxpayer money to real estate development corporations." Glenwood, while not charged with any wrongdoing, was one of the largest recipients of the 421-a tax benefit for dozens of buildings across New York City. Prosecutors maintained in the indictment of Skelos that the now-convicted former majority leader regularly supported legislation that Glenwood sought, including bills extending and amending 421-a. Meanwhile, in the Silver indictment, Glenwood was described as a client of a relatively little-known law firm that allegedly gave the former assembly speaker millions of dollars in alleged kickbacks. From 2000 to 2015, Glenwood legally channeled more than $12.8 million in legal contributions to leading Albany elected officials of both parties through numerous LLCs.[14]

In this overheated atmosphere, where heavy campaign contributions and extensive lobbying are coordinated, imagine the odds facing one legislator's thought-provoking proposal in 2014 affecting the real estate industry. The proposal called for a tax surcharge on pieds-à-terre worth over $5 million that are the properties of foreign buyers and other non-city residents who pay no income taxes and, due to exemptions as well as the city's outdated tax code, incur low property taxes. A Democratic senator from the West Side of Manhattan, Brad Hoylman, based the bill on an analysis by the nonprofit Fiscal Policy Institute. The think tank estimated that such a surcharge could generate as much as $665 million a year for the city's coffers, money that could be used, perhaps, to help create affordable housing for low- to moderate-income people currently struggling to maintain their homes in an increasingly gilded metropolis where gentrification and displacement are common concerns.

"A lot of these individuals are using New York as a tax haven," Hoylman told *Crain's New York Business*, referring to nonresident investors in Manhattan luxury real estate. Hoylman contended that the surcharge, if enacted, would "bring New York in line" with other global-crossroads cities that have established similar tax levies, citing London as one of them, adding, "This isn't viewed as punitive." He contended that many economically hard-pressed, hard-working New Yorkers would support it.[15]

Of course, the powerful real estate sector, and Albany itself, was not as enthused. For reasons that can be guessed but never fully known, the bill was soon swallowed up by the compromised Capitol, its relative merits and shortcomings never subjected to a committee hearing, a floor debate, or a vote in either chamber. Despite a flurry of media coverage, it faded away.[16]

As in any statehouse, money and lobbyists lubricate the Capitol, but far more business is conducted in New York's statehouse than in perhaps any other. During the 2013 Moreland Commission's investigation of the state government, the case of a lawyer who was pushing a bill in Albany for a client was explored. The lawyer advised the client in an email that an active capital lobbyist "strongly suggests a contribution" to a particular elected official because "the ball is in the hands of the assembly and [the elected official] has a lot of say" on a bill of special interest to the client.

The attorney followed up with another email to this business client, stating that while the elected official had indicated he might support the legislation, it was advisable to continue making campaign contributions because he—the attorney—was a "believer in not counting the chickens until they hatch, as well as knowing from experience with the NYS Legislature it is not over until the fat lady sings."[17]

Access to lawmakers can be expensive. Former U.S. Senator Alfonse D'Amato, who plucked George Pataki from relative obscurity and drove him to statewide victory over Governor Mario Cuomo in 1994, was paid $500,000 by a business client in 1999 for making a single lobbying phone call to the MTA, which helped his client secure a loan of $230 million from the agency to continue building its new headquarters in Manhattan. At the time, the building project had fallen behind schedule and was plagued by millions in cost overruns.[18]

Though the agency's inspector general found nothing illegal, the scenario was about as cozy as it gets, even in a state where upward of $120 million a year was then being spent on lobbying state government and local governments of New York (a figure that would rise to $205 million in 2012 according to JCOPE).[19] D'Amato was Pataki's political mentor and ally, and Pataki as governor had of course a substantial measure of control of the MTA, and the state-run agency's executive director, Katherine Lapp, was Pataki's former coordinator of the Division of Criminal Justice Services.

Albany's response to the public's evident dismay over the $500,000 phone call was ultimately a nonresponse. Investigative reporter Wayne Barrett recalled the lobbying scandal in a June 14, 2015, op-ed piece for the *New York Daily News*.[20] As he wrote, the senate seemed poised, in the wake of the revelations about D'Amato's well-placed phone call, to approve a Republican-backed bill to strengthen Albany lobbying disclosure requirements. But "at the last minute" the senate quickly offered an alternate bill with language waiving strengthened disclosure in situations in which the lobbying concerned "vendor disputes"—the issue linked to D'Amato's half-million-dollar fee.[21] The measure further required that the legislature's ethics review mechanisms would be required to demonstrate "intentionality" before moving to penalize a lobbyist for doing something unacceptable. In the end, the bill's emergence helped keep the senate from reaching an agreement with the assembly, which had passed its own bill.[22]

The message? Given the tight orchestration of both chambers, voters without the capital—political or financial—to hire an enormously influential former U.S. senator for access to leading decision makers, are out of luck and left with no information. So are the rest of the legislators, who usually have to read the morning newspapers or check Google to try to find out what is going on and who are handed complex bills to vote on with just hours before the predetermined voting. In my time, legislators' ignorance of the contents of bills on which they were asked to vote was striking, and little has changed since then. We were lucky when we had two days to read hundreds of pages of a piece of legislation. We were expected to give our approval without having thought much about the legislation in an environment where people were only allowed to refer to us deferentially.

Senator Liz Krueger of Manhattan tells the story of approaching the Republican leadership in the senate in 2003 with enough formal commitments, or buck slips, from Republicans for a bill that would require health insurers to cover mental health services for children. The bill, Timothy's Law, was named for a twelve-year-old boy who killed himself after his cash-strapped parents could not afford his drug treatment and counseling. It was modeled after similar coverage available in thirty other states. The leadership refused to carry it, heeding the interests of the insurance companies. Indeed, just one man, Majority Leader Joe Bruno, prevented it from ever reaching committee for debate or a floor vote. The Democrats in Albany, Krueger noted, had been supportive of such legislation for years.[23]

As she remembered, "I went into the doghouse for twelve months, and I can tell you, it's not a good place to be." None of her bills were allowed in the wake of the legislative episode, nor were member items allocated to her district. She became almost an outcast for daring to go against Bruno. "Alice in Wonderland" was how she characterized the experience, and it understandably left her feeling more resolved to work the electoral system with other Democrats to eliminate the Republicans' majority hold on the senate in the coming years and try to create a fully Democratic-led legislature.[24]

A long tussle over the composition of the senate Democratic conference leadership in 2002 reflects, in another way, the counterproductive character of Machiavellian Albany. It is also why I continue to believe that reformist energies need to go into ending legislative members' powerlessness—the root cause of widespread irresponsibility—as well as redistributing the leaders' powers throughout their chambers. Bringing vastly more sunlight and disclosure must also be reformers' immediate goals, rather than aiming to put Democrats into the majority position in the senate by electoral means in an effort to achieve the objectives.

I initially supported the efforts that year of the incumbent Senate Minority Leader, Democrat Martin Connor, to remain in power. Indeed, I gave Connor my word only after then–Senator David Paterson of Manhattan himself telephoned me at home on a Friday and told me—for motives I did not know and could not discern—that he was not seeking this significant Democratic post, he was really interested in supporting Connor instead, and he advised me to do the same.

At the time, it was rumored that Paterson was seeking the post himself. "Don't believe it, it's not true," Paterson, who was the deputy minority leader of the senate, told me. "I am supporting Senator Connor for the leadership." I asked Paterson, to whom I felt close personally and professionally: "David, are you saying I should support Connor?" He replied, "Absolutely."

Over the weekend, I received phone calls from many people, including then–Manhattan Democratic Senator Eric Schneiderman, asking me to support what they said was *Paterson's* push to seize control of the Democratic leadership post in the senate—all in the name of reforming the legislature. A donnybrook was getting under way, despite Paterson's assurances to me to the contrary. Schneiderman called, as did other important politicians, to seek my vote for Paterson, saying the vote was going to be close and if I could help put Paterson over the top, it would be helpful to my future in Albany. He intimated that I would be in line for a more influential position under new leadership.

I had already pledged my support to Connor at the recommendation of Paterson. I felt, as a matter of my own sense of integrity and not out of any limited political alliance I might have had with Connor at various junctures—he had represented Brooklyn in the state senate since 1978— that I could not easily go back on my word at that advanced stage. Besides, I believed I had been misled by the very man whom Albany's reform-minded newer legislators, including Schneiderman and Liz Krueger, were supporting. Also among the earliest supporters of Senator Paterson was Senator Carl Kruger, whom Senator Connor had threatened with expulsion from the Democratic conference because he had supported the candidacy of Republican Martin Golden, the former city council member who had gained a senate seat with the help of Republican senate leaders' gerrymandering.

I mentioned to Schneiderman (who would go on to become the state's attorney general in 2011) that I had spoken with Paterson on Friday, and what he had told me. Why had Paterson not called me back to say he was in fact seeking the post? Schneiderman responded that the situation had become increasingly difficult.

Not good enough, I said. Nor was I interested any longer in a promotion or perks.

Paterson finally called me on Tuesday. He said my vote was important to him now. Most of Connor's allies in our party had fled to Paterson as soon as they sensed Connor had encountered difficulties. I did, too, with some reluctance because of the process some of my colleagues used. This was a day before the Queens County Democrats, who had originally committed to Connor, switched their allegiance to Paterson because their support would likely make Paterson the winner. Before I did so—if only to salvage what was left of my pride—I called Connor to let him know of my change of mind. I felt that a vote for Connor at that point would have done nothing but consign me to irrelevancy for the rest of my tenure. However, I also believed that Paterson would be more inclusive and collegial than Connor, and I had always been closer to Paterson than to Connor. More senior colleagues later informed me that Connor had used similar tactics to defeat then–Deputy Minority Leader Emanuel Gold when they were both running to succeed then–Minority Leader Manfred Ohrenstein.

Depressed because he had been outmaneuvered, Connor told me that I was the only senator who had given him the courtesy of a warning and explanation. The rest had simply deserted.

I was not exactly left in good standing with the triumphant pro-Paterson legislators. Most of them, I suspect, got behind him because, at least in part, they believed that the Democrats could do things better than the Republicans if only they could one day take and hold control of the senate, thereby controlling both houses in Albany. While that partisan goal was understandable from their point of view, and perhaps was seen as realizable before the next redistricting scheduled for 2012, it is deep structural change that is so desperately needed in Albany, and it is the only thing that is capable of making a meaningful difference, regardless of which party has the majority. No leader in either party will voluntarily give up control—and it is the mandatory ceding and dispersal of their power that is required. I began thinking of a constitutional convention as early as then as constituting the best way of bringing about substantive reform of the legislature.

I have no doubt that the reformers wanted to see the legislature changed. It was only their strategy to try to win control for the Democrats that I quarreled with. It should be noted that other strategies, too, were pursued to empower the ordinary lawmakers vis-à-vis their legislative leaders. The late Assemblyman Thomas Kirwan of Newburgh, along with Senator Liz Krueger, deserve great credit for suing Governor Pataki and the leaders of both houses, along with a third coplaintiff, the Urban Justice Center in Manhattan. Though unsuccessful, their previously mentioned, bipartisan lawsuit of 2005—Kirwan was a Republican and former state police officer and Drug Enforcement Agency officer, and Krueger a Democrat and former antipoverty advocate—charged that the rules and practices of the two legislative bodies made a mockery of state and federal constitutional principles by denying minority-party representatives (Democrats in the senate like Krueger and Republicans in the assembly like Kirwan) a "fair opportunity" to represent their constituents and allow the voices of their constituents to be heard. In a word, they were effectively disenfranchised.[25]

The lawsuit's complaint pinpointed a central problem: hypercentralization of power in the hands of the majority-party leaders of each chamber, of which lack of disclosure in lobbying, campaign contributions, and legislative deal-making were all convenient handmaidens. As Greg David of *Crain's New York Business* summed it up years later, "New York State is hopeless because legislators are powerless."[26]

"In New York," the complaint against the Big Three correctly asserted, "the Speaker and Majority Leader effectively control the funds available for each member's staff. In addition, they control the members' use of office space. The Speaker and Majority Leader also effectively control each member's necessary expenses, such as computers, mailing and printing costs for newsletters, and travel reimbursements. They even have the power to sensor a member's newsletter. The majority party leadership also imposes content restrictions on minority members' publications as a condition to funding the printing and postage of such publications, in an effort to deter vigorous debate of legislation."[27]

The suit continued: "The Speaker and Majority Leader make more funds and resources available to members who are members of the majority party, than to members of the minority party who have equal responsibility. The differences in stipends and other resources are gross and are not reasonably related to differences in need, but rather related solely to differences in party enrollment. They are adopted with the purpose, intent, and effect of punishing constituents who elected a representative in the Assembly who is a Republican or a representative in the Senate who is a Democrat."[28] Although the suit was eventually dismissed because courts are reluctant to get involved in the internal operations of the legislative branch, the trial court noted, "studies and newspaper editorials describe New York's Legislature as 'dysfunctional,' and as the worst state legislature in the country."[29] The issues that Krueger and Kirwan raised in this case remain problems to this day. Kirwan lost his seat by a narrow margin of fifteen votes in 2008 though he later regained it. Sadly, he passed away in 2011.[30]

In the late 1980s a series of major scandals centered on New York's city hall under Mayor Ed Koch led to the formation of a state panel of experts appointed to investigate the issue, which demanded and helped bring about numerous permanent and powerfully effective structural reforms.

"In our view," the New York State Commission on Government Integrity, the Moreland Commission chaired by Fordham's John Feerick, said in response to the "city for sale" scandals involving payoffs to elected officials, and state and city dollars, "the leaders of both major parties have failed the citizens of New York by not insisting upon much-needed ethics reforms. . . . Instead, partisan, personal and vested interests have been allowed to come before larger public interests."[31] And much was done, not least of it the creation, through a public referendum, of a model campaign finance system for city elections only, one of the strongest and most effective in the country. New York State did not, however, follow the city's important lead.

In Albany, as I found out in my time and have observed since I left, repeated scandals with recurring patterns, and many inquiries and reports that result from a particularly scandal-ridden period, have little impact on transactional business-as-usual. In the fevered competition for contracts and legislation to benefit individuals, unions, organizations, industries, and other interest groups, Albany puts up few obstacles to prevent conflicts of interest, favoritism, and legal or illegal bribes.

The system continues to let the campaign money flow from moneyed, organized interests with few impediments or rules. It often rewards the most generous givers, which, closer to my tenure, included in part the 450 PACs that contributed more than $13.5 million in 2004, with half of that total coming from just sixteen PACs, the organizations that usually spend their money on advertisements, mailers, canvassing, wages, and polling. The impact of the 2010 U.S. Supreme Court decision in *Citizen United* and other court decisions has made the situation even less equitable and small donors comparatively less important. The so-called independent expenditure committees currently may raise and spend unlimited funds as long as they do not coordinate their spending directly with particular candidates or campaigns.

In the 2014 election cycle in New York State, PACs poured in $17.8 million, with about $14 million designated to races that could decide the majority party in the closely contested state senate. As reported by Capital New York (now Politico New York), the PACs included entities such as Jobs for New York, an extension of the powerful Real Estate Board of New York; Balance New York, operated by members of the senate Republican Campaign Committee and funded by the Republican State Leadership Committee in Washington, D.C.; New Yorkers Together, linked to the Communication Workers of America, a union allied with Democrats; Friends of Democracy, largely funded by Jonathan Soros, son of liberal donor George Soros; and the New York League of Conversation Voters PAC.[32] As the Albany *Times Union* wrote of the $17.8 million in PAC spending in 2014, "Too much of that money comes from shadowy entities—many of them based out of state—that hide behind post office boxes and names like 'Common Sense Principles.'" Still other PACs tied to the state teachers union; the health-care workers union; and trade groups for lawyers, physicians, and insurers have long been part of the fray, joined of late by environmentalists, hydraulic fracturing proponents, the gambling industry, charter school advocates, and many other interests with typically specialized, narrow agendas.[33]

Independent spending is hardly limited to traditional PACs. A plethora of organizations whose funders are not publicly known have proliferated along with SuperPACs since the U.S. Supreme Court's 2010 *Citizens United* decision. Some of them support elected officials, while most do the bidding of special-interest donors who remain hidden from the public. As the Brennan Center for Justice argued in its 2016 report *Secret Spending in the States*, strong lobbying, campaign finance, and disclosure laws, along with rigorous enforcement of those laws, are needed to reduce the influence of these moneyed interests.[34]

While corporate contributions are barred from federal elections as well as those in New York City, there seems to be no limit for businesses that seek to influence New York State's elections. True, a state law theoretically restricts corporations to aggregate contributions of $5,000 per calendar year, but corporations can get around the cap by establishing subsidiaries to give contributions. During my tenure, I also observed that numerous legislators, both Democratic and Republican colleagues, ignored the rules for ethical conduct by accepting free travel and other gifts from lobbyists and interest groups.

Additionally, corporate entities also lavish the party organizations' so-called housekeeping accounts with donations, which can be embarrassing, such as when some of the donors' money was paying the $50,000 annual salary of a personal assistant, food shopper, and an actual housekeeper for then–Governor Pataki's wife, Libby, as *New York Post* state editor and columnist Fredric Dicker reported in early 2005.[35] There are no limits to the amount an individual, group, or corporation can give to political organizations' housekeeping accounts, which are supposed to be used only for noncampaign expenditures. The state Board of Elections says that these checks are only to be used to maintain a party's headquarters and staff or to conduct "ordinary activities that are not for the express purpose of promoting the candidacy of specific candidates." The requirements for reporting these kinds of political contributions are lax and not precise, however; voters have difficulty finding out how the cash is being spent. "That, of course, is what makes these accounts so wildly popular with both contributors and recipients," an October 2011 *New York Times* editorial noted, advocating that housekeeping donations be abolished.[36]

The system for keeping track of direct contributions to candidates is also capable of frustrating the reformer's goal of transparency because the Board of Elections' centralized database on campaign donations was, for many years, not searchable and still only includes the campaigns of candidates for state, not local, offices. This afforded politicians and their campaign contributors an untoward degree of privacy. When Common

Cause New York and NYPIRG tried to follow the money back in 2003, they found that ninety-six companies had, intentionally or not, gotten away with topping the $5,000 annual corporate cap by disbursing their contributions throughout the state. One engineering company wrote $17,646 in checks disbursed to sixty-five election committees. A firm in Nassau County spread $18,575 among twenty-one election committees. The Board of Elections could not keep up.[37]

What did the state Board of Elections do after it received the report by the good-government groups? It began to investigate, but then dropped the matter, citing lack of staff. The legislature did nothing to address the shortage.[38]

In part because following the money is so difficult, the issue of campaign finance tends to arouse little public outcry. "Pay-to-play" arrangements, in which money is exchanged for favorable treatment by elected and other public officials, are after all based on tacit understandings. If you want a state agency or a state elected official to return your phone call or consider your request for a state contract, a regulatory change, or a piece of legislation, you make a contribution of some significance to an incumbent, show up at a campaign fundraiser, or hire the right lobbyist, lawyer, or consultant. While, as noted, lobbyists' gifts to state lawmakers were restricted to a maximum of $75 per year starting in early 2006, contributors' donations were not. I recall that a prominent physician who had contributed $250 to my campaign wanted to donate the same amount to the assembly speaker's campaign fund; he was told by a mutual friend of ours to add an extra zero and make it $2,500 if he wanted to have any input at all with the speaker.

"The loopholes and soft money contributions are the dark side of New York's political system," a *New York Daily News* editorial pointed out more than a decade ago, in a complaint often reprised in the years since. "The public may clamor for reform, but if the big money boys balk, reform dies aborning."[39]

If anyone still thinks that the fault lies with either party alone, and not equally with both of them, consider that the senate has long viewed the cash-flush doctors' lobby as their client. The assembly, meanwhile, has looked on personal-injury lawyers as theirs. Before his conviction in November 2015, Speaker Silver was "of counsel" to one of the state's largest personal injury law firms in the state. Former governor Pataki had scrambled those long-standing arrangements by handing the state's largest, and traditionally Democratic, health-care workers union a raise during his 2002 reelection campaign, depriving his Democratic opponent, state Comptroller H. Carl McCall, of the union's normally expected political support. The cost of the low-paid workers' raise to taxpayers exceeded $1 billion, and came during a decline in the state's budgetary strength. The raise also came as a surprise to most, lacking legislative input or public debate.

Neither party, moreover, really believes in fair and competitive legislative elections, evidenced by the unbridled, poorly tracked influence of campaign money, year after year. Why did Governor Pataki insist on listing campaign contributors in his campaign finance filings alphabetically by first names instead of by surnames?[40] Why, for that matter, did Governor Andrew Cuomo keep under wraps the donors to his Committee to Save New York, which raised money to advance his policy agenda, a maneuver that drew strong criticism from good-government groups.[41] In their own way and for reasons only known to each of them, both governors made following their financial backing more challenging for good-government groups, journalists, and the public. Fortunately, the outcry was loud enough, and once these divisive tactics became well-known, Pataki switched to listing by surname and Cuomo redirected donors to the state Democratic organization.

To a striking extent, the voters over many decades have been left without information as a result of many factors, including the state's meaningless campaign contribution limits; easy transfers from one political committee to another; mushrooming campaign fundraising during the legislative session; late, limited, or deliberately scrambled disclosure of contributors; poor enforcement by the lackluster and low-staffed Board of Elections; the frequent use of campaign donations for junkets, country club memberships, flowers, swimming pool covers, and even cat food and trips to the veterinarian (as *Newsday* reported in 2000);[42] growing influence of lobbyists (who spent a record $140 million lobbying the legislature in 2004); and a lopsided reliance on special interests for election funds. It shocked even some seasoned politicians when it was discovered in the summer of 2005 and the winter of 2006 that several *former* elected officials were still using their campaign funds for personal items such as car payments, meals, and cell phones. Campaign funds are often used to pay the *legal* tabs of state lawmakers fighting allegations of wrongdoing, another dubious category of campaign spending. A *New York Times* examination of the spending of forty-one elected officials who were linked to a scandal or investigation sometime between 2005 and 2015 found that they had collectively spent at least $7 million of campaign funds on legal fees, as recorded on their mandatory filings at the state Board of Elections.[43] I doubt donors expected their campaign contributions to be used to keep incumbents out of jail, but the practice is not illegal in New York State, one of the few states in the nation permitting it.

I should not have been surprised by the coda to former state senator Guy Velella's long political career in politics, or the then–senate majority leader's response to that coda. But I, like many others, was indeed taken aback by what I beheld as the sheer arrogance of these powerful individuals.

Senator Velella had been a high-ranking and well-liked Bronx/Westchester Republican state senator and the Bronx county Republican leader. Throughout his three decades in elected office, he wielded his influence, without incident, to garner contracts for political allies, while bringing home government funds for projects benefitting his district. He held a safe senate seat for eighteen years. He was a fixture and a classic insider. And so it remained until Velella and two associates were charged in 2002 with a twenty-five-count indictment alleging the senator had taken at least $137,000—and allegedly solicited $250,000—in return for steering public works contracts to those who paid bribes.[44]

The indictment covered 1995 to 2000. In 2004, Velella pleaded guilty to one count of bribery and agreed to serve a year in jail. But he was abruptly released after less than twelve weeks, when a virtually unheard-of New York City panel called the Local Conditional Release Commission granted him freedom. Even then–Mayor Michael Bloomberg initially commented that he had never heard of the commission or even that his office appointed members to it. It had never been the focus of press coverage. Still, someone did know of its existence and exerted some influence over its members for Velella. After weeks of embarrassing headlines and outcry following Velella's release, it was rescinded, and he was forced to return to prison.[45]

With the blessings of then–Majority Leader Bruno, much of the $292,500 Velella had paid his lawyer by the spring of 2004, and as much as $100,000 additional thereafter, was given to him in individual donations of $7,500 from many fellow legislators who had dipped into their own campaign war chests a year before he pleaded guilty.[46] The senate leadership also added $10,450 to Velella's annual pension while he was serving his prison term.[47] Bruno was among nearly three dozen people who wrote to the Local Conditional Release Commission requesting Velella's release, stating that he suffered enough as a result of his legal ordeal. "He is no longer a senator, he is no longer able to practice law, he has been financially hurt, and really publicly disgraced," asserted Bruno.[48]

From time to time, we Democratic senators were asked by our conference leaders to contribute to the Democratic Senate Campaign Committee. When, in 2000, I decided to give $10,000 from my campaign committee instead of the $30,000 that my leader wanted, a member of the minority leader's staff told me that my contribution had been a disappointment. The member also told me that in the future when the minority leader and others were making committee assignments, member-item allocations, and other grants, my action would be viewed unfavorably.

When Republican legislators in the senate and assembly were asked to ante up even for an indicted member of their party, such as Velella, most, but not all, did what they were told without complaint. The Board of Elections issued an opinion asserting it was perfectly fine to pay legal defense bills with campaign funds when charges against a public servant were related to the "holding of public office."[49] The Rochester *Democrat and Chronicle* asked rhetorically in an editorial, "Is that a loophole?" Then it replied to its own question: "No. It's a hula hoop."[50]

As Bruno passed the hat for his indicted colleague, Senator Krueger and other legislators decided it was time to bring attention to the absurd fact that elected officials in Albany who commit felonies are still entitled to receive their pension—Velella's amounted to $80,000 a year. "This is about making a simple statement to present and future New York elected officials," she said in announcing a bill inspired by the Velella episode. "It is simply unconscionable for elected officials who violate their oaths of office by committing felonies to receive pensions that are funded by taxpaying New Yorkers. You broke the law. You forfeited that right."[51]

Naturally, the bill, a fair-minded proposal certainly worthy of debate, did not get very far. Such is the fate of all independently generated measures, unless the leadership of both houses feels there is no way to avoid passage. By 2015, according to *Newsday* reporter Michael Gormley, convicted New York State elected officials were eligible for a total of $604,000 annually in pension payments, among them former state Comptroller Hevesi (with his $126,132-a-year in pension payments), former Senator Nick Spano ($70,332), former Assemblywoman Davis ($63,282), former Senator Carl Kruger ($58,008), former Senator Libous ($57,744) former Assemblyman Norman ($44,172).[52] Gormley's front-page article noted that in 2011 the legislature had agreed that a right to a pension must be forfeited if a senator or assembly member is convicted of a felony, but the law only applied to those legislators elected after 2011.[53] The legislature can change this loophole, but probably it never will, short of a constitutional convention.

Indeed, a subsequent effort by newly elected members to extend the pension forfeiture measure to all senators and assembly members on conviction, regardless of when they were elected, failed in part because it came as the top leaders of both chambers—then Silver and Skelos—were themselves facing indictments, the same article explained. Finally, in 2015, the Big Three held closed-door talks on the pension issue, from which nothing resulted. The proposal the three sides worked out would have eliminated pensions of any state employee convicted of a felony, while giving judges the leeway to protect innocent spouses from losing benefits. Before the measure could gain final approval in the assembly, however, public employees unions objected to the inclusion of all workers in the penalty scope. The assembly, in response, modified the bill to include only elected officials as well as high-level policymakers, largely from the executive branch. The senate, though, stuck with the original version of the bill. The two chambers could not find a middle ground, and so former public servants remain eligible for retirement support from the very taxpayers they cheated.[54]

Blair Horner, one of the Capitol's most effective and experienced government watchdog professionals, happened to be in Minnesota attending a 1998 conference on Big Tobacco, after the tobacco industry had deposited records of its lobbying and gift giving nationwide as a result of the industry's lengthy legal battles with the states. Horner, more than six feet tall, boyish-looking and bespectacled, came of age in the politically progressive 1960s, the decade of take-it-to-the-streets (and to-the-courts) activism. He is the executive director of NYPIRG, which, in additional to organizing on issues that include consumer protection, the environment, higher education, and social justice, is one of the state's leading government reform groups with Horner as its advocate at the Capitol almost continuously since the mid-1980s.

Horner recalled that he wanted to look at the tobacco files and went to the warehouse where the industry documents were archived. What he discovered in that Minnesota warehouse touched off one of Albany's more illuminating scandals.[55]

One "astonishing" document, as Horner would later write in a lengthy account for NYPIRG with his colleague Michelle Stern, was a Tobacco Institute budget indicating that in 1995 the trade group had spent $287,700 on the "New York Preemption Plan"—an expenditure that was not reflected in legally required reports of legislative lobbying expenses filed with New York State.[56]

In the 1980s and early 1990s, the administration of Governor Mario Cuomo had been unfriendly to the tobacco industry. The conservative Pataki's election in 1994 represented a possible opening for the industry to stave off and reverse the antismoking momentum in New York and around the country. Not surprisingly, the company quickly deposited $25,000 in Pataki's inaugural account, which at the time was secret, and launched a lobbying effort to roll back the state's antismoking ordinances.

Then, in May 1995, Bruno had a meeting with Philip Morris Chief Executive Officer Geoffrey Bible, Senior Vice President Ellen Merlo, and the company's top Albany lobbyist, Sharon Portnoy, at Philip Morris's New York City offices. In a follow-up letter to Senator Bruno, Merlo wrote, "Sharon has been singing your praises for quite some time, it's wonderful to know that the leadership in this state is taking a pro-business approach. As said in our meeting, working together we can accomplish a great deal. We all took comfort in the message that you had to deliver."[57]

Of course, as Horner and Stern recounted, the public would never know how Joe Bruno reacted or what his supposedly comforting message was. Nevertheless, on June 12, 1995, the senate's all-powerful Committee on Rules, which Bruno totally controlled at the time, introduced a bill to extinguish all previous local laws and regulations "concerning the sale, distribution, use or display of tobacco products."[58]

When health advocates drew the media's attention to the bill, there was confusion over who had initiated it. Bruno was quoted as stating that Pataki had requested the bill. The Pataki administration demurred. A Bruno spokesperson ultimately claimed that some senators had requested the bill's introduction, but he refused to reveal who they were. Due partly to its late introduction and the controversy health and consumer groups created, the legislature adjourned without taking action on the measure.

After the tobacco industry documents came to Horner's attention in 1998, NYPIRG, Common Cause New York, and the League of Women Voters of New York State filed a complaint with the New York Temporary State Commission on Lobbying about illegal gift giving by the tobacco industry's lobbyists. The commission investigated and found that the Tobacco Institute had indeed failed to disclose its expenditures. Lawyers for the Tobacco Institute admitted that it had spent $443,072 on lobbying in New York State in 1995 that it did not report and that it had funneled those funds largely to the New York Tavern and Restaurant Association to advocate on its behalf before state and local governments.[59]

In July 1999 the *New York Times,* basing an article on additional documents from the Philip Morris document archive, revealed that from 1995 through 1997, the tobacco giant had spent tens of thousands of dollars on gifts for Albany lawmakers. The *Times*'s examination of Philip Morris lobbyist Sharon Portnoy's credit card receipts, on which she had recorded the names of her guests, showed that at least 115 current and former legislators of the then 211-member New York legislature had accepted gifts from Philip Morris, ranging from meals at fine restaurants to seats at the men's finals of the U.S. Open tennis tournament, hotel accommodations, and tickets to the Indianapolis 500 and Yankees and Mets games.[60] I was not among those so feted (and I do not smoke).

Interestingly, the *Times*'s coverage of the growing scandal also revealed that in 1995, Philip Morris contributed $10,000 to the Hungarian-American Chamber of Commerce, shortly before it underwrote the cost of Governor Pataki's trip to his ancestral Hungary. The cigarette company dispatched lobbyist Tina Walls to dine with him and others in Budapest, though the governor denied knowing anything about the company's contribution.[61]

Philip Morris was fined $75,000 by the Temporary State Commission on Lobbying for its failure to disclose its lobbying activities as required by law. Portnoy was fined $15,000 for her role and banned from lobbying in the state for the next three years.[62]

In the end, in 2000, the legislature and governor parried over bills to ban members from accepting any gifts from lobbyists, but nothing else happened. Even so, the protracted Big Tobacco lobbying scandal was beneficial in that it neutralized the tobacco industry's efforts to weaken public-health legislation, and once the scandal had pierced broad public consciousness, a flurry of tobacco-related laws passed in Albany, including raising the cigarette tax, setting fire safety standards for cigarette manufacturers, and extending the indoor smoking ban. The reason, wrote Horner and Stern, was that the legislature now needed to demonstrate to the public that it was not under the industry's influence.[63]

It took a similar frustrating experience for the legislature in 2004 to eliminate a policy that effectively granted suspect state employees immunity from investigation when they leave the state payroll in most cases. This was passed at Governor Pataki's beckoning. Until then, any employee who stole money or steered contracts could not be prosecuted under the ethics code, because as soon as the employee came under investigation, he or she could quit, and state officials could no longer pursue the matter. The catalyzing situation involved the 2004 resignation of a state university college president—to deal with family matters, she explained at the time, though the Albany *Times Union* and the *New York Times* reported that she might have faced a state ethics inquiry into accusations that she allegedly had offered to steer a campus construction contract to a developer, who in return would pay to endow a university professorship that she could take over once she left her job as college president. Her lawyer denied the allegation, and it was never proven; her resignation effectively ended the investigation.[64]

Consider, too, Albany's secretive, backroom government from another perspective—that of the relatively open state Department of Transportation, as reported in June 2005 by the *New York Daily News*'s Greg B. Smith. From June 2003 to June 2005 in that department alone, "lobbyists schmoozed the agency on nearly $1.3 billion in contracts," Smith reported. Smith obtained Department of Transportation records through the Freedom of Information Law.[65] He discovered that "only a handful" of these contracts were awarded competitively with sealed bids, a process that significantly restricts influence peddling. Rather, nearly all the contracts—for everything from monitoring bicycle traffic to painting bridges to producing economic and demographic forecasts—were "negotiated," which allowed lobbyists to influence who won.[66]

It was not until after the article appeared, however, that Albany leaders reluctantly agreed to require lobbyists to register and report any activity relating to winning contracts for clients. Up until then, the requirement applied only to lobbyists' efforts to influence the legislature.

Anyone who questions whether Albany is still a place where money is exchanged for favorable treatment by public officials should consider how much money poured into the capital in 2014 from supporters and opponents of the charter school sector alone—an estimated $30 million, according to lobbying reports and campaign finance data gathered by the website Capital New York (now Politico New York). The pro-charter and school-reform groups even outspent the politically active teachers' unions known to have extensive financial resources.[67]

Probably no account of life in Albany would be complete without mention of the abysmal intern sex scandal that roiled the Capitol in spring 2004. That year would come to mark the twentieth consecutive late passage of the state budget. It was also distinguished by such paramount legislation as a bill to let dry cleaners keep clothing left behind by customers for more than six months.

I had seen the fraternizing between some legislators and some of the 150 or so college students interning for state assembly and senate members and had frowned on it. Not only the Albany political culture but also the social one struck me at times as unseemly. In such a context, the $800,000-a-year legislative internship program for college students learning about government should have included rules or restrictions on sexual contact and special protections against improper sexual advances. It did not. Then–Albany County District Attorney Paul Clyne was so disturbed by the improper fraternizing that he actually advised that parents steer their college-age children clear of Albany—advice the *New York Times* would echo in a May 2004 editorial, saying the students deserved a safer and more wholesome environment.[68]

"Any father," Clyne told the *New York Post*'s Fredric Dicker:

> who would let his daughter be an intern in the State Legislature should have his head examined. . . . I'm not going to call the place a cesspool, but I can say there is a group of legislators who, quite honestly, are here to get paid $80,000 a year and party three nights a week and who don't contribute anything to the process. . . . Everyone knows that for some people, legislators and some of the other staff people in the Legislature, the

constant flow of young women in and out of the Legislature
is viewed as an opportunity for them. . . . Lots of legislators
feel that carousing is the main part of their job.[69]

Clyne's comments were not made in a vacuum. In 2002, in one of
the more heavily covered incidents of its type during my tenure, Assembly
Speaker Silver's then–chief counsel, Michael Boxley, was removed from
the statehouse in handcuffs on charges of having sexually assaulted a
twenty-two-year-old woman who worked on the assembly staff. A similar
date rape accusation had been made against Boxley by another young
staffer in 2001, but that woman did not file a criminal complaint. The
second woman did. The year following his arrest, Boxley pleaded guilty to
one misdemeanor count of sexual misconduct, admitting he had engaged
in sexual intercourse with the woman at her apartment without her consent. He was fined $1,000 and placed on probation for six years and on the
state's sex offender registry. Under the guilty plea, prosecutors dismissed
four felony rape charges against him. In March 2006, the Appellate Division of the Supreme Court reinstated Boxley because he had fulfilled the
provisions of his sentence. However, in 2008 was once again convicted
and forced out of his position.[70]

The assembly's institutional response was to modify its sexual harassment policies and require that all verified complaints of harassment be
kept on file for seven years. In early 2006, the speaker's office agreed to
pay $500,000 in public funds to settle a lawsuit brought by the victim,
bringing the matter to a close; for me and others, however, it was just
another reminder that Albany remained a broken place—one that robbed
the state of a more hopeful future.

The perverse apotheosis of the legislature's predatory behavior may
be the case of former assembly member Vito Lopez, a heavy-handed
political boss in Brooklyn's Williamsburg section. The shabby, drawn-out
episode involved allegations by two female assembly aides that Lopez, a
legislator for twenty-eight years and the chairman of the assembly Housing
Committee, had repeatedly groped and made unwanted advances toward
them. Speaker Silver had tried to put the matter to rest without publicity
in 2012 by authorizing $103,080 to settle the sexual harassment claims
confidentially.[71] After the New York Times revealed the case, the secret
offer—the result of months of private negotiation—was withdrawn, and
Silver said he regretted the deal "from the perspective of transparency."[72]

Following a rare state Ethics Commission report on a legislator's antics, Lopez, under fire, was fined $330,000 by the commission[73] and resigned from the assembly in May 2013.[74] (Later that year, Lopez lost the Democratic primary for a city council seat.)[75]

The matter was finally resolved in February 2015 when the women accepted a settlement award in civil court totaling $580,000, and all but $35,000 of it came at taxpayers' expense. Lopez admitted no wrongdoing.[76]

The Overcoat Development Corporation

"Taxes," Justice Oliver Wendell Holmes Jr. declared in one of his U.S. Supreme Court decisions, "are what we pay for civilized society."[1] True enough—except that elected officials are wary of levying or raising taxes, lest we find ourselves voted out of office.

More than seventy-five years ago, New York State pioneered an ingenious mechanism to pay for the vast infrastructure of roads, bridges, tunnels, airports, and public transit needed to get millions of people to work and home again each day, without officially and directly placing the burden of constructing and maintaining these facilities on taxpayers' shoulders. That mechanism is called the public authority, a nonprofit corporation, owned and operated by state, regional, or local government, and funded by issuing tax-free bonds on a scale of tens or hundreds of millions of dollars.[2]

Public authorities are attractive to voters and politicians alike because everyone gets the benefits at seemingly no cost to taxpayers. Bond buyers pay for construction and maintenance; the bonds are paid off with tolls and other fees collected from those who use the facilities. No one raises or pays extra taxes. It is all neat, simple, and clean.

Or so the authorities and the public officials who create them would like taxpayers to believe. Just as everything always has a cost, the proliferation of public authorities in New York State threatens to sink us under an avalanche of debt—totaling in excess of $154 billion in 2014, according to the state comptroller's office[3]—which most taxpayers are unaware that they are expected (though not legally obligated) to pay off if the public authority cannot.

In February 2004, after I decided to leave the state senate, then–Comptroller Alan Hevesi began calling attention to this political and fiscal vulnerability.[4] One of the comptroller's duties is to monitor the performance of state agencies and public authorities, ensuring that the authorities comply with state laws regarding contracting and personnel practices and that their expenditures are prudent and aboveboard. To do this, the comptroller's staff periodically conducts audits that focus on selected programs and projects, checking items such as how well contractors fulfill their contracts, whether projects come in on time and on budget, and whether sufficient internal controls are in place to prevent fraud and corruption. The operative word about these audits is *periodically*. Another word is *narrow*.

When Hevesi began to highlight the state's "authorities problem," as his predecessor H. Carl McCall had also often done, and as his successor, Thomas DiNapoli, would also do, he and his staff tried to count them, only to revise the figure upward on subsequent recounts. For a staff as large as the comptroller's, it was still too arduous a task to acquire an understanding of just how many authorities really existed.

And if determining the total number was difficult, using its auditing powers to monitor the authorities' staff and programs effectively was also impossible for the comptroller's office. Hevesi pledged that in an effort to provide greater oversight, his office would increase its annual auditing to cover three dozen of the state's public authorities—which amounted to 6 percent of the total, a standard subset—but that was hardly reassuring. One observer estimated that a battalion-sized team of auditors would be required to undertake annual audits of each state-run authority.

Consequently, reviews the comptroller's office conducts usually focus on only a segment of an authority's operations, and only a handful of public authorities are annually subjected to audits.

Legislative oversight, too, has been extremely weak, to the point of being nonexistent for entire sessions. The senate and assembly each have committees with oversight power to investigate public authorities. I served as a member of the senate's Committee on Corporations, Authorities and Commissions during my first term in Albany and can attest that its activities were akin to those of a worn-out rubber stamp, barely able to register an impression.[5]

As a member of the Democratic minority, I had virtually no say on any matter that came before the committee. The chairman and his chief of staff prepared the agenda and consulted with Bruno and Bruno's top assistants to arrange the votes beforehand on what usually proved to be innocuous issues. No major issues ever came before the committee for discussion, inquiry, or investigation. This meant that the vast majority of its members, Republicans and Democrats alike, never attended its meetings. As was the way of Albany, they proxied their votes beforehand to ensure that the majority leader had the votes needed to pass (or veto) any measures he wished to. A session's worth of such meetings threatened to put me to sleep. At the end of my second term in Albany, I decided to drop that committee and apply my time and energy to another committee that showed some potential for actually having some positive effect on the public good.

Of course, at the time I did not realize that the role and impact of public authorities on state government and state spending would explode as a major issue in 2005, a few months after I retired from the senate. The subsequent chair of the committee, former Republican state senator Vincent Leibell, responded to some of these growing concerns, together with three Democrats, namely, then–Comptroller Hevesi, then–Assemblyman Richard Brodsky, and then–Attorney General Spitzer. Brodsky, always the thoughtful and assertive legislator, once out of office became a senior fellow at the think tank Demos and an adjunct assistant professor of public policy at NYU's Robert F. Wagner Graduate School of Public Service. He had been bringing attention to concerns about public authorities and the lack of oversight for quite some time, having given up the chairmanship of the Committee on Environmental Conservation for that of the committee that oversaw public authorities because he believed they would be a growing issue.[6]

Indeed, Brodsky's work as chair of the assembly's Committee on Corporations, Authorities and Commissions is an example, albeit rare, of how legislative oversight works when allowed to. Committee hearings conducted in October 2003 revealed that staff members of the state's Canal Corporation, a subsidiary of the New York State Thruway Authority, had engaged in bid rigging to steer rights to develop land along the canal system's right of way for a ludicrously paltry sum of money.[7]

In theory, oversight by the state comptroller and the legislature should be a formality, since each public authority is governed by a board composed of private citizens appointed to represent and safeguard the public's interest in managing authority programs. The governor nominates these board members, who are then confirmed by the senate. Their primary task as board members is to set goals and policies for how their authority accomplishes its tasks and to review how those goals and policies are implemented.

The Canal Corporation scandal revealed, however, numerous weaknesses in this public-member governance model. First, unlike directors of private-sector corporations, board members of public authorities receive no compensation for the hours they put in. Therefore, of necessity, they serve on a part-time basis. Moreover, their part-time attention to governance issues may be further diluted by serving on the board of one of the authority's subsidiaries.

Indeed, one factor in the origin of the Canal Corporation scandal was, as one member of its board later acknowledged, that it had spent 90 percent of its time on Thruway Authority matters and only 10 percent on canal affairs.[8]

A second weakness in the authority governance model is that because they serve on a part-time basis, board members depend on authority staff to provide accurate information on which they use to make decisions about policies and programs. When the staff is determined to cover up activities such as favoritism and corruption that are at odds with the public's interests, keeping such embarrassing—not to mention possibly illegal—activities buried for years is possible.

As reconstructed by then–Attorney General Spitzer and Inspector General Jill Konviser-Levine, the scandal began in 1992, when control of the state's canal system was transferred from the state's Department of Transportation, whose operating costs are appropriated annually from tax revenues, to the Canal Corporation. Under this new arrangement, the cost of running the canals was shifted from the state budget's balance sheets to those of the Canal Corporation's parent, the Thruway Authority, a move that amounted to fiscal deception. While it allowed the governor and legislature to claim that New York's taxpayers were being relieved of the cost burden of operating the canals—since the money to do so would no longer have to be appropriated each year as part of the state budget— the burden simply popped up on the books of the Thruway Authority, whose budget is also paid for by taxpayers, albeit indirectly in the form of Thruway toll revenues.[9]

Shifting responsibility for operating the canals to another arm of the state was merely cosmetic. Doing so did not address, much less solve, the fact that the canal system was a money loser: it cost roughly $70 million to operate annually, but took in less than $2 million in users' tolls and fees. The authority was faced with the problem of absorbing those increased operating expenses while still meeting its fixed expenses of repaying bondholders.[10]

In September 1995 the authority approved a plan to generate revenue that it expected would help defray this added expense: areas along the canal system would be opened to residential and commercial development. Rights would be sold to entrepreneurs who would create canal-side communities featuring upscale homes and boat marinas. Eight months later, in May 1996, the Canal Corporation's chairman sent a letter to 200 companies and individuals soliciting possible participation in developing the canal.[11]

Richard Hutchens, who eventually won the Canal Corporation's approval to proceed with such development, did not appear on the initial solicitation list. His name was added after he contacted Donald Hutton, the Thruway Authority's deputy director of planning. Though he had no direct experience in developing canal-side properties—other than as a manual laborer during the 1940s for an uncle who developed a community near Orlando, Florida, and as a foreman in the 1950s at a drainage canal construction site at an Air Force base in Texas—Hutchens quickly emerged as the Canal Corporation staff's favored candidate.[12]

As Spitzer and Konviser-Levine detailed in their seventy-five-page investigation report, which partly relied on state Comptroller Hevesi's fiscal oversight work, during the next three and a half years Canal Corporation staff members failed to perform due diligence background checks that would have revealed: Hutchens's nonexistent qualifications for the project; routinely passed along, and sometimes embroidered, Hutchens's renditions of his qualifications; and made few, if any, efforts to check whether similar canal communities existed (they did) in order to determine an accurate fair-market price for the rights Hutchens sought. Hutchens failed to inform the corporation board that he had defaulted on a riverboat tourism project for which he had no experience. Regardless, the staff somehow managed to present Hutchens as the sole viable bidder. The board staff members steered Hutchens to lobbyists to influence corporation board members to approve Hutchens's proposal after some members expressed doubts and tabled consideration of it, and the staff placed him in contact with campaign fundraisers who solicited donations for Governor Pataki.

The staff also misled board members about precise details of Hutchens's development proposal.[13]

At several points during the Hutchens negotiations, Nancy Carey Cassidy, one of the three Thruway Authority public members who served on the Canal Corporation's three-person board, raised questions or objections that momentarily derailed the deal. Carey Cassidy, daughter of former Governor Carey, was appointed to the board in 1993 by her father's successor Mario Cuomo. As a partner in a commercial real estate development firm, she brought great expertise to the board and her colleagues relied on her counsel when land development proposals were brought to the Canal Corporation. Therefore, in late 1997, when Carey Cassidy expressed her concern that the corporation was undervaluing the development rights it was being asked to sell to Hutchens, the deal came to a standstill. But only briefly.[14]

Rather than compelling Hutchens and the Canal Corporation staff to create a more financially feasible proposal, Carey Cassidy's objections served to goad the staff first into advising Hutchens to buy political influence by making a contribution to a state official whose campaign manager happened to have taken a leave of absence as the Canal Corporation's director of operations and second engaging a lobbyist to meet with Carey Cassidy in December 1998 in an attempt to overcome her objections. To her credit Carey Cassidy remained unconvinced about the financial arrangements, and a decision was again postponed.

Nonetheless, in the end Hutchens—with the complicity of the Canal Corporation's staff—got what he wanted: exclusive rights to develop all of the Canal Corporation's developable land along the canal for $30,000, a price much lower than normal market price. On January 27, 2000, the corporation board approved handing over development rights to Hutchens—who immediately started renegotiating the terms of a formal contract, again with covert assistance from Canal Corporation staff.[15]

The final contract, which Thruway Authority representatives signed in December 2001, contained provisions favorable to Hutchens that had never been presented to, much less approved by, the Canal Corporation board. The final, failed links that allowed the deal to blossom into a scandal were approvals of the contract made by the Office of the Attorney General and the Office of the State Comptroller, in January and May 2002, respectively. Only with Brodsky's oversight hearings to air the irregularities involved in the Hutchens deal was the deal finally halted.[16] In the process, New Yorkers were afforded a glimpse into the problems we now confront for having abdicated our responsibility for controlling the state's finances and development.

The explosive growth of public authorities as a tool to manage all varieties of what were once functions of state and local government, and therefore subject to voter oversight, is essentially a postwar development.

New York's pioneering public authority, a cooperative venture with its neighboring state, New Jersey, is an interstate compact approved by the U.S. Congress. The Port Authority of New York and New Jersey was established in 1921 (as the Port of New York Authority) to develop shipping and rail facilities in the two states' common harbor area at the mouth of the Hudson River. Proponents of the project came up with the public authority model as a way to insulate harbor development from the vagaries of state legislative budgeting and appropriations processes. Efforts of such enormous size had in the past frequently foundered or suffered long delays when recessions, depressions, and cost overruns threatened to outstrip legislatures' abilities to raise sufficient revenues to proceed on an annual pay-as-you-go basis. The harbor project was so large and was expected to take so long to complete, the legislatures of both states surrendered their direct say as a way to avoid straining their states' annual budgets.[17]

In the 1930s, in the depths of the Great Depression, Robert Moses brought public authorities to everyone's attention. Hailed at the time as "the man who can get things done" without falling prey to the pitfalls of fraud, inefficiency, and waste that Tammany Hall's patronage demands had imposed on previous public works projects, Moses engineered the consent of beleaguered state and local officials to create public authorities as a means of capturing tens of millions of dollars in federal appropriations intended to provide employment and restart the state and the national economy. Using federal funds as start-up capital, Moses's authorities then raised additional funds on the bond market. Banks and other financial institutions willingly bought authority bonds because Moses's projects were self-financing: highways, bridges, and tunnels that charged users tolls, which were earmarked for maintenance and paying off bondholder debt. New York State and New York City, limited by their constitution and charter, respectively, regarding the amount of debt they could accumulate, and severely constrained in the amount of revenue they could raise from taxpayers reeling from the Great Depression, viewed Moses as a miracle worker. Until the 1960s, they rarely challenged his suggestions for creating yet more authorities to tackle yet more massive job-producing public works projects.[18]

By 1956, with prosperity returned, New York legislators decided to assess the number and scope of the state's authorities as part of a review of state government activities. The Hults Commission, formally known as the Temporary State Commission on Coordination of State Activities, identified fifty-six authorities and recommended eliminating twenty.[19] However, the state's creation of authorities was only temporarily abated. During the 1960s, authorities proliferated, mainly to establish financing for housing and urban development projects without having to go to the voters with statewide referendums that asked taxpayers whether they wanted to assume the cost burdens of the projects.[20]

With the state having found a way around the prospect of taxpayer revolts by technically keeping this form of financing from appearing on the state's budget ledger, even more authorities have been created since the 1970s, mainly for the purpose of issuing debt for state and local government projects and services. By 1987, when a Moreland Act Commission on Government Integrity was appointed to review Albany's operations, state officials had lost count of the number of authorities. In "Underground Government: A Preliminary Report on Authorities and Other Public Corporations," the panel acknowledged, in a tone of exasperation rarely vented in such documents: "At present, so far as Commission staff has been able to determine, no one has even an approximate count of how many of these organizations exist, where they are, much less an accounting of what they do." (In a footnote, however, the report cited a 1985 *Local Government Handbook,* published by the governor's office, which cited forty-six statewide or regional authorities, and "about" 529 local authorities.[21])

My favorite example of New York State's zest for creating public authorities at the slightest provocation is the Overcoat Development Corporation. Established in 1986 in an attempt to encourage an Indiana clothing manufacturer to relocate its operations to the Mohawk Valley town of Amsterdam, the corporation led a mysterious existence. In 2004, a *New York Times* reporter attempted to uncover what success, if any, this rather specialized authority had achieved and went to 633 Third Avenue in Manhattan, its address of record. No "Overcoat Development Corp."

appeared in the lobby's directory of the building's tenants, and no one in the building could be found who had ever heard of it; it appeared as though it was dormant and no longer functioning.[22] As of February 2005, however, when Hevesi enumerated at least 733 existing authorities, the Overcoat Development Corporation was still listed among them, as a subsidiary of the ESDC mega-authority. A useless appendage, it was finally dissolved in May 2007.

Deriding the Overcoat Development Corporation as an example of Albany's infatuation with authorities is easy. Dismissing the frequent use of authorities as a mere foible runs the risk of failing to understand that reliance on authorities is an admission on the part of state officials that the very functioning of state government has long been deeply dysfunctional in meeting its most elemental responsibility, which is sound fiscal management.

The Local Government Assistance Corporation (LGAC) is a case in point. Established in June 1990, the LGAC had the power to issue up to $4.7 billion in bonds, whose debt service costs are covered by appropriations provided by one-quarter of the state's 4.5 percent tax levied on all sales transactions. A fine example of bureaucratic obfuscation, the LGAC was created as an integral part of an overall program of state fiscal reform to eliminate the state's practice of financing substantial amounts of local assistance payments during the first quarter of the state's fiscal year through the issuance of short-term tax and revenue anticipation notes, also known as the "Spring Borrowing."[23] Bonds were issued to cover payments to local governments and school districts in a timely manner as had once been the state's practice, and LGAC was created to take on the role of issuing those bonds.

In order to properly decode LGAC's account of its creation and raison d'être, one needs to be aware of the most outstanding symptom of state government dysfunction, which until April 2005 had plagued Albany for two decades: the inability to pass a state budget by the constitutionally mandated April 1 start of the fiscal year. This has changed since Andrew Cuomo became governor in 2011. On-time state budgets are one of his major accomplishments, but for decades, late budgets—sometimes months late—were the norm.

The late budget agreements meant that no one in Albany could authorize release of state revenues to local governments and school districts for social services programs and education. There was a constant threat that lack of a budget agreement in Albany would stop the flow of funds, and that the local programs New York's citizens relied on would gradually come to a standstill or end.

Rather than solving its dysfunction head-on, Albany resorted to a quick fix. Instead of letting everything come to a standstill while the legislature and governor dithered and dickered, they agreed on a system whereby the state would be allowed to take short-term loans from banks and other sources, and these loans would allow local governments and school districts to continue operating until a budget was passed. These loans were secured by promising to pay back the borrowed money—with interest of course—from the proceeds of future tax collections (the "short-term tax and revenue anticipation notes" cited above). Since New York State's budget is supposed to be agreed on in early spring, and because it had not been for twenty years, and because the state had to borrow funds to keep the state's local government and education entities operating, this became known as the "Spring Borrowing."

As is often the case, though, a quick repair for one dysfunction soon led to another dysfunction: the Spring Borrowing unavoidably drove up the cost of state government, which spelled potential higher taxes for state residents. Rather than enhancing the budget process to reduce the need for spring borrowing, Albany resorted to yet another quick fix, another public authority—LGAC—with the power to issue bonds and notes up to $4.7 billion. Now the eyesore of those Spring Borrowing short-term tax and revenue anticipation notes disappeared from the state's budget ledger, and the cost of repaying the LGAC's bonds and notes was buried in internal transfers from the state's sales tax collections to the LGAC. Albany's inability to pass a budget on time continued to exact a toll on taxpayers—except, this time, the aim was to make it harder for taxpayers to tell that they were losing money.

The LGAC has had its defenders, and sometimes in unexpected places. Writing in a January 1998 paper issued by the Manhattan Institute, ordinarily a politically conservative scourge of New York State and New York City mismanagement follies, William J. Stern and Edwin Rubenstein noted, "Admittedly, the LGAC is a regrettable expedient, made necessary by the irresponsibility of leaders in Albany. Given the political reality of New York, however, such borrowing is a reasonable way to ensure that the state's residents are not forced to endure regular interruptions in basic services. Moreover . . . LGAC bonds account for only a small fraction of overall state indebtedness."

That is true. Yet the LGAC exists largely because our legislature and some of our governors had not found the means to properly do the jobs for which they were elected. The ultimate losers are the New Yorkers who elected them and whose taxes continue to be diverted to fund an authority whose ultimate, if unintended, function is to permit the state's elected officials to grandstand each year over the state's budget and to insulate them from being held accountable for the consequences of perennially late budgets.

On paper and in theory, the New York State Constitution invests budgetary authority in those who pay the taxes that give the state money to spend on services for its residents. And it provides a safeguard to prevent state officials from spending wildly without taxpayer approval. If state officials want to go into debt to pay for a project that cannot be paid for out of current or prudently anticipated revenues, and if they want to pay off that debt by adding to the taxes that New Yorkers already pay, then state officials have to give voters an opportunity, through a general obligation debt referendum, to vote "yes" or "no" about whether they are willing to pay more taxes for the project. Because New York residents are among the most heavily taxed in the nation, obtaining voter approval in such referendums is a notoriously uncertain proposition.

Creating a public authority is a way to raise and spend taxpayer money—more than $20 billion a year—without being required to ask taxpayers whether they want to pay higher taxes. That is because, in theory, public authorities pay for their projects by selling bonds to bondholders, and then pay back those bonds with revenue produced by the project. In the midst of the Great Depression, Robert Moses demonstrated that this proposition worked with the bridges and tunnels his authorities built. In fact, revenues from tolls were so much greater than originally projected that, had he been so inclined, he could have paid off debts to bondholders years before the bonds were due to mature. However, only a few New Yorkers at the time cared. The tolls taxpayers paid seemed reasonable, bondholders were happy, and no state taxes were increased.

Today, however, the Moses-model public authority does not describe the vast majority of the total 1,182 authorities that have been created by the state (325), the local governments (847), or through interstate or international acts (8), encompassing what the state comptroller's office in a 2014 report accurately described as "an increasingly large and influential sphere of government."[24] Many of the authorities established since the 1960s after Robert Moses was eased out of power do not generate steady streams of revenue from their projects. Since bondholders want some sort of security that their bonds will be paid back, New York State provides that guarantee. Because the state cannot guarantee that, as a last resort, it will pay off the bonds from general-obligation tax revenues without first obtaining voter consent, however, most authority bonds are backed by the state's moral obligation to pay off the bonds if the authority fails to do so.

Though "moral obligation" sounds like a weak and perhaps vaguely worded guarantee, state officials familiar with the circumstances surrounding the near failure in 1975 of the Urban Development Corporation (UDC)—the state public authority financed by billions of dollars in bond borrowing—are unlikely to forget the havoc that moral obligation bonds can wreak on those who do not take the obligation seriously. The UDC's near collapse coincided with a recession-softened dip in the real estate market that threatened to push New York City over the brink of fiscal insolvency and into bankruptcy and default on its city-issued bonds. When the federal government balked at providing loan guarantees to keep the city operating through its threatened default, the state was called on to provide assistance. This was the time that one of New York's greatest governors, Hugh Carey, rescued New York City and New York State from possible insolvency.[25]

The only source of funds to meet these twin threats was private money markets, and the price was steep. Funds were made available, but interest rates to service the debts—paid out of state taxpayers' pockets— skyrocketed. Had the UDC been financed through general-obligation debt, the state's taxpayers would have had a collective choice whether to vote on raising their taxes to pay for its projects. As it was, the UDC's creation as a public authority robbed them of that choice, and they paid anyway—and at higher-than-anticipated rates once the prospect of default became real. (Part of the procedure that staved off UDC's default was to subsume it as a subsidiary of, yes, yet another authority, the ESDC, created to take over UDC's obligations and debt.) The UDC debacle, and New York State's near-collapse in its wake, was memorable and a cautionary event for public officials who had to regroup and deal with the state's fiscal issues. But memories fade with time, and with renewed prosperity for the past few decades, Albany embarked on a period of unchecked spending fueled by the proliferation of public authorities with authority to borrow money—without voter approval—by issuing moral obligation bonds.[26]

In 2014 Comptroller Thomas DiNapoli's office reported that state and local public authority spending had risen to $59.6 billion in the 2012–2013 fiscal year. Although the state-created authorities represented 28 percent of the total number of authorities statewide, they accounted for $38.1 billion, or 68 percent, of the total spending.[27]

The cost of servicing the state authorities' debt—that is, paying the interest—*is* part of the state budget. The interest payments on the $59.6 billion in the debt carried by the state-run public authorities (the debt service for an astonishing—and growing—$257 billion in total local and state authority debt principal, a figure that includes both the borrowing by the authorities for their own purposes as well the borrowing they incurred as a conduit for other state entities), requires the state to pay an estimated $5 billion a year in interest in 2014, up from $3.5 billion annually when I was in office.[28]

Virtually all of this debt, and the annual payments necessary to service it, has been incurred without the state's voters having been given a chance to decide whether they agreed to assume the "moral obligation" that accompanied its accumulation.

An example of how New York's public authorities have been subverted to respond to political demands, rather than to the public interest, was the 2005 rise and demise of former New York City Mayor Michael Bloomberg's plan to build a 75,000-seat football stadium on Manhattan's West Side.

Bloomberg, throughout the first term of his mayoralty, championed the idea of a stadium as a project that would repatriate the New York Jets professional football team from neighboring New Jersey and at the same time stimulate building on the West Side by bringing thousands of construction and services jobs to the city. He also touted the project as a central venue for the 2012 Summer Olympic Games, until the International Olympic Committee, in July 2005, chose to award the games to London.[29]

Initially the stadium project's anticipated costs were estimated at $1.4 billion, but they rose to $1.7 billion and then $2 billion before settling in at $2.2 billion. The mayor and then–Governor Pataki made equal pledges of $300 million in city and state funds to underwrite the project, with the state's share to come from the ESDC. Securing the state's

$300 million proved to be the stadium's downfall in spite of the strong backing, although this did not become apparent until very late in the process.[30]

Citizens' groups, fearing traffic congestion, pollution, and construction-related disruption, opposed the stadium, as did good-government organizations, which voiced skepticism about job creation and other purported economic benefits that stadium advocates said would follow in the project's wake, yet neither deterred the mayor and governor who were both determined to see the stadium built. Their confidence in their ability to prevail was based, in large measure, on their belief that they could bypass both the city and state legislatures and finance the measure through the state's public authorities. Of course, this meant there would be no public referendum. Such confidence represents a remarkable demonstration of the extent to which the state's public authorities, originally designed to act as nonpoliticized tools of the public's interests, have become important tools of politicians.[31]

Robert Moses was haughty in his dealings with elected officials with regard to public works projects between the 1920s and the 1960s, and the politicians were generally forced into the role of supplicants who begged for his attention and largesse. The state, however, no longer has a public works czar—in part due to elected officials' determination never again to suffer the humiliations Moses imposed on their predecessors. Public authorities' chairpersons and boards are now more responsive when the governor makes his wishes known because the governor has the principal role in appointing them to their posts. Moreover, the longer a governor serves, the more likely the authorities are to accede to the governor's wishes because the governor will have had a hand in appointing increasing percentages of the chairs and boards of all the state's authorities. At that point, there is a risk that an authority's decisions will no longer be based on independent, nonpolitical assessments of the public's interests but instead on the political calculations of the person who appointed a majority of its board. The dynamic is in clear opposition to the reason states and municipalities supposedly establish public authorities: to insulate decisions about massive public works spending and indebtedness from political calculation and interference.

The stadium proposal, which gathered momentum throughout 2004, hinged during 2005 on how much money the MTA would ask from the football team's owners as the price for selling development rights to construct a stadium above the authority's West Side Rail Yard. Initially, the Jets offered $100 million. This soon rose to $210 million after critics of the MTA, which had recently announced its intention to reduce services on the city's subway system in response to a projected budget deficit, charged that the authority was acting in a fiscally irresponsible manner by offering the site at less than the market price. Research into the MTA's records subsequently uncovered an internal report showing that the authority's property appraisal staff had estimated the value of the site's development rights to be $923 million.[32]

The MTA, not quite recovered from earlier revelations that its board had, in effect, been keeping two sets of accounting ledgers—one showing an operating deficit, which it used when attempting to justify fare increases for the city's subway and bus lines, and another, internal set, which showed that the authority's fiscal position was not nearly so dire as publicly proclaimed[33]—reconsidered its asking price for development rights to its West Side yards. The Jets subsequently raised their offer to $250 million.[34]

Additional pressure descended on the MTA when Cablevision, a Long Island-based company that owns Madison Square Garden, offered $400 million for the rail yards' development rights. Cablevision said it intended to use the site to build a residential complex of 5,800 new moderate-income apartments, which, the company projected, would create 3,200 construction jobs over twelve years and generate $100 million in state and city taxes by 2012. Supporters of the stadium contended that the cable operator's proposal was a cynical ruse designed to thwart competition for sports and other arena revenue, which Cablevision feared would be drawn away from Madison Square Garden, where their Rangers, Knicks, and Liberty play, and which also hosts other lucrative events including concerts, the circus, college basketball, and rodeos. Yet another company, Transgas, entered the fray, offering the MTA $700 million for the development rights in return for the authority's promise to support its plan to build a power plant in Brooklyn and to purchase its power for twenty years.[35]

On March 31, the MTA board announced its decision, accepting the Jets' offer of $250 million, to be paid in five $50 million installments over four years—or $210 million in a lump sum. Authority officials justified their decision by citing the football team's pledge to pursue an accelerated construction schedule and its commitment to hire minority- and woman-owned businesses as subcontractors. Then–MTA board member John Banks told the *New York Daily News,* "All of that equals greater than $400 million [the total offered by Cablevision]."[36] Transgas's offer was reportedly rejected on grounds that its bid had been accompanied by extraneous and burdensome conditions.

The MTA's decision momentarily buoyed Bloomberg's and Pataki's hopes, but a final obstacle loomed: approval by a crucial but relatively little-known state agency called the Public Authorities Control Board (PACB).

The PACB was created in 1976 in the wake of the UDC's technical default "to receive applications for approval of the financing and construction of any project proposed" by any of eleven of New York's public authorities, including UDC successor ESDC. Technically, the PACB consists of five members appointed by the governor. Four of them are appointed at the direction of each of Albany's main legislative fixtures: the senate majority leader, the assembly speaker, and the minority leaders of each chamber. The fifth, the chair, is the governor's pick. In true Albany fashion, however, only representatives of the governor, the senate majority leader, and the assembly speaker are empowered to cast votes; representatives of the senate and assembly minorities can listen and ask questions but cannot vote on items that come before the board. Strip away the camouflage of its nonvoting members, and the PACB is yet another example of New York's perennial rule of "three men in a room" because it requires a unanimous vote for any request to pass, gaining approval of any measure offers maximum leverage for hard and shrewd bargaining among Albany's triumvirate—another subversion of the original aim of creating public authorities in order to insulate decisions about massively expensive public works projects from political pressure.

Thus, it was a disagreement among the triumvirate—Governor Pataki, Senate Majority Leader Bruno, and Assembly Speaker Silver, with the latter two abstaining—that prevented a unanimous vote to approve the ESDC's expenditure of $300 million in state funding for construction of a West Side stadium. When the PACB met on June 6, 2005, to consider the ESDC's request, the governor's representative voted in favor, and Bruno's and Silver's representatives were instructed to abstain—which had the same effect as casting a negative vote. Though Bruno did not explicitly state a reason for his vote, he was reported to have been seeking an equal $300 million in funds for economic development projects in areas outside of New York City, especially upstate. Silver was more direct, stating his belief that the stadium would draw funds and future economic development from lower Manhattan and reconstruction of the World Trade Center site destroyed in the 9/11 terrorist attack—a site in Silver's assembly district.[37]

How much revenue New York State and New York City might have realized had the stadium proposal been approved is simply impossible to determine. The projections offered by the football team as well as by various elected officials who supported the project were not precise. The out-of-pocket cost to state and city taxpayers, however, can be calculated with greater accuracy: $300 million in ESDC funding for the stadium, $300 million from the ESDC for Bruno's wish list to secure his support, $300 million in city commitments, and another $673 million, representing the difference between the $923 million at which the MTA's appraisers valued development rights to the West Side rail yards site and the $250 million for which the MTA board agreed to sell those rights to the Jets football team. That total comes to $1.573 billion of public funds financed through New York State's public authorities—$1.573 billion of public funds on whose expenditure state and city officials assiduously tried to make sure taxpayers would not have an opportunity to vote, regardless of whether they thought a football stadium was how they wanted to spend their tax dollars.[38]

Clearly the prospect of a new stadium needing an obscure state board's approval was primarily a windfall for lobbyists for the New York Jets and the Cablevision media giant of Long Island. While it was an extremely important matter at that moment in New York's struggle to regain its footing in the wake of 9/11, the question of the stadium, and the broader economic considerations also at issue, occasioned remarkably little involvement by the 210 other legislators in Albany. The majority leader, the speaker, and the governor were the ultimate audience for the blizzard of lobbying—a record, in fact—for television ads and direct cajoling, along with additional courting efforts by Mayor Bloomberg.

Long before the stadium came before the PACB, Governor Pataki and Senator Bruno designated representatives in their stead to attend its brief monthly meetings held in an unmarked room in the Capitol. The board, in turn, seemed to do little to keep in check the large grouping of authorities under its fiduciary purview. (The current three men in a room also have designated representatives to attend the board meetings).[39]

That the two men—Silver and Bruno—who directed their representatives to abstain from casting votes can determine so much without public hearings or expert testimony about the potentially enormous implications of a historic land-use decision speaks volumes about the need to restore democracy to Albany.[40]

It was said of the Bourbon kings that, individually and collectively, they neither forgot anything nor learned anything, which contributed to their demise as the most prominent reigning family of Europe. Albany's three men in a room—and their successors—may well share the Bourbons' fate should they continue to avoid facing the fiscal liabilities presented by the reliance on public authorities to finance the state's long-range indebtedness.

The few measures Albany has adopted to address the public authorities have amounted to initial half-steps, followed by a more forceful measure (though not a panacea). In February 2005, then–Comptroller Hevesi issued the "Public Authorities in New York State: Accelerating Momentum to Reform" report. Late in June of that year, in the wake of scandals at the Canal Corporation, the MTA, and other authorities, the legislature authorized appointment of an inspector general and creation of a separate budget office to provide oversight of the authorities' operations, and Governor Pataki created a Commission on Public Authorities Reform, chaired by Ira Millstein. As might be expected, Albany's major actors hailed these moves as significant steps toward reform. Assemblyman Richard Brodsky, who brought the Canal Corporation scandal to light, proclaimed, "We have recaptured these Soviet-style bureaucracies."[41] Outside the confines of the statehouse, however, longtime observers remained skeptical, noting that the governor, who appoints members of public authorities' boards, would now also appoint both the inspector general and the chief of the new budget office charged with supervising his appointees. But Brodsky, demonstrating in effect that the legislature does indeed possess the power to be a leader when it comes to government reform, pressed on. His further work at the committee level and public opinion helped to push through, more than three years later, the Public Authorities and Reform Act of 2009. The law helped nudge the authorities at least partly out of the shadows by establishing statutory mechanisms for increased oversight by the Office of the State Comptroller, an Independent Authorities Budget Office, and expanded lobbying reporting requirements.

Albany, though, has also not confronted its penchant for fiscal deviousness. Rather, it has continued to pile yet more debt onto the books of the state's public authorities. When necessary, the state authorizes the transfer of funds from the authorities' own ledgers to the state budget for state purposes. This is an unofficial method, especially because authorities typically operate with less oversight and transparency than traditional state agencies and are not subject to the state's restrictions on the issuance of public debt and the requirement that bond issues be approved by the voters. For legislators, though, it is better than asking voters to approve tax increases. The political benefits of maintaining so many public authorities were evident in 2006, when a record $112.5 billion state budget was passed, a surplus of as much as $4.5 billion declared, and New York City was given $11.2 billion to construct and rehabilitate schools. The budget also included a round of tax cuts for the state's wealthier taxpayers, just in time for legislators to ask voters to reelect them in November. To be this effective, however, required authorizing New York's Dormitory Authority (whose purview was long ago broadened to finance construction of hospitals) to issue $2.6 billion in bonds for the city's school projects. Another $9.4 billion for capital construction was to be raised by the state's guarantee to back debt issued by city-controlled public authorities.[42] Perhaps when the bill for this and subsequent borrowing comes due, Albany will once again attempt to resort to what it has done with increasing frequency during the past fifty years: authorize public authorities to go even more deeply into debt by issuing still more bonds designed to pay off New York State's off-the-books debt, in an ever more desperate attempt to delude taxpayers into believing that sometimes they can get something for nothing.

Ultimately, the state's public authorities must be severely restricted in number and powers, and the state comptroller must be given the staff and resources needed to audit their functions. In releasing a December 2014 report on the public authorities, state Comptroller Thomas DiNapoli said that their spending had increased $3.5 billion in a year's time, and their debt had grown to more than a quarter of a trillion dollars overall.[43] In essence, what he depicted was a galaxy of "shadow governments," too many of them characterized by inaction and being ineffectual as well as an outsize sense of entitlement, yet none readily accountable to the public.

9

Other People's Money

The legislature's leaders almost always prefer keeping their rank-and-file legislators as fully dependent on them as possible. The unhealthy dynamic contributes to the now-epidemic levels of irresponsibility and stifles policy advances and new directions.

The overall dysfunction relates to three key areas: the legislative law-making process; the annual budget negotiations, shrouded by secret deals and arcane nomenclature; and the loose campaign finance system and noncompetitive arena of legislative elections. Many legislators usually make do with power arrangements as they find them and are little deterred by often-ambiguous rules of conduct and ethically flexible role models. In Albany's inherently transactional environment, the individual legislator, and sometimes the aggressive prosecutor, are left to sort out the difference between the expected practice of exchanging favors—appropriate give-and-take in negotiations over a bill, a policy, or an appropriation—and the trading of an official act for private benefit, which *is* a crime. Does the bill a legislator voted for offer a benefit to a private client? Is that a conflict of interest? Should the legislator recuse himself from voting in such borderline cases when doing so would effectively deprive his constituents of representation? The answers are not always so easily decided.

All of which makes it unfortunate that the recent state Moreland Commission was not permitted to complete its extensive review of the state and bring greater clarity to Albany's responsibilities. It is especially unlucky when one considers that JCOPE, the state's permanent and primary oversight vehicle, seems to offer little in the way of guidance and has enforcement powers over the executive branch but not over the legislative branch. Cases of alleged wrongdoing in the legislative branch are referred for enforcement to the Legislative Ethics Commission, which is controlled by the leaders of the legislature. Here again, as in too many other areas, the problem comes down to an excessively top-down legislative structure. Despite JCOPE's "independent" status, it too is ultimately controlled by the same political leaders that it is tasked with monitoring, with its members all appointed by the governor and the majority and minority conference leaders of the legislature. Additionally, the Albany *Times Union* and reform voices have criticized it as inscrutable, its deliberations and the basis for its decisions largely opaque.[1] Its effectiveness has also been challenged. Other than the alleged sexual harassment charges against former Brooklyn Assemblyman Vito Lopez, which had made numerous headlines by the time the panel looked into it, JCOPE has failed to bring a single important case of legislative wrongdoing to light.[2] It has no power to make legislators obey—none, that is, that it is willing to use.

The two legislative committees that are supposed to address ethics, the senate's Committee on Ethics and the assembly's Committee on Ethics and Guidance, do not play much of role in addressing corruption, preferring to look, occasionally, at internal complaints about conduct, such as sexual harassment accusations, or attendance.[3] As of early 2016, neither had held a hearing for nearly seven years.[4]

If one were to improve the ethical atmosphere in the state legislature, one would need first to break up the monopoly on decision-making held at this writing by Assembly Speaker Carl Heastie of the Bronx and Senate Majority Leader John Flanagan of Suffolk County, reenfranchise the minority party in each chamber as part of the process and not principally as reluctant pawns, and reinvigorate the moribund committee hearing system and floor debates. All of these also require ending the enormous problem of excessively free-flowing cash on "Planet Albany."[5]

The LLC loophole discussed in chapter 3 exemplifies the way wealthy interests are capable of getting what they want in Albany regardless of the ramifications to taxpayers. That the Board of Elections voted not to address the LLC issue in mid-2015 suggests the strength of Albany's attachment to all this free-flowing cash. The LLCs are treated under state election law as individuals, an absurd designation that allows them to make donations far above the corporation cap. The existence of this gaping loophole tempts legislators to vote on a bill, a member-item grant, or the appropriation of public funds or policy to help a private benefactor with extensive resources.

Funding nonprofits that they control is tempting for legislators, as in the prosecutions of Senator Pedro Espada Jr. in connection with his Soundview Health Center and Senator Shirley Huntly in connection with her education nonprofit Parent Workshop.[6] Both lawmakers were convicted of embezzling from the groups that they founded and funded through legislative earmarks. Similarly, former senators Larry Seabrook and Hiram Monserrate were each convicted of improprieties involving nonprofits that they funded as members of the New York city council, where they served before and after their senate terms, respectively.[7] The ties between community nonprofits and legislators were a significant part of the inquiries of the recent Moreland Commission to Investigate Public Corruption.

"With only limited success, the [Moreland] Commission has attempted to reverse-engineer the *somewhat inscrutable* [emphasis added] process of determining which legislator was responsible for the allocation of particular non-profits," the panel wrote in its December 2013 preliminary report.[8] To that end, the commission "used all the investigative tools at its disposal—including issuing numerous subpoenas, conducting surveillance, and deploying undercover agents to place recorded phone calls and conduct site inspections—in an effort to track questionable grants and check the sponsorship of the funding, the propriety of the grant, the controls in place to prevent abuse, and the ultimate use of state funding."[9]

Special interests, meanwhile, contributed large and virtually unlimited donations to the campaigns of legislative incumbents even though questions have arisen about some candidates' suspect use of campaign funds for personal expenses. According to the Moreland Commission report, a common goal of major donors, in many cases, is not so much to ensure the reelection of an incumbent, which is usually anticipated, but rather to ensure continued access to that legislator after the election.[10]

The limits that do exist for contributors, however, do not exist with regard to donations to so-called housekeeping accounts of the political parties. Although these kinds of accounts may be used only to maintain a permanent headquarters and carry on ordinary activities that are not for the express purpose of promoting the candidacy of specific candidates, according to election law, the Moreland Commission wrote that party housekeeping accounts "have become a device for raising virtually unlimited sums for campaign use."[11] A study by Common Cause New York cited in the commission report found that fifty-nine donors gave $200,000 or more and twelve donors gave $1 million or more to these accounts between 2006 and 2013.[12] The commission served at least eleven subpoenas related to party housekeeping accounts before it was ended.

The commission also looked at so-called independent expenditures by individuals and organizations engaged in "electioneering" activity independently of candidates and political parties. Such individuals and organizations are required under state law to register with the Board of Elections, but the board makes it easy for them not to because it has a restricted definition of *electioneering*. Only when a campaign message that expressly calls for the election or the defeat of a candidate is deployed does the board's disclosure requirement come into play, and thus public disclosure is circumscribed and the sources of donations remain hidden.

"Fundamental reform is required to create a campaign finance system that promotes public trust and democracy, changes our pay-to-play political culture, and empowers ordinary New Yorkers. This means lowering contribution limits, closing loopholes, improving disclosure, and creating an independent and vigorous campaign finance law enforcer," the Moreland Commission report said.[13] This is what New York City has done for municipal elections to great effect. The city, in the late 1980s, also adopted a small-donor match system of public funding, empowering ordinary individuals, and lessening the impact of large donors and special interest money. The majority of Moreland Commission members recommended a similarly robust campaign finance program for the state level.

What legislative action was taken on campaign finance reform as a result of the Moreland Commission's preliminary findings? The distressing answer: none. Thus, year after year, fundamental reform issues loom, and, while much is discussed, they are legislatively all but ignored in the once-pioneering and now-dysfunctional New York legislature. Major problems fester. However, many far less significant issues provided me with reminders of Albany's culture of group and individual misconduct in the years I served in the senate's minority.

A case in point: It is "well known in legislative circles," the late former Assemblyman Thomas Kirwan of Newburgh said in 2005, that legislative staffers are paid to perform campaign-related activities.[14] Although using taxpayer funds to pay for reelection efforts is illegal, legislative employees are routinely used for campaign tasks nonetheless. Staff members earn compensatory time for hours worked on regular duties beyond their base workweek. This makes sense for Albany staff, who may have to work long hours during the session from January to June and not as many after session ends. For them, it all averages out. Many employees who earn compensatory time, however, are expected to use it to "volunteer" during campaign season while still drawing their regular legislative staff salaries. This loophole is abused by designating some employees as part-time at a full-time salary, with the minimum hours required for receiving benefits. Those part-time employees, by working full-time for part of the year, can work on campaigns for months at a time while still earning their legislative paychecks. At one point, Assemblyman Kirwan had a simple solution to curb this routine abuse: pay the workers cash for overtime and do not allow compensatory time.[15] Legislative leaders denied any abuses, however. Characteristically they did not seek to tamper with a practice that caters to the perpetuation of incumbency and the top leadership's grip on power.

The legislature's hidebound and defensive posture was also evidenced by an earlier episode. In 2000, a small group of Democratic assembly members including Brooklyn's James Brennan, concerned about the fertile ground for financial mischief, had announced at a news conference that they had traced numerous state grants to a variety of hidden accounts in the New York State budget. The legislators called these murky accounts "slush funds," and they were collectively worth hundreds of millions of dollars. They existed under the virtually exclusive control of Albany's top two legislative leaders and the governor, noted the lawmakers.

The first of the funding items that they described was the Community Facilities Enhancement Program. This program, which sounded very official, was begun as a $425 million appropriation in the 1997–1998 state budget.[16] While it was known that the appropriation was designed to help finance new sports stadiums across the state—such as a $93 million arena for Buffalo—and that then–Governor Pataki, Assembly Speaker Silver, and Senate Majority Leader Bruno contributed equally to the full $425 million amount, the additional projects subsidized from this appropriation were never identified within the budget. Any fair and complete reckoning of how or whether all of this appropriation was used, and what happened to any unspent balance, became one of those enduring and commonplace mysteries that characterized the budgeting of billions of dollars of public funds in New York State.[17]

It was also an example of the business-as-usual fiscal practices that would never measure up to the required standards in any respectable company or any self-respecting, professionally staffed state legislature. New York, after all, has arguably the nation's heaviest tax burden; inordinately heavy and growing debt; and many serious, looming issues that the lackluster committee hearing process rarely examines. The entire state budget, which totaled more than $142 billion in 2015, is so large that few elected representatives ever bother to ask many questions about major appropriations or try to find out whether and how the money is to be spent. Under the master/serf dynamic that prevails in the legislature in Albany, most lawmakers seem to recognize that such conduct would be construed by their house leadership as rebellious, and could jeopardize their status in the hierarchy.

When one lawmaker did ask such questions loudly, as James Brennan and his colleagues did in issuing their "slush fund" critique back in 2000, the answers that came from the top were less than complete. But there was more to their report. The other "major slush fund" Brennan's group traced was known as the "Education Lump." The 1999–2000 state budget contained two such education lump-sum appropriations, which totaled $27 million. Listed as "grants-in-aid," they did not specify the recipients. "Behind the scenes," Brennan stated, "the legislative leaders choose which projects get funded."[18]

Of course he was right. While Assemblyman Brennan was not saying that tax money was improperly pocketed or illegally spent, he assailed the murkiness surrounding so many millions of dollars budgeted in accordance with accounting "principles" that were not worthy of a state legislature. The intentional vagueness increased the possibility of favoritism, real or perceived conflicts of interest, or even outright theft of public money.[19] Following his understandably daggered questions about how the public's money was being spent, as well as his speaking against Silver during the Michael Bragman "coup" attempt, the outspoken Brennan was demoted from his committee chairmanship. It took years before Brennan was apparently back in Silver's graces, when he was named chair of the assembly Committee on Corporations, Authorities and Commissions, and became the assembly majority representative on the PACB.

Mary Louise Mallick, who worked as a budget director for the senate majority under Majority Leader Joe Bruno during the Pataki years, says some innovative efforts were made to involve more senators and assembly members in developing the budget in response to legislators' complaints about being shut out or caught unaware of the final version. These staff-led initiatives, well-intentioned in the years they were tried, may have been doomed from the start because of the leadership-controlled budget process that has evolved in New York, she added in an interview.[20]

The real budget power, as I and everyone else in Albany knew, emanated from the three men in a room. In addition, in my experience the pressure of getting the budget done on time, or as close to the deadline as possible, made wider deliberation over budget details difficult and impractical. Legislators like me were advised how and when to vote to approve the aggregate budget package—or Big Ugly as some call it—and neither we nor even at times the experts of the budget staff knew the financial rationale for particular appropriations or cuts. It all contributed, just as much as loose or nonexistent campaign finance laws did, to an atmosphere of secrecy and unaccountability.

Take the issue of pensions, as E. J. McMahon and the Albany-based Empire Center for Public Policy did in July 2005, when it put out one of a regular series of red-flag reports that come and go in New York, too often unread and all but ignored. The research center's study began by noting that state retirement costs were straining state and therefore county budgets, to which many costs were shifted, with more than $4 billion in pension enhancements having been added to the state's retirement costs in the five years prior to the Empire Center for Public Policy report.[21]

The legislature's response to what many argued were structural weaknesses that could eventually cause problems in a lasting economic downturn—pension costs had risen faster than even the costs for the state's then–$45 billion and now $54 billion Medicaid program, the second costliest item in the budget after education aid—was to pass a series of hundreds of measures designed to increase pensions for unions and workers whose financial support and votes the legislators counted on at no immediate cost for which the legislature had to pay.[22]

This dependable generosity, driven by election-year dynamics and obscured by the secretive style in which the state budget is assembled (with its predictable coda of closed-door negotiations among the three top leaders), burdened both the state's finances and those of county governments. These growing obligations contributed to the strain on the public employee pension fund, which covers both state and local government retirees.[23]

Should the state government be using its enormous pension reserve differently? That is hard to say, partly because the tightly controlled, undemocratic process of passing a budget or doing just about anything of consequence in the Capitol does not allow time on the floor or in committees for public debate or expert input. Yet there are few topics more complex, politically fraught, or worthy of open discussion and vigorous debate than the subject of public pensions, given how many people depend on them and their cost to the state compared with other essential public priorities.

Because of the way the budget is assembled in Albany, access is often the thing that matters most for anyone seeking to influence the process from outside. The gradual cultivation of favors resulting in a backroom deal is the currency in Albany, as much now as ever, and probably more so.

Former Common Cause New York Director Rachel Leon has noted that many of the lobbyists the gambling industry hires in the state have been individuals who once exerted strong political or economic influence in state politics, people such as Patricia Lynch, the former chief of staff to assembly Speaker Sheldon Silver; Bill Paxon, a former New York congressman, now a lobbyist with a Washington law firm whose clients included the Seneca Nation of Indians; and Bill Powers, the former head of the state Republican Party. They provided access to key decision makers for those wealthy enough to afford them.[24]

John O'Mara, according to Common Cause New York, was a good example of how average citizens and their elected representatives were marginalized compared to those with personal ties to the Big Three. O'Mara is former chairman of the New York State Public Service Commission, which oversees the location of power plants and other state energy matters. He served on Governor Pataki's campaign and transition teams, and Pataki appointed him to the state Public Service Commission. O'Mara later became a lobbyist on behalf of energy giant Niagara Mohawk (now National Grid). Even as he lobbied legislators for the power corporation, he continued to serve as the governor's lead negotiator with Native American tribes and chaired Pataki's advisory council on federal judgeships. "No wonder he's called the 'ultimate insider,'" wrote Common Cause New York, discussing how power companies have sought to stave off grassroots pressure to close down old plants and reduce toxic emissions.[25]

One could spend a great deal of time, as Leon laudably did, to synthesize all these disparate facts in order to show cause and effect. It was, and is, a necessary but difficult chore, due to the many ways that those in power have connived and conspired to safeguard their power. But it is not easy. In New York State, even a landmark ruling on education funding by its highest court, the Court of Appeals, can be virtually ignored. The ruling in favor of the grassroots Campaign for Fiscal Equity required the state to come back to the court with a formula for funding public schools that did not penalize New York City and other low-income urban school districts with the highest proportion of economically and educationally disadvantaged students.

As much as $30 billion was supposed to flow to city schools over five years due to the court's 2005 decision. But then–Governor Pataki chose to appeal the court decision in order to leave in place a school funding process that all but guaranteed unequal school funding between cities and suburbs in violation of the court's interpretation of the state constitution and in particular its requirement that every child is entitled to a "sound, basic education." The necessary legislative debate on where the money would come from and how it would be spent did not materialize. The court decision was not considered in the 2005 budget.

In 2007, with the court decision still pending, an agreement was worked out among the governor, the legislature, and the Campaign for Fiscal Equity that increased classroom operating aid to many schools around the state by $5.5 billion over five years, with three-quarters for high-need school districts and one-quarter for average-need school districts. The state met its obligation for the first two years, but when the global recession hit in 2009 causing innumerable budget woes during Governor Paterson's administration, state education aid was frozen. Then, over the next two years, the state enacted $2.7 billion in school cuts, in effect undoing the Campaign for Fiscal Equity agreement. The issue headed back to trial in 2015, with eight small cities with high poverty rates in upstate New York pressing for the school aid they believed they were constitutionally entitled to receive. No decision had been reached at the time of this writing.[26]

Why the state government feels it can sidestep a Court of Appeals ruling, or at least determinedly postpone doing what it should be doing, certainly has something to do with the executive branch's enormous power over the state budget and, as it turned out, the governor's political goals. Governor Pataki, who had appealed and reappealed the court ruling to no avail, announced in August 2005 that he would not seek a fourth term after public opinion polls suggested the principal Democratic challenger,

Eliot Spitzer, might beat him. Clearly, dismissing the enormously important, expensive, and controversial school funding issue—as did then–Senate Majority Leader Bruno, whose political base was outside New York City—was certainly easier than complying with the spirit if not the letter of the court decision.

In the arena of education and in many other areas, Speaker Silver and Majority Leader Bruno contended that they were up against an extraordinarily powerful executive branch and thus their own sway was limited. This was to some extent true. Unfortunately, though, their contention was that they could not therefore permit too much independence of action or thought by their members so that they could show the governor a united front as often as possible.

The fact is, legislators are unable to serve their constituents adequately or fairly as long as their behavior is controlled by the leaders. Their fawning subservience does not necessarily strengthen their leaders' hand in annual budget negotiations with the governor, as is often argued by proponents of the status quo. In fact, if individual legislators were empowered, then a leader could use possible dissent from the ranks to their benefit in negotiations with the other house and the governor.

"Governor, I'd like to give you that $1.5 billion highway widening grant," an assembly speaker might be able to credibly say, "but I'm not going to be able to sell that one to my New York City members. I want to keep my job, thank you very much. So how about some additional mass transit aid to keep them happy? Then we can talk about your upstate highways."

In the meantime, the leader will have gotten better advice, a broader and, perhaps, more complex sense of the considerations and interests at issue from a more active and representative group of lawmakers. If the price of that is more contentiousness in his body, well, we live in a democracy.

A constitutional amendment that would have significantly revised the state budget process was put before the voters in November 2005. The amendment included a procedure for a contingency budget if the legislature failed to act on the governor's budget by the start of the fiscal year, which would have been moved from April 1 to May 1. While the amendment had some good features—it would have created an independent budget office and changed state school aid to two-year appropriations—it was criticized for giving the legislature the power to pass its own budget after a contingency budget was in place. The referendum was voted down by nearly 2 to 1.[27] If the objective was to give the people more say through their elected representatives, it was not likely to be realized. If the referendum had been approved, the result would have been to give additional power to only two of the three men in the room; at least now, the third man, the governor, a statewide official, could be voted out of office. The governor faces a sometimes volatile and uncertain *statewide* contest, of course, while the individuals who are promoted by their houses to senate majority leader or assembly speaker are elected in local contests comprising a sliver of the statewide electorate and a legislative district where they can, and do, dominate politically. In a state of 19 million people, approximately 129,000 people are in each of the 150 assembly districts and 307,000 in each of the 63 state senate districts.

If a choice has to be made between whether the governor or the legislature should control the budget introduction and approval process, then the governor should continue to have more power than the legislature. The legislature simply cannot be trusted due to structural lack of accountability because of the lack of transparency in the way it raises and spends the taxpayers' dollars it controls.

In relation to this concern, the citizens of New York State amended the state constitution in 1927 to implement the "executive budgeting system," an overhaul of the way New York was governed and the way in which the budget was put together. The system imposed new responsibilities on the governor to ensure that at least one person in the process was accountable to voters statewide. It gave the governor what was thought to be a reasonable degree of power to be more effective, and it has been the subject of court decisions over the decades.[28]

"The Governor is the constructor or the architect of the budget," explained John M. Caher, who was the Albany bureau chief of the *New York Law Journal*, during a 2005 Rockefeller Institute of Government forum on budget powers in New York. "The Legislature is the critic. Under the Constitution, the Legislature has budgetary authority to only approve an appropriation in its entirety; delete an appropriation in its entirety; reduce the amount of an appropriation without changing the when, how, and where conditions on how that money is to be spent; or it can add a new separate item of appropriation subject to gubernatorial veto."[29]

"What it can't do," Caher continued:

is substitute its judgment for the Governor's. It cannot delete the Governor's appropriation for X, vote that down, and then conjure up its own version and put it in place. As long as legislation is related to the appropriation, the Governor can condition the appropriation on the legislation. In other words, the Governor could for instance add language to a Medicaid appropriation bill. He could appropriate X number of dollars and put a line in there to say, "None of these dollars are to be used for abortion."

The Legislature's option then would be to accept the appropriation with the limiting language, or reject the entire appropriation and shut down Medicaid. Those are the only two options. . . . That leaves the Legislature with the power to create chaos, to do nothing—to refuse to pass the Governor's budget, to leave things hanging, and hopefully induce him by political pressure to negotiate. That is really the check and balance on the Governor's power.[30]

The U.S. Congress has not followed the same path. Checks and balances are not simply a theory in Washington. There are lengthy hearings and debates each year on the federal budget, despite the fact that the White House has enormous influence including the power of a presidential veto, which can only be overturned by a two-thirds vote of each house of Congress.

Citing the way legislators are shut out of the budget and lawmaking processes may sound like jealousy and resentment from a former minority Democrat in a Republican-majority house, and if that were all it was, it would be easy enough to dismiss. But only by considering the unremittingly self-serving logic of Albany can one even begin to understand how badly things work there—or how, to name one big example, Medicaid, in 2014 a $54-billion program to provide health care to the poorest New Yorkers, more than Texas and Florida combined,[31] is little scrutinized by the state legislature, year after year.

It is true. Medicaid, the half-century legacy of Lyndon B. Johnson's Great Society, has become a barn-sized target for unscrupulous people in the medical industry in New York, partly because the state came to provide just fifty civil servants and a few outside contractors to investigate recipients of Medicaid funds. One of the prices paid for limiting government's role was a diminution in the public regulatory and watchdog apparatus to keep track of government spending.

"It's like a honey pot," a former senior Medicaid prosecutor in Albany told the *New York Times* in its scathing, two-part exposé by reporters Clifford Levy and Michael Luo, which appeared in July 2005. The articles estimated that Medicaid fraud in New York State could amount to billions of dollars.[32]

Not surprisingly, some opportunistic New Yorkers in the medical industry realized they could act with relative impunity to tap into Medicaid's federal, state, and city billions—including dental and medical clinics, hospitals, transportation services, and pharmaceutical enterprises.

Several other states' health departments have antifraud offices that are larger than New York's in proportion to the size of their Medicaid budgets, the *Times* article pointed out. Therefore, New York's 301 employees in anti-fraud efforts recovered less than half as much money from Medicaid fraud prosecution as those in Texas, Florida, and New Jersey. Of those 301, only fifty were fully dedicated to anti-fraud work, as noted above. The rest shared that task with other jobs, such as administrative duties. "The decline of fraud control in New York," the second of the two *Times* articles said, "contrasts sharply with the situation in other states. In 1998, California, which had several high-profile Medicaid fraud cases in the 1990s, added about 400 employees to an existing staff of about 40 charged with rooting out abuse. The number of fraud cases referred to prosecutors has since doubled."[33]

The *Times* articles caught many Albany regulars by surprise, including key members of the governor's staff and the legislative leaders as well. There had been no probing hearings during my tenure on Medicaid spending. Then–Comptroller Hevesi, like his predecessor H. Carl McCall, was never invited to testify on the issue. Willful ignorance was the norm, which was nothing new. An earlier state comptroller, Erie County Republican Edward Regan, once reported that during his fourteen years as the state's chief financial officer no legislative committee asked him to testify on any topic, especially such an important a one, despite his repeated offers to do so.[34]

Then–Governor Pataki might have assumed that Medicaid has such a strong liberal constituency and that so many financial interests were invested in its bloated condition, that no one would bother to look closely at its enormous price tag, at least for the remainder of his time in office.

In addition, as with the last decade's Court of Appeals decision requiring fairer formulas for state education aid, Pataki resolved that Medicaid was one highly contentious situation he did not want to address.

The assembly speaker and senate majority leader had little to say about the Medicaid system too, having failed to charge a committee with addressing the issue of Medicaid oversight, though the more than 4.2 million poor people who depended on Medicaid clearly would have benefitted if fraud and waste were reduced—particularly when considering those tens of thousands of illegal claims for reimbursement that were approved. Since the state's legislative and executive branches preferred to operate without independent oversight, an independent review of the state Health Department was just as unwelcome. Nor do the legislative leaders want a separate entity of any kind to help determine how much money will be available for spending on any large line items in the budget in the next year—as many states allow.

Rather, the Big Three want to retain their power to argue and deal. In more recent years, slowing the rapid growth of the program took the involvement of Governor Andrew Cuomo, who had focused on Medicaid fraud as the state's previous attorney general. Starting in 2011, his first year as governor, he moved as much of the program as possible into managed care in collaboration with health-care industry leaders. Comptroller DiNapoli's auditors found that Medicaid's annual spending increases from 2010 to 2013 averaged just 1.7 percent—a drop from 5.3 percent the previous decade.[35] DiNapoli's review suggested that the governor's action had been strikingly successful. The legislature itself had no way of knowing or apparent desire to find out: it neither conducts long-term financial planning, nor has it created an independent budget office, such as the one New York City voters created in the late 1980s. The Albany legislative leaders do not want any type of oversight. The legislature has never even agreed to establish a four-year financial plan, a fundamental facet of how other states and cities, or any enterprise, manages its books.

Should we be surprised, then, that New York State does not conform to generally accepted accounting principles?

After a record late budget in August 2004, the legislature passed on-time budgets in 2005 and 2006, albeit budgets with many details left to be filled in later. Former Governor Mario Cuomo was critical: "It's not a real budget if, when the legislature adopts it, they know there are a billion and more dollars they have to add to it to meet their important needs," he told the *New York Times*. "It sounds to me like a Potemkin Village of a budget—it has the facade of a budget, it looks like a budget, but it's not a budget."[36]

Finally, from the halls of the Empire State's executive branch during my tenure in the legislature came surreptitiously recorded conversations. The subject matter was related to an important issue for any governor, whether Democrat or Republican—and that is patronage.

Regardless whether the conversations may or may not have been illegally taped, they ended up with Fredric Dicker of the *New York Post* in August 2005.[37] Gossip they may have been, but they were of genuine significance because New York is a state, like most, where the public gets only glimpses of their leaders speaking at carefully staged and controlled settings. In this instance, Thomas Doherty, one of Pataki's top aides in his first term, and various other people close to the governor were taped in private chats on Doherty's line. The snippets, while incomplete, should remind voters that the government needs to be more transparent and accountable.

With regard to patronage, a voice on the tapes, recorded shortly after Pataki won office in 1994, is that of Alfonse D'Amato, then a U.S. senator from New York. Doherty described his difficulties placing a Republican patron in a $60,000-a-year Department of Motor Vehicles job. A less than enthusiastic Department of Motor Vehicles official had told Doherty that the requested appointment would be a "heavy lift."

Pataki's response to the *Post* report was to call angrily for a federal inquiry into the unknown source of the recordings. On the matters of patronage, the doling out of jobs to political allies, and the involvement of a top aide and a U.S. senator who was his patron, the then governor of course said nothing.[38]

What should have been readily discussed, but was not, was "that the Pataki crowd has used Albany as its personal hiring hall," a *Times* editorial stated.[39]

Wiretapping in Albany returned to the headlines almost a decade later, when federal prosecutors used them on legislators and others to try to ascertain what was really going on behind closed doors and whether some state legislators were trying to profit privately from their public service.

In over ten years' time, lamentably, we have returned to the original state of affairs, and in so many ways—from the unbridled purchase of proximity to decision makers, to lack of transparency in budget decision making, to furtive maneuvering by legislative leaders and their minion—the situation was no better as of 2016.

10

The Road to Reforming a Failed State

Sometimes Albany's corrupt practices warrant jail, and sometimes they are difficult to discern, such as when officials use their influence to ensure that large political contributors receive lucrative state contracts or favorable legislation. Small matters, such as legislators requiring their staff members to "volunteer" on political campaigns, are considered business as usual, legal under New York's lax ethics laws and rules. Large ones sometimes attract headlines, as they should, and outrage often ensues.

While no regulations or government framework will ever be able to prevent corrupt individuals from stealing from the public purse, much more could be done to constrain the almost unbridled power of personal ties and big money in connection with Albany's Big Three and their many supplicants, thereby reducing instances of misconduct.

Why, one should ask, is there no truly independent budget office as in the New York City local government or Washington, a public authorities watchdog, or autonomous and empowered executive and legislative ethics commissions to keep a sharp eye on public officials?

The answer is simply that the state's leaders have not wanted to create a climate of transparency and oversight. When monitoring mechanisms have nominally been allowed to come into existence, such as in JCOPE and the Legislative Ethics Commission (to which JCOPE refers cases for enforcement), they have not been provided with the legal and financial means to eliminate criminal and unethical behavior. This is why, for example, JCOPE has no enforcement authority over the legislature, and the Legislative Ethics Commission lacks significant budgetary support and a truly nonpartisan staff. The senate's and assembly's standing ethics committees do not provide leadership, either. They neither hold hearings on reform topics nor consider legislation proposed to tighten ethics.[1]

Those of us who have served in the legislature and call ourselves reformers face a major dilemma. During my service in Albany, many items in the state budget could be considered essential for our district constituents or those of the state as a whole, whether they concerned education, transportation, the economy, social issues, or community needs. Individual items in the budget could not be voted on independently within either chamber, however, after the three men in a room had made their decisions. Nothing could be removed for separate consideration after the governor issued his "message of necessity" for the agreed-on budget bills. Each budget bill remained in the package. We were able only to vote "yes" or "no" on the package. Anyone who dared to vote "no" on this budget, approved by the governor, the assembly speaker, and the senate majority leader, was considered unpredictable and marked as one who could not be trusted. Vote "yes," however, and a legislator was seen as a one who works well with the other members and one who could possibly advance in his or her party ranks and in a few years or so become a chair or a ranking minority member of an impressive committee, which gives the legislators a larger stipend on top of their salaries.

Yet, legislative leaders still tended to view ethics reform proposals as a veiled attempt by the executive branch or outside reform groups to weaken the assembly and senate bodies. They often complained that the governor was not willing to impose reciprocal restraints on the executive branch, which at times was the case.

Then, as now, ethics reform was given less importance than immediate budgetary and policy issues, and it was lower on the agenda of whoever happened to be governor. In recent years, reform has continued to be used as leverage during the budget negotiations among the three men in a room—not as an end in itself. The issue of improving the way the legislature functions has been readily deferred in return for concessions and compromises on immediate spending issues, policies, and laws. Sometimes, when what resulted was considered a good-government measure by editorial writers, they did not write about a missed opportunity for serious ethics reform. For example, after Andrew Cuomo's 2010 campaign pledge to make ethics reform his top priority resulted in only compromise ethics legislation in his first year as governor, and when that, in turn, was followed the next year by legislation reducing the cost of pensions for prospective state and city workers[2]—a goal of many editorial pages around the state—there was no flurry of newspaper editorials lamenting that good-government measures were abandoned, including the potential introduction of an independent, nonpartisan system of decennial redistricting. Instead the public outrage over the governor's record on cleaning up Albany came later, when Cuomo was running for reelection. Editorials charged that he bargained away the important Moreland Commission probe (much supported by the editorials) for an on-time budget and relatively minor ethics changes.[3]

As I look back now, my years in the legislature were disturbing, especially after I came to know how the institution takes care of its own at all costs and blindsides the voters. I have concluded that only top-to-bottom reform can bring more transparent and democratic processes to the Capitol; certainly nothing that has happened in the years since *Three Men in a Room* was published in 2006 has caused me to change my views. In light of the events of the ten years that followed, I realize that the magnitude of the problem in Albany is greater than I ever imagined. On further reading, interviews, and reflection, I have come to understand that structural reform is necessary to end the concentration of power in the two top legislative leaders—whoever they happen to be at any given time and without regard to party affiliation. What can result from serious reform of the legislature, I believe, are much more dynamic and publicly accountable senate and assembly members, freed to dissent if necessary from their leadership and able to represent the interests of their districts and the state as a whole.

Decentralizing the all-controlling power wielded by the two legislative leaders, regardless of who they are or what their party affiliation, is the surest road to a stronger, more vibrant, and representative legislature. The shackles and strictures of lockstep leadership control that characterize Albany squelch debate and innovation, as well as public interest in what goes on there. It also leads to self-inflicted legislative paralysis. Empowering all members will embolden, not weaken, the legislature, as a counterbalance to the power of the strong New York governorship.

As noted, legislators stand little chance of being unseated, even when targeted for defeat at the polling booths by opposing forces. By 2004, however, I decided that after nearly a decade in office, I would voluntarily abandon my salary and perquisites, staff assistants, and all the public attention. Simply ending my quest to help right the legislature did not seem adequate, however, so I decided to add my voice to all those committed men and women throughout the state then, and now, clamoring for change.

Initially the important Brennan Center for Justice 2004 comparative analysis of New York and other states (discussed earlier) recommended that the senate and assembly leaders take it upon themselves to improve their procedures and make them more democratic. More than one-fourth of the Democratic assembly members signed a resolution in support of many of the reforms proposed in the detailed study.[4] At issue then was the dysfunctional budget and legislative processes. Now, in 2016, in response to the Dean Skelos and Sheldon Silver convictions, and the growth and magnitude of corruption within the environment of New York State's still dysfunctional legislature, there sadly has been no similar resolution or response of any kind.

The reforms that have been enacted since the Brennan Center for Justice report and its follow-ups and in the wake of the Silver and Skelos scandals have been piecemeal, partial, and even counterproductive. Legislators have chosen to remain in the same disempowered condition in which I had encountered them when I was first elected in 1996. Their reluctance to institute genuine democratization underscores, for me, that the legislature and even executive branch will not and cannot be relied on to reform themselves, except in incremental ways. The Big Three, whoever they are at any given time, will not *voluntarily* make Albany more ethical, more democratic, more open to public scrutiny, or fundamentally more accountable to the voters.

Indeed, even the recent criminal convictions of the two major leaders from two different parties failed to prompt the legislative leaders to amend the major rules, activities, and political culture of the senate and assembly.

Strong remedies, such as a state constitutional convention, which some think may be risky, are urgently needed, especially given that courts are reluctant to interfere in the other branches of government, public pressure increases and decreases, and the situation sometimes appears hopeless and intractable.

Nevertheless, we must seriously consider this remedy because what happens in Albany affects every man, woman, and child in the Empire State: a constitutional convention. A constitutional convention could potentially open the entire system of state governance to reexamination. It appears to be the only way that substantial restructuring of the legislature can come about, given both the legislative branches' entrenched pattern of corruption, refusal to reform, and reflexive instinct for self-preservation.

No one should underestimate the legislative instinct for survival and deeply entrenched, seemingly intractable nature of Albany's problems. Reporter Michael Cooper wrote in the *New York Times* in June 2005 that so-called soft-money contributions, which the federal government had banned, inundated state campaigns—sometimes in $100,000 installments. Those nearly unlimited contributions were made to political party organizations' innocuously named "housekeeping accounts."[5] Frighteningly, they still are, a decade later, in 2016.

Unrestrained soft-money contributions help parties protect incumbents who face strong challengers in much the same way that legislative leaders use hundreds of thousands of dollars in discretionary public funds, known as member items, to ease incumbents to victory in potentially close races. They carve out irregularly shaped districts to protect or enhance their party's control of their house in the legislature. Legislative turnover in New York remains one of the lowest of any state legislature in the nation.[6]

Over a quarter century ago, the New York State Commission on Government Integrity (the Moreland Commission chaired by Fordham University School of Law Dean John Feerick) pointed out the campaign finance loopholes and laxity.[7] In order for these self-serving campaign finance laws to change, however, a three-way agreement from the senate, the assembly, and the governor is necessary. The laws were never changed, and, therefore, the system remains unchanged.

"First," the 1980s Feerick commission recommended, "New York State's existing campaign finance laws are wholly inadequate to disclose and monitor, much less to limit, contributions to powerful legislators or legislative races by moneyed interest groups. . . . Second, interest group money plays an undesirably significant role in legislative campaign fundraising, particularly for party committees and individual legislators."[8]

Just as fundamental as campaign finance reform, there remains a critical need to introduce a nonpartisan redistricting process to prevent the parties from tailoring district lines to suit their political needs. Several states, notably Iowa, have taken up this reform, but not New York.

Rather than creating districts that are geographically compact and keeping communities and neighborhoods together, New York's districts are drawn largely for political purposes.

"The legislature's redistricting task force is armed with detailed data on population and voting characteristics that allow it to tailor a district to an incumbent's needs with block-by-block precision," wrote Mark Berkey-Gerard in an article for the online *Gotham Gazette*. "They are drawn to favor the majority party and ensure that each majority incumbent gets reelected."[9] As NYPIRG has noted wryly, the districts often resemble coffee stains on a map or bugs squashed on a windshield.[10] That is no accident, to be sure, but a calculated manipulation.

Albany also needs to do away with its "shadow government" of public authorities. The sprawl of state authorities—public benefit corporations acting independently of the flawed process by which money is raised and spent by the legislature—operate with little scrutiny. What exactly does each of them do? How do they operate? Why so many? Who is hired to run them? On what basis? Who scrutinizes their daily activities or their spending—equivalent to nearly one-quarter of the state budget if it were included?[11] One is hard-pressed to find the answers to such questions, given the layers of secrecy and lack of oversight under which they function.

These entities are generally exempt even from what few controls exist in the legislative and executive branches to limit favoritism, influence peddling, fraud, and waste. They are also exempt from civil service requirements and from many restrictions on how contracts are awarded, auditing and financial reporting requirements, and conflict-of-interest rules. Yet the taxpayers cover the interest payments on the massive and mounting long-term bonds.

Not only authorities but also the legislature, state agencies (including the Office of the State Comptroller and the Office of the State Attorney General), and the governor's office hold great potential for malfeasance, mismanagement, and conflicts of interest. They are all the focus of the law firms, bond underwriters, banks, engineering firms, contractors, and consultants—many of them former state employees—that interact with them. Mechanisms such as tough laws and ethical codes are needed to control and make more accountable and transparent the many governmental branches, agencies, and offshoots.

Term limits are both one of the most controversial and one of the most popular policies in the country. A poll the Empire Center for Public Policy commissioned not too long after I left the legislature found that approximately two-thirds of New Yorkers favorably viewed the introduction of term limits for state lawmakers and governors.[12] Term limits have improved the competitiveness of New York City council elections and reduced the concentration of power in that body.

Between 1990 and 2000 voters backed term limits for state legislatures in twenty-two states by an average popular margin of 2 to 1. They have gone into effect in fifteen states. Nebraska voted for term limits three times between 1992 and 2000, persisting when state and federal courts struck down their first two attempts. Their objective was realized. Senators are term-limited after putting in two consecutive terms and must wait four years before running again.[13]

Unfortunately, getting rid of incumbents in any other way than term limits is difficult in most states because of gerrymandering. Nebraska and other states that voted for term limits hope that it will lead to more "citizen legislators." A Nebraska official said that some of the state's veteran politicians had been playing golf with lobbyists for a generation. Interestingly, the legislatures of a few term-limiting states such as Arizona and California have become more ethnically diverse, boasting greater numbers of Latinos. Arkansas and Michigan have had more African Americans. California can claim a dozen more women in the assembly since term limits started. In some cases, the newcomers are more wary of lobbyists—at least initially—than their predecessors.

In the 1990s, New York City voters twice approved term limits for not only city council members but also the mayor, the public advocate, the city comptroller, and the five borough presidents. Those term limits first had an effect on those elected officials in 2001. I initially opposed term limits, but I now favor them as a means of lessening the entrenched power of the leadership as well as the dysfunctional state legislature. This is based in part on New York City's experience. Term limits have been relatively successful in achieving their goal to make public officials more responsive to the people. When elected officials can serve twenty, thirty, or more years, as in Albany, they sometimes lose contact with reality. Some then begin to feel that they are part of a permanent elite and accept the institutional inequities, relative ineffectuality, and corruption of the legislature as normal. In the years since the inception of term-limit law in the New York City, new faces and new leadership have risen, and the city council is fairer and as strong if not more so than it had been previously. Fears of political chaos were not realized. There is also no sign that special interests, wealthy contributors, and bureaucrats were more controlling over temporary lawmakers—or that the council speaker was enfeebled vis-à-vis the constitutionally more powerful mayor's office in the annual budget negotiations. New York State's term limits would not have to be the same as New York City's. The state's can and probably should include staggered terms in order to prevent an almost complete turnover (and with it the loss of much of institutional knowledge all at once). Additionally, having the terms for each legislator extend to a maximum of three terms of four years each might be better since moving up in any legislature requires patience and time served. This kind of approach could also make staggering their terms and giving them time in office to accrue influence and accomplish things easier.

The Need for a Constitutional Convention

If a state constitutional convention were held in New York, many delegates would probably agree that state legislators should not be able to continue to hold an office for an open-ended period of time because turning their jobs into lifetime sinecures simply by serving the leadership in a submissive, ineffectual manner is already too easy. And because the governor is more accountable and given to turnover—serving longer than three terms is almost unheard of in contemporary politics because the voters inevitably want someone new—a gubernatorial term limit is probably not needed. Others may feel differently. New Jersey, for example, has a two-term limit for its governor, as do many other states. Virginia governors may only serve one term. In New York, however, only one governor in seventy-five years, Nelson Rockefeller, was elected to a fourth consecutive term, and he left in the middle of that term in hopes, perhaps, of running successfully for president but was appointed vice president by President Gerald Ford.

Standing in the way of any solutions to the permanent crisis in Albany is the lack of a real legislature, one that would be permitted to do all the things that many legislators have done for decades in Washington and in many states: debating and proposing and holding hearings. That kind of enlivened, representative body, to which the public is entitled and on which a healthy democracy depends, does not exist now in Albany.

The route of a constitutional convention is not recommended frivolously. I am well aware that a convention could open the entire state constitution—any part of it—to possible amendment by the voters based on the recommendations of the elected delegates. Our current state constitution contains, for example, some of the best protections for the poor of any state. But as we have seen with welfare policy, federal policy determines the shape of state policies concerning poverty relief.

New York is one of fifteen states with existing mechanisms for calling a constitutional convention. At any time, the legislature may put the question of holding a convention before the voters. The legislature may limit the scope of the convention in the language of the referendum, but need not do so. If voters then approve it, delegates are subsequently elected by the people. This provides a reasonable opportunity for delegates to consider the needed revisions. As with constitutional amendments the legislature proposes, any revisions to the constitution the delegates approve then go on the ballot for voters' final approval or rejection. In 1965 the legislature placed an unrestricted constitutional convention on the ballot, and the voters supported it. The 1967 constitutional convention proposed a vastly revised constitution as a single revision, which the people then voted down.[14]

"I think it's a risk worth taking," former Westchester Democratic Assemblyman Richard Brodsky said at a 2004 forum on Albany sponsored by the Rockefeller Institute of Government. "I think the people of the state can be trusted to be fair and sensitive to a variety of needs."[15] In a September 2016 interview, Brodsky said he was committed to his long-held view that a constitutional convention remained the best opportunity for the kind of "civic discussion on government reform" that New York State sorely needs.[16]

I believe that there is no viable alternative to a constitutional convention today. The legislature cannot be trusted to create, via the constitutional amendment mechanism, a nonpartisan redistricting panel to strengthen ethics rules and enforcement, to curtail and abolish superfluous state authorities and their back-door borrowing, or to institute debt reform and budget reform. Because any of these needed measures would dilute the power of the legislature's leadership, they are unlikely ever to be placed before the voters as a ballot referendum.

There is indeed a crisis of governance and of public confidence, born of decades of institutional failure. Only a bold remedy can possibly cure the patient. New Yorkers must look to a constitutional convention for the serious changes needed to revitalize our governing institutions, and many, including the late Governor Mario Cuomo and the current Governor Andrew Cuomo have argued that a constitutional convention offers voters the opportunity to achieve lasting reform in Albany.[17]

The New York State Constitution provides that voters be asked every twenty years whether a constitutional convention should be convened. "Shall there be a convention to revise the Constitution?" is the wording of a ballot measure voters will, by law, see in 2017, twenty years after the majority of state voters had last considered holding a convention in 1997, turning it down. Leaders across the state, citizens of all political persuasions, and the media can exert influence—more readily and consequentially than many may think—toward convening this historic convention, come the 2017 referendum. Remember, the people have no power to petition directly for a convention; this opportunity comes around only once every twenty years.

In 1992, in advance of the 1997 vote, Peter Goldmark, who was New York State budget director under Governor Carey and later president of the Rockefeller Foundation, was appointed by Governor Mario Cuomo to head a commission to examine the need for a constitutional convention. Goldmark ended up opposing a convention in 1997 because he believed that reform of state institutions could best be achieved by a series of state commissions. Under Governor Pataki, Speaker Silver, and Majority Leader Bruno, few if any of the desired reforms took place. The highly respected Goldmark now believes that a convention is needed to achieve meaningful reform,[18] as does former Lieutenant Governor Richard Ravitch.[19]

Former state Senator Richard Dollinger once reminded me that I was hardly alone among former and current state legislators in my then-growing belief about the importance of a convention sooner rather than later. Dollinger, who was the county chairman for the Democratic Party organization in greater Rochester, left the New York State senate after the 2001–2002 term and later became a judge of the New York State Court of Claims. He saw campaign finance reform as essential to reinvigorate Albany, yet he believed it would probably never come about without a constitutional amendment, whether that amendment is placed on the ballot by the legislature or a constitutional convention. He said some years back that the "signs of collapse" in the Capitol will create the conditions for something as dramatic as a constitutional convention.[20] Those signs of collapse have increased significantly over the past decade.

The state constitution is not a static document, having been substantially revised at least four times in New York history. The original New York State Constitution was drafted and approved in 1777, a decade before the U.S. Constitution. Major rewrites took place in 1821 (when a Bill of Rights was inserted), 1846 (enshrining a referendum process for determining whether a new convention should be held every twenty years), 1894 (establishing the right to an education for every child in the state), and 1938 (providing for social services for the poor, public health programs, labor and housing rights, and four-year instead of two-year gubernatorial terms).[21] It has been amended more than 200 times in all, either following a constitutional convention or after legislative passage in two consecutive sessions, both of which required approval by the voters of a ballot question on the suggested amendment.[22]

Since 1964, at least eleven states have adopted new constitutions,[23] while other states have substantially revised their constitutions.

As I see it, the statewide editorial-page outcry and the defeat or near defeat of some incumbents might have been the lead-in to a decisive new movement for reform. Public pressure has grown in the wake of U.S. Attorney Bharara's successful prosecutions of Silver, Skelos, and Libous. Similar indictments and convictions of consecutive senate Democratic leaders such as Malcolm Smith, Pedro Espada, and John Sampson have added to the momentum.

Recommendations to Reform the New York State Legislature

The following reforms would go a long way to improving New York State's government, through the necessary vehicle of a constitutional convention:

◆ **Ethics enforcement:** Establish a nonpartisan, independent commission to oversee ethics in the legislative and executive branches. Unlike the current bipartisan JCOPE, whose members are appointed by the governor and the leaders of the majority and minority legislative conferences, this commission would be truly independent of both the legislature and the executive. It would also have enforcement power over the legislature, which JCOPE lacks. The commission could be appointed by the chief judge of the New York State Court of Appeals and the presiding justices of the four departments of the Appellate Division of the Supreme Court in order to create a nonpartisan rather than bipartisan commission. The governor should also establish a new commission under the Moreland Act to investigate corruption and make recommendations designed to ensure public integrity including the scope of powers for the independent state ethics agency.

◆ **Redistricting:** Similarly, New York State needs to have a politically independent, nonpartisan redistricting board for both legislative and congressional districts as a number of states have successfully done. For decades senate and assembly leaders have used New York's redistricting process to prevent truly competitive elections and protect their house majorities. The legislature has a 98 percent reelection rate.[24] The assembly has been under Democratic control since 1975 while the Republicans have controlled the state senate for all but three years since 1939. The 2014 constitutional amendment establishing a bipartisan redistricting commission appointed by the legislature, whose proposals must be approved by both houses of the legislature, is not sufficiently independent.

◆ **Reduce the power of the legislative conference leaders:** The current system in which the leaders of each conference have control over committee assignments, leadership titles, and staff budgets must be reformed. The leaders should be accountable to their conference members, not vice versa. And, the conference members must be given power for decision-making to make the state legislature an inclusive and deliberative body. We want an environment in which power is more diffuse throughout government and not held by three men in a room.

◆ **Fair distribution of legislative resources:** All members of each house, regardless of party or seniority, should be given comparable staff allocations and Albany office space, as well as funding for district offices sufficient to serve their constituents, in accordance with geographic size, population, local rent, and other costs. The ability to provide basic constituent services should not depend on a member's party and seniority.

◆ **Empower committees:** The current legislative committee system in both houses is largely a sham. The committees serve as puppets of the assembly speaker and senate majority leader, accomplishing little through their powers to hold hearings or review proposed legislation except at the stipulation of their house leader. Committee chairs should be appointed by the individual members of the committee—not just the leaders of each house. This will give all committees some autonomy from legislative leaders to devise and debate legislation. Committees should be empowered to hold hearings on pending legislation, allow bill markups and amendments, and decide which bills are sent to the floor of each house for a vote without fear of retribution from the leaders, thereby ensuring that every bill voted out of a legislative committee be presented for a vote by the entire house and not selectively buried by the house leader. Finally, we should establish conference committees as a mechanism to resolve legislative differences concerning bills passed in the senate and the assembly.

◆ **Procedural reforms:** All members of both parties should be allowed to offer motions to discharge bills that have not been reported out of committees as well as to propose amendments for bills being considered on the floor. Governors' messages of necessity, which allow for the immediate consideration of bills on the floor without the normal three-day waiting period, should be used only in the case of actual emergencies (such as addressing a natural disaster) and not as a means of quickly adopting a deal made by the three men in a room without review by the rest of the members as a deadline approaches.

◆ **Transparency:** Make the legislature subject to both the state Open Meetings Law and the state Freedom of Information Law so that residents can know what their representatives are doing. All legislative sessions, hearings, and committee meetings should be broadcast, as is the practice in the U.S. Congress and New York City's city council.

◆ **Four-year terms with term limits:** Extend the legislative term from two to four years with term limits of three or four terms. Having four-year rather than two-year terms would change the current practices of congressional representatives and state legislators who claim that they must fundraise and campaign as soon as they are elected or reelected for two-year terms. The constant pressure to campaign every two years and raise money for reelection undermines members' ability to act in the best interest of the people. Unlimited terms lead to entrenched leadership with excessive power and increase the possibility of corruption at the top, as exemplified by the recent spate of arrests of legislative leaders.

Long Island U.S. Representative Steve Israel in 2016 announced that he would not run for reelection for another two-year term, saying that "I don't think I can spend another day . . . begging for more money. I always knew . . . the system was so dysfunctional. Now it is beyond broken."[25] This is an appropriate comment about what exists in the nation's capital, but the federal government is still less dysfunctional than many state governments. In New York, the two-year terms of both assembly members and senators mean that legislators are perpetually raising money, campaigning, and making legislative decisions based on fundraising and elections and not necessarily working in the best interests of the people.

• **Make the legislature full-time, with higher pay, and ban or significantly curtail outside income:** Legislators frequently claim that their $79,500 salary, which has not been increased since 1996, is insufficient, especially for the members of the legislature who do not have outside employment. They cite the low salary as a justification for the system of tens of thousands of dollars in stipends given for the numerous conference leadership positions and committee chair and ranking minority member positions. They also cite it to justify maintaining often lucrative outside employment, sometimes in conflict with their legislative positions. We should provide for a full-time state legislature just as we have a full-time U.S. Congress[26] and, as provided in a 2016 pay increase bill signed by Mayor Bill de Blasio, a full-time New York City City Council.[27] I would recommend a full-time legislative salary of between $125,000 and $150,000 per year. Future salary increases should be limited to those recommended by an independent commission and not at the legislature's discretion. Members should be working in the best interest of their constituents and the people of New York State, not on behalf of outside interests to whom they are financially linked. This outside income should be no more than 10 percent of their full-time salary. The information should also be completely transparent and reviewed by an independent ethics commission. While some have said that members of the legislature do not have enough to do in Albany to justify full-time status along with a ban on earning outside income,[28] robust and active committees conducting bill markups, issue hearings, and oversight would require considerably more hours than the current part-time legislature in which the governor, the assembly speaker, the senate majority leader, and their staffs do most of the work.

• **Strengthen conflict-of-interest laws and establish a fiduciary oath:** As the recent federal convictions of Silver and Skelos have shown, New York's weak conflict-of-interest laws along with the prevalence of outside employment by members of the legislature have allowed members to benefit financially from the offices they hold. Members of the legislature must be expressly prohibited from exploiting conflicts of interests for their own or their families' financial gain. Similarly, former Assemblyman Richard Brodsky has proposed that all public officials swear a fiduciary oath in which they pledge primary allegiance to their office and the people of the state rather than self-interest. Such an oath, already required of members of public authorities, would give prosecutors an additional means of addressing conflicts of interests that otherwise may not violate ethics and bribery laws.[29]

◆ **Per-diem reform:** Replace the current unverified system of per-diem payments for food and lodging when in Albany, which a growing minority of legislators has abused, with a new system limited to reimbursement for proven food and lodging expenses while on official business in the state capital. Require both receipts of payments and proof that the member was at work in Albany, which will prevent members from collecting per-diem payments for time they are in Albany but not working, such as weekend days before a session week, as well as from collecting lodging reimbursements in excess of their actual housing costs.

◆ **Budget reforms:** Prohibit special budget allocations from being worked out only by the three men in a room for different projects. The final budget bills must be made available to all legislators well in advance for review and not voted on without the necessary time to read these items.

◇ **Earmark reform:** Eliminate unitemized lump-sum budget lines and slush funds under the control of the governor and the two legislative leaders. Require transparency for all member items and other designated grants regardless of the nomenclature. These kinds of grants are intended to serve community needs, not the electoral agenda of the house leaders, and they should be vetted to ensure that the member does not have a personal or financial interest at stake. Where appropriate, community organizations should be funded in the baseline budget and granted funds objectively by state agencies through an application process based on the merits of the proposal rather than at the discretion of any of the three men in a room. The ability to designate expenditures should be allocated equally to all members of the legislature, not as a way to reward some members, especially those in the majority party, and to punish others. Members should be encouraged to adopt participatory budgeting processes in which members of the community propose and vote on the projects to be funded by discretionary funds.

✧ **Independent budget office:** Establish a nonpartisan, politically independent budget office to monitor the state budget and state finances, including debt accumulation and taxation. New York City's Independent Budget Office has been very successful, and there is every reason to expect such success with a state independent budget office.

• **Public authority reforms:** Sharply reduce the number of public authorities, concentrating on support for essential services such as economic development and transportation; eliminate most of the rest and incorporate their functions into executive agencies that are part of the state budget and subject to constitutional debt restrictions. At the same time, establish a nonpartisan commission to work with the state comptroller on oversight of public authorities, which will report on their expenditures and borrowing levels to the legislature and make its findings public. The state's use of public authorities creates significant public debt beyond constitutional limits, leaving to future generations additional obligations to pay for benefits we receive now while pretending that these expenditures have no cost.

• **Pension reforms:** The laws governing public officials' pensions need to be changed. Currently, officials elected before the passage of PIRA are permitted to collect their pensions even after being convicted of corruption. This must end. One consequence of an elected official being convicted of corruption must be the forfeiture of his or her pension, and the state must pass a constitutional amendment such as the one Governor Andrew Cuomo proposed to achieve this.[30]

Another outrage is sitting members of the legislature submitting retirement papers at the end of one term, only to be sworn back into office for the next term and collecting both a legislative salary and a legislative pension. Since the legislature ended this practice for members first elected after 1995,[31] more than twenty veteran members have "retired" and returned to office since then and collected both the salary and pension.[32] This "double-dipping" must also end.

- ◆ **Campaign finance reforms:** Critically, New York State needs sweeping campaign finance reform. New York City's successful experience with campaign finance reform provides a roadmap.

    ◇ **Lower contribution limits with matching public financing:** New York State has the highest campaign contribution limits of any state that limits contributions.[33] Legislators' campaign committees should be subject to contribution limits of $1,000 with prohibitions on transferring funds to any other committee. With the new system of lower contribution limits, the state should establish public campaign financing in the form of small-donor matches along the lines of the successful campaign finance system for all New York City elected officials. This system should not only cover the legislature but also the executive branch, which includes the governor, lieutenant governor, the attorney general, the state comptroller, and the district attorneys in all of the state's sixty-two counties, as well as the elected judiciary.

    ◇ **Close the LLC loophole:** An LLC, a business entity similar to a corporation or a partnership, is allowed to contribute to campaigns the maximum amount allowed for individuals. This LLC loophole makes no policy sense and is exploited to give some wealthy interests undue influence. It must be closed. LLCs should be treated like partnerships with their contributions attributed proportionally to their owners and subject to the owners' contribution limits.

◇ **Eliminate party housekeeping accounts:** The housekeeping accounts of party committees serve as conduits for unrestricted contributions by entities with interest before the state and localities and should be banned.

◇ **Require full disclosure of independent political spending:** In the years since the 2010 *Citizens United* U.S. Supreme Court decision, political spending by independent organizations has dramatically increased, often with the sources of the money spent hidden. Campaign finance and lobbying laws must be amended to require that these groups disclose both their spending and the sources of their funding.

When the Silver and Skelos trials ended at the end of 2015, the new senate Republican leadership consisting of Majority Leader John Flanagan and Deputy Majority Leader John DeFrancisco downplayed the state's need for additional ethics reform, publicly stating that further redistricting was unimportant and opposing the elimination of outside work for elected officials. Senator DeFrancisco even went further than his colleague did by saying that the Silver and Skelos convictions show that new laws on ethics reform are not necessary: He asserted that the existing laws that deal with unethical and illegal behavior are sufficient at leading to their arrest and convictions. He was quoted in his hometown paper, the Syracuse *Post-Standard*, stating, "whether it is failing to report certain things on expense reports, bribery, using their office for their own personal benefit, that's all in the existing law."[34]

Yet, in addition to misreading the legislature's flourishing corruption and its systemic causes, DeFrancisco was woefully out of step with public sentiment. There is widespread public concern about corruption and support for many of these reforms. A Siena Research Institute poll released in February 2016 found that 89 percent of New Yorkers believe that corruption is a serious problem whereas more than 60 percent supported making the state legislature full-time.[35]

We have seen thirty-three members of the legislature fall to corruption scandals in approximately fifteen years. Many were prosecuted by

U.S. Attorney for the Southern District of New York Preet Bharara under federal statutes, although, as Bharara told *City and State* in September 2016, reform cannot be left to prosecutors alone.[36] Few errant legislators, in any case, were prosecuted by district attorneys or the state attorney general. State laws and rules, and particularly the enforcement of these rules, are clearly inadequate and so is the legislature's interest in doing anything about it.

Failed State: Dysfunction and Corruption in an American Statehouse should be viewed, therefore, as part of a process of getting "we, the people," as well as our elected leaders, to move quickly toward a meaningful conversation on democracy and decision-making in the Empire State.

As U.S. Supreme Court Justice Louis Brandeis noted more than a century ago, "Sunlight is said to be the best of disinfectants."[37] New York State needs to pry open its governance system, let in fresh ideas and new blood, and usher in disinfecting sunlight. Instead of remaining in a state of disgrace, the legislature can move steadily toward becoming a national model of transparency, democratic engagement, and effective policymaking. The languid pace of reform of the past fifteen years simply will not be sufficient given the state's enormous complexity and daunting concerns. The time has come for fostering a higher standard of government ethics and performance to which all New Yorkers are entitled. As Peter Goldmark mentioned to me, the reforms recommended above "are comprehensive and tough, and almost all of them are things that other states have done or used well—so it would be hard for anyone to say they're 'Pollyannaish' or 'dangerous.' And of course we've got to try a Constitutional Convention. . . . What we have in Albany is an unholy confluence of leader tyranny, corrupt campaign financing, insidious gerrymandering, and no real oversight on integrity, due process, and transparency."[38]

To defer major, structural reform of the New York legislature, year after dysfunctional year, could be the worst crime of all. George Santayana said, "Those who cannot remember the past are condemned to repeat it."[39] The time to start reform is now. The recent past has been a disaster that must be changed dramatically so that New York State is restored to the heights it once occupied—a beacon of light, progress, and integrity that other states will seek to replicate.

Notes

Chapter 1
When Poetry Met Prose

1. Prudence Katze and Susan Lerner, *Outside Income Brief—December 2015: Common Cause/NY Compiles a Major Review of Outside Income for NYS Lawmakers*, Common Cause New York, http://www.commoncause.org/states/new-york/research-and-reports/ccny-2015-review-of.pdf, p. 2.

2. Charles D. Lavine, "After Skelos and Silver, How to Save Albany," *New York Times*, Dec. 12, 2015, p. A25.

3. The number of Senate members was increased from sixty-one to sixty-two in 2003 and to sixty-three in 2013.

4. Citizens Union of the City of New York, "Turnover in the NYS Legislature Due to Ethical or Criminal Issues, 1999 to 2015" (updated Dec. 11, 2015), Dec. 2015; 17 of the 117 members that served in the New York State Senate from 2000 to 2014 have faced charges of corruption or malfeasance as of this writing. They represent 16.4 percent of senate membership at any given time during that period.

5. Andrew Cuomo, *The New NY Agenda: A Plan for Action*, 2010, http://s3.documentcloud.org/documents/7206/the-new-ny-agenda.pdf.

6. New York State Joint Commission on Public Ethics, "New York State Public Integrity Reform Act (PIRA): An Overview for Public Officials," http://www.jcope.ny.gov/training/NYSPIRA%20-%20A%20Guide%20for%20Lobbyists%20Clients%20Pub%20Corps%20FINAL.pdf; "Governor Cuomo Signs Ethics Reform Legislation," Aug. 8, 2011, https://www.governor.ny.gov/news/governor-cuomo-signs-ethics-reform-legislation.

7. Jen Benepe, "Lobbying Reforms Hit Real Estate Board," *Real Deal*, Oct. 25, 2007; Thomas Kaplan, "Renaming the Ethics Bill, and Asking for Money," *New York Times*, "City Room" (blog), June 8, 2011, http://cityroom.blogs.nytimes.com/2011/06/08/renaming-the-ethics-bill-and-asking-for-money/.

8. "New York State Public Integrity Reform Act (PIRA)"; Blair Horner, email to Seymour P. Lachman, Jan. 13, 2016.

9. Thomas Kaplan, "Cuomo Creates Special Commission to Investigate Corrupt Elected Officials," *New York Times*, July 3, 2013, p. A22.

10. New York State Commission to Investigate Public Corruption, *Preliminary Report*, Kathleen Rice, Milton Williams Jr., and William Fitzpatrick, cochairs, Dec. 2, 2013, http://publiccorruption.moreland.ny.gov/sites/default/files/moreland_report_final.pdf.

11. Moreland Act of 1907, New York Executive Law § 6.

12. Moreland Commission on Utility Storm Preparedness and Response, http://utilitystormmanagement.moreland.ny.gov/, retrieved Sept. 19, 2016.

13. New York State Commission to Investigate Public Corruption, http://publiccorruption.moreland.ny.gov/, retrieved Sept. 19, 2016.

14. Glenn Blain, "NY Gov. Cuomo Says Moreland Commission Can Look at Whoever It Wants—Even Him," *New York Daily News*, "Daily Politics" (blog), Aug. 29, 2013, http://www.nydailynews.com/blogs/dailypolitics/ny-gov-cuomo-moreland-commission-blog-entry-1.1696093.

15. John Caher, "Legislators Hire Counsel to Guide Response to Potential Ethics Probe," *New York Law Journal*, Sept. 20, 2013.

16. Nick Reisman, "Moreland Commission Officially Withdraws Its Subpoenas," *Time Warner Cable News Capital Region* (Albany, NY), "State of Politics" (blog), Apr. 24, 2014, http://www.nystateofpolitics.com/2014/04/moreland-commission-officially-withdraws-its-subpoenas/; Nick Reisman, "Moreland Commission's Lawsuit Is No More," *Time Warner Cable News Capital Region* (Albany, NY), "State of Politics" (blog), May 6, 2014, http://www.nystateofpolitics.com/2014/05/moreland-commissions-lawsuit-is-no-more/.

17. Susanne Craig, William K. Rashbaum, and Thomas Kaplan, "Governor's Office Hobbled Corruption Investigations," *New York Times*, July 23, 2014, p. A1.

18. Zephyr Teachout, *Corruption in America: From Benjamin Franklin's Snuff Box to Citizens United* (Cambridge, MA: Harvard University Press, 2014); Ginia Bellafante, "A Cuomo Opponent Tilting at Corruption," *New York Times*, Aug. 3, 2014, p. 1 (Metropolitan section).

19. New York State Board of Elections, "Statewide Democratic Gubernatorial Primary, September 9, 2014," http://www.elections.ny.gov/NYSBOE/elections/2014/Primary/2014StateLocalPrimaryElectionResults.pdf.

20. New York State Board of Elections, "Governor/Lt. Governor Election Returns, November 4, 2014," (rev. Apr. 3, 2015), http://www.elections.ny.gov/NYSBOE/elections/2014/general/2014Governor.pdf.

21. William K. Rashbaum and Susanne Craig, "U.S. Said to Subpoena Records of Anticorruption Panel," *New York Times*, May 6, 2014, p. A18.

22. Ibid.

23. Benjamin Weiser, Thomas Kaplan, and Susanne Craig, "Leaders of Anticorruption Panel Felt Cuomo Intervened, Prosecutors Say," *New York Times*, Sept. 13, 2015, p. A31.

24. Benjamin Weiser, "No U.S. Charges against Cuomo on Ethics Pan," *New York Times*, Jan. 12, 2016, p. A1.

25. Chris Bragg, "Cuomo on Moreland Tampering: 'It's my commission,'" *Crain's New York Business*, "Insider" (blog), Apr. 24, 2014, http://www.crains newyork.com/article/20140424/BLOGS04/140429924/cuomo-on-moreland-tampering-its-my-commission.

26. Aaron Short, Carl Campanile, and Leonard Greene, "Silver, Donor under Investigation Are Longtime Friends," *New York Post*, Dec. 31, 2014, http://nypost.com/2014/12/31/silver-donor-under-investigation-are-longtime-friends/; Anna Sanders, "Staten Island Attorney Reportedly Tied to Criminal Charges against Sheldon Silver," Jan. 22, 2015, http://www.silive.com/news/index. ssf/2015/01/staten_island_attorney_reporte.html.

27. Short, Campanile, and Greene, "Silver, Donor under Investigation Are Longtime Friends"; *United States of America v. Sheldon Silver*, U.S. District Court, Southern District of New York, 15 Cr. 93, "Indictment," https://assets.document-cloud.org/documents/1671632/indictment-of-sheldon-silver.pdf, pp. 3–6.

28. Stephen Rex Brown, "Sheldon Silver Told Dr. Robert Taub to Keep Scheme a Secret, Feds' Witness Says at Corruption Trial," *New York Daily News*, Nov. 4, 2015, http://www.nydailynews.com/news/crime/dr-robert-taub-testifies-sheldon-silver-trial-article-1.2423558.

29. Erica Orden, "Attorney Testifies about Sheldon Silver's Perks," *Wall Street Journal*, Nov. 11, 2015.

30. William K. Rashbaum and Thomas Kaplan, "Landlord Tied to Law Firm that Paid Assembly Chief," *New York Times*, Dec. 31, 2014, p. A15.

31. Susanne Craig and Benjamin Weiser, "U.S. Introduces Letter Showing a Potentially Lucrative Deal for Silver," *New York Times*, Nov. 13, 2015, p. A27.

32. *United States v. Sheldon Silver*, "Indictment," p. 8; Charles V. Bagli, "Real Estate Executive with 'Access to Politicians' Is at Center of Scandal," *New York Times*, May 25, 2015, p. A15.

33. Colby Hamilton, "At Silver's Corruption Trial, Veteran Lobbyist Recalls Phone Call," *Politico New York*, Nov. 13, 2015, http://www.capitalnew york.com/article/albany/2015/11/8582840/silvers-corruption-trial-veteran-lobbyist-recalls-phone-call.

34. Citizens Union of the City of New York, "Turnover in the NYS Legislature."

35. Thomas Kaplan and William K. Rashbaum, "Secret Taping by 2nd Official Rattles the State Legislature," *New York Times*, May 4, 2013, p. A1.

36. Errol Louis, "Sheldon Silver's Army of Enablers," *New York Daily News*, Jan. 26, 2015.

37. Jesse McKinley, "Field Thins Quickly in Contest for New Assembly Chief," *New York Times*, Jan. 30, 2015, p. A20; Yancey Roy, "Heastie elected, Bronx Democrat Is First African-American Assembly Speaker," *Newsday*, Feb. 3, 2015.

38. Russ Buettner and David W. Chen, "Assembly Speaker Benefited from His Mother's Embezzlement," *New York Times*, Apr. 21, 2015, p. A1; Russ Buettner, "Speaker's Tab Includes Cars, Clubs and 'Other,'" *New York Times*, June 9, 2015, p. A1.

39. Josefa Velasquez, "Heastie's First Budget Is a Departure from Silver," *Capital New York*, Apr. 1, 2015, http://www.capitalnewyork.com/article/albany/2015/04/8565156/heasties-first-budget-departure-silver.

40. Jim Dwyer, "Charming, Ruthless Andrew Cuomo," *New York Review of Books*, Aug. 13, 2015, http://www.nybooks.com/articles/2015/08/13/charming-ruthless-andrew-cuomo/.

41. Governor Eliot Spitzer's one budget in 2007 was passed one day late.

42. Thomas Kaplan, "Cuomo Gets Timely Budget but Pays Price," *New York Times*, Mar. 31, 2015, p. A1.

43. Benjamin Weiser and Susanne Craig, "Lawyers Offer Contrasting Views of Ex-Speaker as His Corruption Trial Opens," *New York Times*, Nov. 4, 2015, p. A22.

44. Benjamin Weiser and Vivian Yee, "Sheldon Silver, Ex-New York Assembly Speaker, Gets 12-Year Prison Sentence," *New York Times*, May 3, 2016.

45. Josh Saul, "Ex-State Senate Boss Dean Skelos, Son Indicted on Corruption Charges," *New York Post*, May 28, 2015.

46. Laura Nahmias, "Skelos Indictment Points to Medical Malpractice Firm," *Capital New York*, May 29, 2015.

47. *United States of America v. Dean Skelos, Adam Skelos*, U.S. District Court, Southern District of New York, S1 15 Cr. 317, "Superseding Indictment," http://online.wsj.com/public/resources/documents/skelos_indictment0730.pdf.

48. Tom Precious, "Skelos Out, Flanagan in as State Senate Majority Leader," *Buffalo News*, May 11, 2015; "Dean Skelos, Adam Skelos Verdict Proves the Dysfunction of New York Politics." editorial, *Newsday*, Dec. 11, 2016.

49. Phillip Anderson, "The Real Reason(s) Why Dean Skelos Wants Rent Laws to Expire Every Two Years," Albany Project, May 4, 2015, http://thealbany-project.com/skelos-rent-control-corruption-arrested, retrieved May 7, 2015; Ashley Hupfl, "Arrest Sheds New Context on Skelos' Call for Rent Regulations to Expire Every Two Years," *City & State*, May 6, 2015, http://www.cityandstateny.com/articles/politics/new-york-state-articles/arrest-sheds-new-context-on-skelos-call-for-rent-regulations-to-expire-every-two-years.html.

50. Thomas Kaplan and Susanne Craig, "Charges of Corruption Topple another of Albany's Leaders," *New York Times*, May 12, 2015, p. A1.

51. Jon Campbell, "Libous to Be Removed from Office after Guilty Verdict," *Press and Sun-Bulletin* (Binghamton, NY), July 23, 2015, http://www.pressconnects.com/story/news/local/2015/07/22/libous-guilty/30531301/.

52. Jesse McKinley, "Thomas Libous, Powerful New York Senator Felled by Scandal, Dies at 63," *New York Times*, May 4, 2016.

53. Reuven Fenton and Bruce Golding, "Terminally Ill Tom Libous Spared Jail Time," *New York Post*, Nov. 24, 2015.

54. Barbara Ross, Victoria Bekiempis, and Dareh Gregorian, "Dean Skelos Guilty in Corruption Case; Former State Senate Majority Leader and Son Now Face up to 130 Years in Prison," *New York Daily News*, Dec. 11, 2015.

55. Benjamin Weiser and Vivian Yee, "Dean Skelos Is Sentenced to 5 Years in Prison in Corruption Case," *New York Times*, May 12, 2016.

56. Benjamin Weiser, "Schumer Aide Is Confirmed as United States Attorney," *New York Times*, Aug. 8, 2009, p. A16.

57. William D. Cohan, "Preet Bharara: The Enforcer of Wall Street," *Fortune*, Aug. 2, 2011.

58. Carl Campanile and Pat Bailey, "Feds Widen Crackdown on New York Political Corruption," *New York Post*, Apr. 30, 2014. See also Jeffrey Toobin, "The Showman: How U.S. Attorney Preet Bharara Struck Fear into Wall Street and Albany," *New Yorker*, May 9, 2016.

59. Glenn Blain and Kenneth Lovett, "U.S. Attorney Preet Bharara's 'Stay Tuned' Warning after Accused Assembly Speaker Sheldon Silver's Arrest Sends Chill through State Capitol," *New York Daily News*, Jan. 24, 2015; Jerry Zremski, "Bharara Sees Corruption 'All Over' New York State," *Buffalo News*, Feb. 14, 2015.

60. Blain and Lovett, "U.S. Attorney Preet Bharara's 'Stay Tuned' Warning."

61. Rebecca Davis O'Brien, "Preet Bharara, in Kentucky, Rails against Corruption," *Wall Street Journal*, Jan. 6, 2016.

62. Susanne Craig and Thomas Kaplan, "Bargain-Hunting Legislators Try to Make the Most of Their Per Diem," *New York Times*, Mar. 27, 2014, p. A25.

63. Casey Seiler, "Heastie Announces New Per Diem Requirements for Members," *Times Union* (Albany, NY), "Capitol Confidential" (blog), June 26, 2015, http://blog.timesunion.com/capitol/archives/237810/heastie-announces-new-per-diem-requirements-for-members/.

64. Kenneth Lovett, "Upstate GOP Assemblyman Racks Up Just over $19G in Per Diem Expenses over First Half of 2015: Controller's Office," *New York Daily News*, July 28, 2015, http://www.nydailynews.com/news/politics/upstate-assemblyman-racks-19g-diem-2015-article-1.2307388; Joseph Spector, "NY Lawmaker Per Diems Rise Again," *Democrat and Chronicle* (Rochester, NY), July 30, 2015, http://www.democratandchronicle.com/story/news/2015/07/30/new-york-legislature-per-diem-expenses/30897911/.

65. Commission to Investigate Public Corruption, *Preliminary Report*, p. 87.

66. J. H. Snider, "Preparing for New York's Next Constitutional Convention Referendum," *Gotham Gazette*, June 4, 2015.

67. Nicholas Kusnetz, *Only Three States Score Higher than a D+ in State Integrity Investigation*, Center for Public Integrity, Nov. 9, 2015, https://www.publicintegrity.org/2015/11/09/18693/only-three-states-score-higher-d-state-integrity-investigation-11-flunk. The only three states that passed the review of transparency and accountability were Alaska, California, and Connecticut. All others, including New York, received a D+ or below. "New York is not remarkable, however, in at least one regard: Only one of those 14 lawmakers has been sanctioned by the state's ethics commission," the report stated.

68. Winston Churchill, Speech in the (United Kingdom) House of Commons (Nov. 11, 1947), *The Official Report, House of Commons* (5th Series), Nov. 11, 1947, vol. 444, pp. 206–207.

69. Quinnipiac University Polling Institute, "Ethics Help Pull New York Gov. Cuomo to New Low, Quinnipiac University Poll Finds; Voters Say 2-1 Clean House to Clean Up Albany," news release, June 3, 2015, http://www.quinnipiac.edu/images/polling/ny/ny06032015_Nu26rhv.pdf.

70. Mike McAndrew, "Poll: 97 Percent of NY Voters Want New Laws to Combat State Government Corruption," *Post-Standard* (Syracuse, NY), May 3, 2016, http://www.syracuse.com/politics/index.ssf/2016/05/poll_97_percent_of_ny_voters_want_new_laws_to_combat_state_government_corruption.html.

71. "It's Broke, Fix It: To Make Government Work, Albany Must Embrace Reform," editorial, *Newsday*, Aug. 5, 2002; "Fixing Albany: Two Ways to Boost Democracy," editorial, *New York Times*, May 26, 2003; Howard Healy, "A Middle Way Makes Sense for State," *Times Union* (Albany, NY), Aug. 18, 2004, p. A13; Fredric U. Dicker, "Albany's Empty Ethics Reform," *New York Post*, June 23, 2005; "Get the Broom in Albany," editorial, *New York Daily News*, Apr. 21, 2007; "Endorsements for a Better Albany," editorial, *New York Times*, Aug. 22, 2008, p. A18; "Where's Joe's Law?: Gross Corruption Shown at Bruno Trial Cries Out for Ethics Reform," editorial, *New York Daily News*, Nov. 22, 2009; "Gov. Cuomo's Next Big Task," editorial, *New York Times*, Dec. 24, 2011, p. A20.

72. See *New York Times*'s "Fixing Albany" series, http://www.nytimes.com/ref/opinion/fixing-albany.html.

73. "It's Broke, Fix It," editorial, *Newsday*; "Fixing Albany," editorial, *New York Times*; H. Healy, "A Middle Way," p. A13; Dicker, "Albany's Empty Ethics Reform"; "Get the Broom in Albany," editorial, *New York Daily News*; "Endorsements for a Better Albany," editorial, *New York Times*, p. A18; "Where's Joe's Law?," editorial, *New York Daily News*; "Gov. Cuomo's Next Big Task," editorial, *New York Times*, p. A20.

74. "The Governor's Primary in New York," editorial, *New York Times*, Aug. 27, 2014, p. A22.

75. Thomas Kaplan and Jesse McKinley, "Cuomo Putting Big Challenges on His Agenda," *New York Times*, Jan. 2, 2015, p. A1; Joan Gralla and Dan Burns, "New York Cuts Pension Benefits for Public Workers," *Reuters*, Mar. 15, 2012,

http://www.reuters.com/article/us-newyork-pensions-idUSBRE82E0OF20120 315.

76. Andrew Cuomo, *Clean Up Albany: Make It Work—The New NY Agenda*, 2010, http://web.archive.org/web/20101008011648/http://www.andrewcuomo.com/system/storage/6/2a/3/1101/andrew_cuomo_clean_up_albany.pdf, p. 1.

77. Mike McAndrew, "One-Third of CNY's State Legislators Facing No Opponent despite Voter Dissatisfaction with Albany," *Post-Standard* (Syracuse, NY), June 16, 2010, http://www.syracuse.com/news/index.ssf/2010/06/one-third_of_cnys_state_legisl.html.

78. Jacob Gershman, " 'Ugly' Process Gets Results, and Rebukes," *Wall Street Journal*, Mar. 16, 2012, p. A15.

79. Karen DeWitt, "Redistricting Prop Passes, but Concern Turns to 2022," *WAMC Northeast Public Radio*, Nov. 6, 2014, http://wamc.org/post/redistricting-prop-passes-concern-turns-2022.

80. Campbell Robertson with Julia C. Mead, "Voters Tell Fix Albany: Heal Thyself," *New York Times*, Nov. 7, 2004.

81. William Murphy, "Suozzi Concedes; Mangano to Take Helm in Nassau," *Newsday*, Dec. 1, 2009.

82. Campbell Robertson with Julia C. Mead, "Voters Tell Fix Albany: Heal Thyself."

83. Joseph Spector, "Independent Democratic Caucus to Get Committee Chairs and $12,500 Stipends," *Journal News*, "Albany Watch" (blog), Jan. 25, 2011, statepolitics.lohudblogs.com/2011/01/25/independent-democratic-caucus-gets-committee-chairs-and-12500-stipends.

84. Lisa W. Foderaro, "Politics; 3 Months + 18 Votes = Spano's 10th Term," *New York Times*, Feb. 13, 2005.

85. Gerald McKinstry, "Nick Spano Prepares for Prison," *Newsday*, June 21, 2012.

86. Nick Reisman, "ASC: 'Stunning' There Hasn't Been a Woman Majority Leader," *Time Warner Cable News Capital Region* (Albany, NY), "State of Politics" (blog), Feb. 29, 2016, http://www.nystateofpolitics.com/2016/02/asc-stunning-there-hasnt-been-a-woman-majority-leader/.

87. Edward I. Koch, interview by Seymour P. Lachman, 2005; New York State Legislative Task Force on Demographic Research and Reapportionment, *Public Hearing, Congressional and State Legislative Redistricting*, New York, Sept. 21, 2011, http://www.latfor.state.ny.us/hearings/docs/20110921trans.pdf, p. 40.

88. William L. Riordon, *Plunkitt of Tammany Hall: A Series of Very Plain Talks on Very Practical Politics* (1905, repr., Whitefish, MT: Kessinger Publishing, 2004), pp. 3, 12.

89. Richard D. Heffner (host), "The Sheriff of Wall Street," *Open Mind*, PBS, July 13, 2004, http://www.thirteen.org/openmind-archive/public-affairs/the-sheriff-of-wall-street/.

90. Celeste Katz, "Eliot, Dad Divvy to Dems. Drop Nearly 400G into Party War Chests," *New York Daily News,* July 18, 2006; John Milgrim, "Baum Is Spitzer's Go-To Guy," *Times Herald-Record* (Middletown, NY), Oct. 15, 2006, http://www.recordonline.com/article/20061015/NEWS/610150340; Nick Paumgarten, "The Humbling of Eliot Spitzer," *New Yorker,* Dec. 10, 2007.

91. Ann Farmer, "Spitzer Backs a Democrat from Nassau for the Senate," *New York Times,* Jan. 13, 2007.

92. Kenneth Lovett, "40 percent of New York State Legislators Earn Outside Income, with Some Making up to $515K," *New York Daily News,* Dec. 18, 2015; 1. Katze and Lerner, *Outside Income Brief,* p. 2.

93. Andrew M. Cuomo, "Built to Lead: State of the State 2016," Jan. 13, 2016, pp. 277, 278, 287–288, https://www.governor.ny.gov/sites/governor.ny.gov/files/atoms/files/2016_State_of_the_State_Book.pdf; Bill Mahoney, "Cuomo's Reform Proposals Feature a Mix of Old and New," *Politico New York,* Jan. 13, 2016, http://www.capitalnewyork.com/article/albany/2016/01/8587969/cuomos-reform-proposals-feature-mix-old-and-new.

94. Jim Tedisco, interviewed by Matt Ryan, *New York Now,* WMHT-TV, aired on Aug. 19, 2016, http://nynow.org/post/tedisco-focuses-water-infrastructure-needs (link includes imbedded video of full episode).

Chapter 2
Son of Immigrant Parents

1. "List or Manifest of Alien Passengers for the United States Immigration Officer at Port of Arrival," *S.S. Paris,* July 22, 1922, http://www.liberty ellisfoundation.org/show-manifest-big-image/czoxNzoidDcxNS0zMTUwMD AzMC5qcGciOw==/1.

2. Allen C. Thomas, *A History of the United* States [Geshikhṭe fun di Fereynigṭe Shṭaaṭen], vol. 1 (New York: Jewish Press, 1916); available from the National Yiddish Book Center at https://archive.org/details/nybc207764.

3. *Brown v. Board of Education of Topeka,* 347 U.S. 483 (1954).

4. Title VI, 42 U.S.C. § 2000d et seq.; Title VI, 42 U.S.C. §§ 1973 et seq; Title VI, 42 U.S.C. § 3601 et seq.

5. Seymour P. Lachman, "A Study of the Church-State Issue as Reflected in Federal Aid to Education Bills, 1937–1950," PhD diss (New York University, 1963).

6. "Class Notes," *Time,* Apr. 1, 1974, p. 3; Leonard Buder, "U.S. Drops Survey of Pupil Attitudes on Race Relations," *New York Times,* Mar. 19, 1974, p. 1.

7. Todd S. Purdum, "New York Adopts Public Financing of Political Races," *New York Times,* Feb. 10, 1988.

8. Michel Marriott, "The 1988 Elections: New York City Charter; Rules on Mayoral Succession and Anti-Corruption Voted," *New York Times,* Nov. 9, 1988;

New York City Charter Revision Commission, *Report of the New York City Charter Revision Commission, December 1986–November 1988, Volume One*, Jan. 1989, http://www.nyc.gov/html/charter/downloads/pdf/1986-1988_final_report.pdf.

9. *Board of Estimate of City of New York v. Morris*, 489 U.S. 688 (1989).

10. Gene I. Maeroff, "Education; For a Change, Cooperation Ruled the Day," *New York Times*, Dec. 10, 1985.

Chapter 3
A Can of Worms

1. Somini Sengupta, "Neighborhood Report: Brooklyn Up Close; Ever the Loyal Democrat, Lachman Reaps His Reward," *New York Times*, Jan. 28, 1996.

2. Campbell Robertson, "Fix Albany Effort Is Rocking No Boats," *New York Times*, Nov. 28, 2004.

3. "The Little Tax that Could," editorial, *New York Daily News*, Apr. 1, 2003.

4. Mario Cuomo, interview by Seymour P. Lachman, 2005.

5. Susan Saulny, "Ex-Legislator Gets 90 Days in Bribery Case," *New York Times*, Mar. 19, 2003.

6. James C. McKinley Jr., "State Senator Quits in Deal over a Bribery Indictment," *New York Times*, May 15, 2004.

7. John Kifner, "Velella, Bronx Powerhouse, Is Sentenced to a Year in Jail," *New York Times*, June 22, 2004.

8. Michael Cooper, "Brooklyn Assemblyman Quits after Admitting False Billing," *New York Times*, June 2, 2004; Michael Cooper, "Democrats Gain Seats, but GOP Retains Senate and Most Incumbents Win," *New York Times*, Nov. 3, 2004.

9. Anemona Hartocollis, "Party's Ex-Boss in Brooklyn Is Convicted," *New York Times*, Feb. 24, 2007, p. B1.

10. Liz Benjamin, "Happy Disco Birthday Clarence Norman," *Time Warner Cable News Capital Region* (Albany, NY), "State of Politics" (blog), Aug. 26, 2011, http://www.nystatcofpolitics.com/2011/08/happy-disco-birthday-clarence-norman/.

11. Fredric U. Dicker, "It Pays ($4.4 Million) to Hire Bruno's Son," *New York Post*, Apr. 25, 2005; Sewell Chan, "Bruno Son Emerges as Key Link in Father's Circle of Connections," *New York Times*, Jan. 11, 2007, p. B1.

12. Michael Cooper, "Legislators Short on Time to Carry Out Reform Vows," *New York Times*, June 20, 2005.

13. Chan, "Bruno Son Emerges as Key Link."

14. "Ex-NY Senate Leader Joe Bruno to Serve 2 Years," *Times Herald-Record* (Middletown, NY), May 7, 2010, http://www.recordonline.com/article/20100507/News/5070349.

15. *United States v. Skilling*, 561 U.S. 358 (2010); Adam Liptak, "Justices Limit Law Used for Corruption Cases," *New York Times*, June 25, 2010, p. A1; U. S. Department of Justice and U.S. Attorney's Office, "Joseph Bruno Acquitted of Honest Services Mail Fraud Involving Bribery Charges," news release, U.S. States Department of Justice and U.S. Attorney's Office, Northern District of New York, May 16, 2014, https://www.fbi.gov/albany/press-releases/2014/joseph-bruno-acquitted-of-honest-services-mail-fraud-involving-bribery-charges.

16. Associated Press, "His Waning Days: Sen. Majority Leader Joe Bruno Will Resign This Week," *New York Daily News*, July 15, 2008.

17. Associated Press, "Espada Defeats Gonzalez in Contentious Senate Race," *Norwood News* (Bronx, NY), Sept. 18, 2008, http://www.norwoodnews.org/id=1455&story=espada-defeats-gonzalez-in-contentious-senate-race/.

18. Benjamin Weiser, "A Former Bronx Senator Gets 7 Years for Corruption," *New York Times*, May 26, 2010, p. A22.

19. Elizabeth Benjamin, "Minus One Assembly Dem; Diane Gordon Convicted," *New York Daily News*, Apr. 8, 2008.

20. Benjamin Weiser, "Ex-Labor Leader Is Sentenced to 10 Years for Racketeering," *New York Times*, May 21, 2009, p. A27.

21. Colin Moynihan, "Former Assemblyman Sentenced to Six Years," *New York Times*, "City Room" (blog), Feb. 4, 2010, http://cityroom.blogs.nytimes.com/2010/02/04/seminero-sentenced-to-six-years/?hp.

22. Anemona Hartocollis, "Hospital Chief Facing U.S. Charges Is Fired," *New York Times*, Mar. 16, 2011, p. A27.

23. "For Senate Democrats Thinking of Switching Parties, Cautionary Tales Abound," *City & State*, Oct. 13, 2008, http://archives.cityandstateny.com/for-senate-democrats-thinking-of-switching-parties-cautionary-tales-abound/; Danny Hakim, "No New Senate Leader until January?," *New York Times*, "City Room" (blog), Nov. 11, 2008; Jim Dwyer, "About New York: Albany Drama Is Tragedy and Farce," *New York Times*, Dec. 10, 2012, p. A23.

24. "For Senate Democrats Thinking of Switching Parties."

25. Mosi Secret, "Ex-Legislator Guilty of Theft Gets 5-Year Prison Sentence," *New York Times*, June 15, 2013, p. A16.

26. Ken Lovett, "Queens Sen.-elect Hiram Monserrate Quits 'Gang of 4,' Deals Eyed with Other Rebel Democrats," *New York Daily News*, Nov. 9, 2008.

27. Nicole Bode, "State Senator Hiram Monserrate Indicted for Assaulting Girlfriend," *New York Daily News*, Mar. 23, 2009.

28. Danny Hakim and Jeremy W. Peters, "In Albany, Democratic Rebel Returns, Leaving Senate in a Knot," *New York Times*, June 15, 2009, p. A1.

29. Cristian Salazar, "Hiram Monserrate's Fate Depends on NY Senate Special Committee," *Huffington Post*, Dec. 28, 2009, http://www.huffingtonpost.com/2009/12/29/hiram-monserrates-fate-de_n_406245.html.

30. Jeremy W. Peters, "Expels Monserrate over Assault of Companion," *New York Times*, Feb. 10, 2010, p. A19.

31. Robert Gearty, "Hiram Monserrate Sentenced to 2 Years in Prison for Corruption," *New York Daily News*, Dec. 11, 2012.

32. Bruce Golding, "Seabrook Guilty of Funneling $1.5M In Taxpayer Funds to Friends, Family," *New York Post*, July 26, 2012.

33. Benjamin Weiser, "Ex-Lawmaker Gets 5 Years in Corruption," *New York Times*, Jan. 9, 2013, p. A17.

34. Benjamin Weiser, "Judge Rules Ex-Politician Must Forfeit His Pension," *New York Times*, May 27, 2015, p. A17.

35. Michael Johnson, "Sampson Elected Leader (Updatedx2)," *YNN Capital Tonight* (Albany, NY), Nov. 29, 2010, http://www.capitaltonight.com/2010/11/sampson-elected-leader/; Joan Gralla, "NY Democrats Win Back Control of State Senate," *Reuters*, July 9, 2009, http://www.reuters.com/article/us-newyork-senate-democrats-idUSTRE5687WO20090709.

36. Thomas Kaplan and Danny Hakim, "Coalition Is to Control State Senate as Dissident Democrats Join with Republicans," *New York Times*, Dec. 5, 2012, p. A26.

37. Kenneth Lovett, "Independent Democratic Conference Tells State Sen. Malcolm Smith He's No Longer Welcome," *New York Daily News*, Apr. 14, 2013.

38. Priscilla DeGregory and Leonard Greene, "Malcolm Smith Sentenced to 7 Years in Prison," *New York Post*, July 1, 2015.

39. Benjamin Weiser, "Ex-State Senator Receives 7-Year Term in Bribery Case," *New York Times*, Apr. 27, 2012, p. A21.

40. Jonathan P. Hicks, "State Senate: Seeming Defeat for Incumbent from Queens," *New York Times*, Sept. 13, 2006.

41. Celeste Katz, "Ex-Queens State Sen. Shirley Huntley Gets Year and a Day in Prison for Looting Charity," *New York Daily News*, "Daily Politics" (blog), May 9, 2013, http://www.nydailynews.com/blogs/dailypolitics/ex-queens-state-sen-shirley-huntley-year-day-prison-looting-charity-blog-entry-1.1694572.

42. New York State Joint Commission on Public Ethics, *Substantial Basis Investigation Report*, "In the Matter of an Investigation of Assemblymember Vito Lopez," JCOPE–127, http://www.jcope.ny.gov/enforcement/2013/lopez/Lopez%20Substantial%20Basis%20Investigation%20Report.pdf.

43. Jesse McKinley, "Lopez Fined $330,000 by Panel over Harassment of Women," *New York Times*, June 12, 2013, p. A23.

44. Benjamin Weiser, "Jury Acquits Assemblyman of Conspiring to Take Bribes," *New York Times*, Nov. 11, 2011, p. A26.

45. Thomas Kaplan, "Brooklyn Legislator to Lose $67,000 for False Travel Filings," *New York Times*, Feb. 8, 2013, p. A20.

46. Mosi Secret, "Assemblyman Is Convicted in Second Corruption Trial," *New York Times*, Mar. 7, 2014, p. A19.

47. Nicholas Casey, "Ex-Assemblyman, Scolded by Judge, Gets a 14-Year Term for Corruption," *New York Times*, Sept. 18, 2015, p. A23.

48. William K. Rashbaum and Nate Schweber, "Blunt Sidewalk Meeting between State Senator and Lawyer Leads to a Guilty Plea," *New York Times*, Dec. 7, 2010, p. A27.

49. Robert Gearty, "Bronx Assemblyman Eric Stevenson Indicted on Charges of Taking $20K in Bribes," *New York Daily News*, May 3, 2013.

50. Thomas Kaplan, "Albany Riveted by Double Life of an Assemblyman and Informer," *New York Times*, Apr. 10, 2013, p. A17.

51. Daniel Beekman, "Bronx Pol Eric Stevenson Gets 3-Year Prison Sentence for Bribe Conviction," *New York Daily News*, May 21, 2014.

52. Kaplan, "Albany Riveted by Double Life of an Assemblyman and Informer."

53. Karen Rouse, "Ex-Lawmaker Gets Probation in Federal Court," *WNYC News* (New York, NY), Sept. 14, 2014, http://www.wnyc.org/story/ex-lawmaker-gets-probation-federal-court/; Ben Kochman, "Tarnished Bronx Politician, Albany Informer Nelson Castro Escapes Prison for Perjury, Vows New Career Selling Lightbulbs," *New York Daily News*, Nov. 17, 2014.

54. Robert Gavin, "Assemblyman William Scarborough Gets Prison Sentence for Cheating Taxpayers," *Times Union* (Albany, NY), Sept. 15, 2015.

55. Jeremy W. Peters, "Formerly Reticent, a Brooklyn Democrat Finds a Voice as a Leader in the Senate," *New York Times*, July 3, 2009, p. A22.

56. Rebecca Davis O'Brien, "New York Sen. John Sampson Found Guilty of Obstruction of Justice," *Wall Street Journal*, July 24, 2015.

57. Brennan Center for Justice, "Closing New York's LLC Loophole," New York University School of Law, https://www.brennancenter.org/closing-new-york-llc-loophole, retrieved Sept. 19, 2016.

58. Ibid.; "Contribution Limits," New York State Board of Elections, http://www.elections.ny.gov/CFContributionLimits.html, retrieved Sept. 19, 2016.

59. Chris Bragg, "State Elections Watchdog Files Lawsuit against 'LLC Loophole,'" *Times Union* (Albany, NY), Aug. 26, 2015.

60. Chris Bragg, "LLC Loophole Penalty Could Hinder NY Donors," *Times Union* (Albany, NY), Sept. 9, 2015.

61. Chris Bragg, "State Elections Watchdog Files Lawsuit against 'LLC Loophole.'"

62. Susan Pace Hamill, "The Origins behind the Limited Liability Company," *Ohio State Law Journal*, vol. 59, no. 5 (1998): 1460–1462, 1517.

63. "The Perks of Being an Albany Leader," editorial, *Newsday*, June 7, 2013; "New York State Legislative Stipends," *Newsday*, http://data.newsday.com/long-island/data/opinion/leg-stipends/.

64. Matthew Hamilton, "Brennan Center, State Lawmakers Sue Board of Elections over LLC Loophole," *Times Union* (Albany, NY), "Capitol Confidential" (blog), July 14, 2015, http://blog.timesunion.com/capitol/archives/238509/brennan-center-state-lawmakers-sue-board-of-elections-over-llc-loophole/.

65. Brennan Center for Justice, "Closing New York's LLC Loophole"; Jesse McKinley and Vivian Yee, "Cuomo Offers $20 Billion Plan to Ease State's Housing Woes," *New York Times*, Jan. 14, 2016, p. A1.

66. Michael Cooper, "New York Is Sued by U.S. on Delay of Vote System," *New York Times*, Mar. 2, 2006.

67. Valerie Bauman, "N.Y. to Miss Voting Act Deadline," *Oneida Daily Dispatch*, Nov. 26, 2007.

68. *Lopez Torres v. N.Y. State Bd. of Elections*, 462 F.3d 161, 171–178 (2d Cir. 2006), overruled 552 U.S. 196.

69. *New York State Board of Election v. Lopez Torres*, 552 U.S. 196 (2008). Associate Justice John Paul Stevens, joined by Associate Justice David Souter, quoted the late Associate Justice Thurgood Marshall saying, "The Constitution does not prohibit legislatures from enacting stupid laws."

70. William F. Hammond Jr., "A 38 percent Increase in Minimum Wage Passes into Law," *New York Sun*, Dec. 7, 2004.

71. Michael Virtanen (Associated Press), "NY Board Upholds $15 Minimum Wage for Fast-Food Workers," Dec. 9, 2015, http://bigstory.ap.org/article/06e14feee9d749d0ad1345a8f973a293/ny-board-upholds-15-minimum-wage-fast-food-workers.

72. Rebecca Davis O'Brien and Joe Jackson, "New York Gov. Andrew Cuomo Wants to Raise Minimum Wage," *Wall Street Journal*, Jan. 18, 2015, http://www.wsj.com/articles/new-york-gov-andrew-cuomo-wants-to-raise-minimum-wage-1421623975; Erica Orden and Josh Dawsey, "Behind Cuomo's Shifting Stance on Minimum Wage," *Wall Street Journal*, Sept. 11, 2015, p. A13.

73. Glenn Blain, "Senate's Independent Democratic Conference Announces End to Alliance with Republicans—UPDATED," *New York Daily News*, "Daily Politics" (blog), June 25, 2014, http://www.nydailynews.com/blogs/dailypolitics/senate-independent-democratic-conference-announces-alliance-republicans-blog-entry-1.1844227; Ken Lovett, "Breakaway Senate Dems Unveil 'Invest New York' Policy Agenda," *New York Daily News*, "Daily Politics" (blog), Jan. 19, 2015, http://www.nydailynews.com/blogs/dailypolitics/breakaway-senate-dems-unveil-invest-new-york-policy-agenda-blog-entry-1.2084096.

74. Andrew Stengel, Lawrence Norden, and Laura Seago, *Still Broken: New York State Legislative Reform 2008 Update*, Brennan Center for Justice at New York University School of Law, Jan. 2, 2009, p. 4, http://www.brennancenter.org/page/-/publications/Still.Broken.pdf.

75. Raymond Hernandez, "Failed Coup in Assembly Leaves Speaker Standing, but Wounded," *New York Times*, May 23, 2000; Raymond Hernandez, "Albany Rebel's Fall from Power; Lawmaker Laments after Failed Coup against the Speaker," *New York Times*, June 8, 2000.

76. Erik Kriss, "Seeds of Overthrow Sown, Speaker Plows 'em Under," *Post-Standard* (Syracuse, NY), May 28, 2000; Hernandez, "Albany Rebel's Fall from Power."

77. Michelle Breidenbach, "Remember Michael Bragman? A Former Assemblyman Reminds Democrats What Happens to Those Who Challenge Speaker Sheldon Silver," *Post-Standard* (Syracuse, NY), Oct. 02, 2012, http://www.syracuse.com/news/index.ssf/2012/10/remember_michael_bragman_a_for.html.

78. William F. Hammond Jr., "Suit Threatened for Change in State Capital," *New York Sun*, Nov. 26, 2004; Patrick D. Healy, "Minority Party Lawmakers Sue," *New York Times*, Feb. 16, 2005; "Suing Albany's Three Men," editorial, *New York Times*, Nov. 27, 2005.

79. Hammond, "Suit Threatened for Change in State Capital"; P. Healy, "Minority Party Lawmakers Sue"; "Suing Albany's Three Men," editorial, *New York Times*.

80. Jennifer Medina, "Censorship Is Alleged in Suit against Leaders in Albany," *New York Times*, Apr. 13, 2006.

81. Nicholas Confessore and Danny Hakim, "Capturing Senate, Democrats Are Poised to Control Albany," *New York Times*, Nov. 5, 2008, p. P15, http://www.nytimes.com/2008/11/05/nyregion/05york.html?_r=0>.

82. Glenn Blain, "Queens State Sen. Malcolm Smith in the Middle of Politicians Revolt," *Daily News*, Nov. 10, 2008.

83. Danny Hakim, "Vying to Be Majority Leader, Minority Leader Gains a Vote," *New York Times*, Nov. 9, 2008, p. A44; Danny Hakim, "No New Senate Leader until January?"

84. Danny Hakim, "Senate Accord Falls Apart, Putting Leadership in Question Again," *New York Times*, Dec. 11, 2008, p. A43; Danny Hakim, "Democrats Reach Pact to Lead the Senate," *New York Times*, Jan. 7, 2009, p. A23.

85. Kenneth Lovett and Glenn Blain, "GOP Coup in Albany: Senators Hiram Monserrate and Pedro Espada Jr. Vote against Fellow Democrats," *New York Daily News*, June 9, 2009.

86. Ibid.; Danny Hakim and Jeremy W. Peters, "Door Is Locked, and Senate Is in Gridlock," *New York Times*, June 11, 2009, p. A23.

87. Danny Hakim and Nicholas Confessore, "Feeling Slighted, Rich Patron Led Albany Revolt," *New York Times*, June 10, 2009, p. A1.

88. Dwyer, "About New York: Albany Drama Is Tragedy and Farce."

89. Ibid.

90. Kenneth Lovett and Glenn Blain, "Different Day, Same Old Dysfunction in Albany: Senate Democrats Locked in Chambers . . . Again," *New York Daily News*, June 24, 2009.

91. Jimmy Vielkind, "'This mess is worse than ever,'" *New York Observer*, June 16, 2009, http://observer.com/2009/06/this-mess-is-worse-than-ever-2/.

92. Danny Hakim, "Paterson Picks MTA Figure as His No. 2," *New York Times*, July 9, 2009, p. A1.

93. Johnson, "Sampson Elected Leader (Updatedx2)"; Gralla, "NY Democrats Win Back Control of State Senate."

94. Richard Ravitch, telephone interview by Seymour P. Lachman, June 25, 2015.

95. Tina Moore, "Republicans Regain State Senate Control after Long Island GOPer Jack Martins Wins in Recount," *New York Daily News*, Dec. 4, 2010; Thomas Kaplan, "Republicans, Outnumbered, Keep Power in Albany," *New York Times*, June 14, 2012, p. A26.

96. Celeste Katz, "Simcha Felder to Caucus with NY Senate GOP; Dean Skelos Pretty Happy with That," *New York Daily News*, "Daily Politics" (blog), Nov. 13, 2012, http://www.nydailynews.com/blogs/dailypolitics/simcha-felder-caucus-ny-senate-gop-dean-skelos-pretty-happy-blog-entry-1.1692747; Casey Seiler, "GOP, IDC Announce Coalition Agreement (Updated)," *Times Union* (Albany, NY), "Capitol Confidential" (blog), Dec. 4, 2012, http://blog.timesunion.com/capitol/archives/170239/gop-idc-announce-coalition-agreement/.

97. Seiler, "GOP, IDC Announce Coalition Agreement (Updated)."

98. Kaplan and Hakim, "Coalition Is to Control State Senate as Dissident Democrats Join with Republicans."

99. Aaron Short, "The Odd Couple: The IDC's Jeff Klein and the GOP's Dean Skelos," *City & State*, July 9, 2013.

100. Karen DeWitt, "NYS Senate, Assembly Reconvene," North County Public Radio, Jan. 8, 2015, http://www.northcountrypublicradio.org/news/story/27130/20150108/nys-senate-assembly-reconvene.

101. Liz Krueger, interview by Ronnie M. Eldridge, May 26, 2015, *Eldridge & Co.* CUNY-TV, aired on May 27, 2015, http://www.cuny.tv/show/eldridgeandco/PR2004174, https://www.youtube.com/watch?v=dlj4tsChdzg.

Chapter 4
Like a Meeting of the Supreme Soviet

1. Liz Krueger, interview by Robert Polner, 2005.

2. Robert J. Freeman, telephone interview by Robert Polner, Mar. 8, 2016.

3. Jeremy M. Creelan and Laura M. Moulton, *The New York State Legislative Process: An Evaluation and Blueprint for Reform*, Brennan Center for Justice at New York University School of Law, July 21, 2004, pp. xi, 30–32, http://www.brennancenter.org/page/-/d/albanyreform_finalreport.pdf.

4. James L. Seward, "Senate Acts on Legislative Reforms," news release, New York State Senate, Jan. 24, 2005, https://www.nysenate.gov/newsroom/in-the-news/james-l-seward/senate-acts-legislative-reforms.

5. Creelan and Moulton, *The New York State Legislative Process*, pp. xiii, 36.

6. New York Legislature, 2015–2016, LegiScan, https://legiscan.com/NY.

7. Timothy Bolger, "Skelos Corruption Trial: State Pol's Reluctance on Reform Aired," *Long Island Press*, Nov. 23, 2015, https://www.longislandpress.com/2015/11/23/47698/; Vivian Yee, "Who's Taking on Ethics in Albany? Not the Ethics Panels," *New York Times*, Jan. 20, 2016, p. A19.

8. Bolger, "Skelos Corruption Trial"; Yee, "Who's Taking on Ethics in Albany?"

9. Benjamin Weiser, Susanne Craig, and William K. Rashbaum, "U.S. Attorney Says Trials Offer Solutions to a Corrupt Albany," *New York Times*, Dec. 14, 2015, p. A1.

10. Yee, "Who's Taking on Ethics in Albany?"

11. Alfred E. Smith, *Up to Now: An Autobiography* (New York: Viking Press, 1929), p 71.

12. Weiser, "Ex-Labor Leader Is Sentenced to 10 Years for Racketeering"; Mosi Secret, "Ex-State Senator Guilty of Theft from Nonprofit," *New York Times*, May 15, 2012, p. A1; Rashbaum and Schweber, "Blunt Sidewalk Meeting between State Senator and Lawyer"; Katz, "Ex-Queens State Sen. Shirley Huntley Gets Year and a Day"; Golding, "Seabrook Guilty of Funneling $1.5M"; Gearty, "Hiram Monserrate Sentenced to 2 Years."

13. M. Cuomo interview.

14. Josh Barbanel, "Legislators Pass New State Budget," *New York Times*, Apr. 1, 1984.

15. "Looking under the Budget Flaps," editorial, *New York Times*, Apr. 9, 2006 (City, Long Island, and Westchester special sections).

16. Franz Leichter, interview by Seymour P. Lachman and Robert Polner, 2005.

17. "Peeking at Albany's Pork," editorial, *New York Post*, Apr. 4, 2006, p. 28.

18. Jimmy Vielkind, "Once a Harsh Critic, Cuomo Now Signs Off on Legislative Earmarks, *Politico New York*, Oct. 7, 2015, http://www.capitalnewyork.com/article/albany/2015/10/8578951/once-harsh-critic-cuomo-now-signs-legislative-earmarks.

19. Karen DeWitt, "Lawmakers Agree on Member Item Reform" (audio), *North County Public Radio*, Mar. 23, 2007, http://www.northcountrypublicradio.org/news/story/8904/20070323/lawmakers-agree-on-member-item-reform.

20. Blair Horner, email to Marc A. Rivlin, Jan. 28, 2015; José M. Serrano, "Serrano/Galef Call for Revamp of Member Item System in Light of Persistent Abuse," news release, Feb. 28, 2013, https://www.nysenate.gov/newsroom/press-releases/jos%C3%A9-m-serrano/serranogalef-call-revamp-member-item-system-light-persistent; Will Brunelle and Jimmy Vielkind, "Senate Republicans Offer Most Budget Pork," *Capital New York*, Apr. 10, 2014, http://www.capitalnewyork.com/article/albany/2014/04/8543511/senate-republicans-offer-most-budget-pork.

21. Colby Hamilton, "Cuomo Says He'll Veto 129 'New' Legislative Member Items," *WNYC News*, "The Empire" (blog), Apr. 11, 2012, http://www.wnyc.org/story/198803-cuomo-says-hell-veto-129-new-legislative-member-items/; Rick Karlin and Chris Bragg "Cuomo Vetoes 'Pork' Items in Budget," *Times Union* (Albany, NY), Apr. 13, 2015.

22. "NY Lawmakers Keep the Secret Spending Alive," editorial, *New York Post*, Oct. 6, 2015.

23. Citizens Union of the City of New York, *Spending in the Shadows: Discretionary Funding in the NYS Budget: FY 2017 Executive Budget Update*, Feb. 2016, http://www.citizensunion.org/www/cu/site/hosting/Reports/FINAL%20CU%20Spending%20in%20the%20Shadows%20Report%20FY17%20Executive%20Budget%20-%202%2029%2016.pdf.

24. Isabel Vincent and Melissa Klein, "New York–Presbyterian was biggest beneficiary of slush fund," *New York Post*, Sept. 27, 2015; Kenneth Lovett, "Billions in Discretionary Funds Set Aside by Gov. Andrew Cuomo Enable Him to Exercise Great Power: Insiders," *New York Daily News*, Feb. 4, 2013.

25. Jimmy Vielkind, "State Pours Subsidies into Staten Island Outlet Mall," *Politico New York*, Feb. 15, 2016, http://www.capitalnewyork.com/article/albany/2016/02/8591022/state-pours-subsidies-staten-island-outlet-mall.

26. Ibid.

27. Ibid.

28. Celeste Katz, "Krueger's Easy Victor in Senate Race," *New York Daily News*, Feb. 13, 2002.

29. Legislative Task Force on Demographic Research and Reapportionment, Map of Senate District 22, 2002, http://www.latfor.state.ny.us/maps/2002sen/fs022.pdf.

30. New York State Board of Elections, "NYS Board of Elections—Senate Vote—Nov. 5, 2002," Certified Election Results, n.d., http://www.elections.ny.gov/NYSBOE/elections/2002/general/2002_sen.pdf.

31. Bill Farrell, "Gentile Is Council Winner by 31 Votes," *New York Daily News*, Mar. 14, 2003.

32. Legislative Task Force on Demographic Research and Reapportionment, Map of Senate District 27, 2002, http://www.latfor.state.ny.us/maps/2002sen/fs027.pdf.

33. Michael Gormley (Associated Press), "NY Senate Leader Joseph Bruno Won't Run Again," *Newsday*, June 23, 2008; Danny Hakim, "Bruno Declines Re-election Bid," *New York Times*, June 24, 2008, p. A1.

34. Hakim, "Democrats Reach Pact to Lead the Senate."

35. N.Y. Leg. Law § 5-a.

36. Weiser, "Ex-State Senator Receives 7-Year Term."

37. Legislative Task Force on Demographic Research and Reapportionment, Map of Senate District 22; Legislative Task Force on Demographic Research and Reapportionment, Map of Senate District 23, 2002, http://www.latfor.state.ny.us/maps/2002sen/fs023.pdf.

38. Legislative Task Force on Demographic Research and Reapportionment, Map of Senate District 21, 2002, http://www.latfor.state.ny.us/maps/2002sen/fs021.pdf.

39. New York State Board of Elections, "NYS Board of Elections—Senate Vote—Nov. 5, 2002."

40. New York State Senate, *Expenditure Report, Oct. 1, 2003–Mar. 31, 2004*, Joseph L. Bruno, Temporary President.

41. Andrew J. Hawkins, "The Budget's Done. But Who Won?," *Crain's New York Business*, "The Insider" (blog), Apr. 5, 2015, http://www.crainsnewyork.com/article/20150405/BLOGS04/150409946/the-budgets-done-but-who-won.

42. Eric Lane, "Albany's Travesty of Democracy," *City Journal* 7, no. 48 (Spring 1997), http://www.city-journal.org/html/albany%E2%80%99s-travesty-democracy-11888.html.

43. Ibid.

44. Ibid.

45. Ibid.

46. Ibid.

47. James Dao, "Ally of Pataki Replaces Marino as State Senate Majority Leader," *New York Times*, Nov. 26, 1994.

48. Nicholas Confessore, "Paterson Is Sworn in as Governor," *New York Times*, Mar. 17, 2008.

49. Creelan and Moulton, *The New York State Legislative Process*.

50. Michael Cooper, "Pataki's Promises of Change Yielded to Custom," *New York Times*, Jan. 5, 2005.

51. Lawrence Norden, David E. Pozen, and Bethany L. Foster, *Unfinished Business: New York State Legislative Reform 2006 Update*, Brennan Center for

Justice at New York University School of Law, Oct. 11, 2006, http://www.brennancenter.org/page/-/d/download_file_37893.pdf; Stengel, Norden, and Seago, *Still Broken*.

52. Stengel, Norden, and Seago, *Still Broken*, p. 1.

53. Ibid.

54. Peter A. A. Berle, *Does the Citizen Stand a Chance? Politics of a State Legislature—New York (Politics in Government)* (Woodbury, NY: Barron's Educational Series, 1974).

55. Manfred Ohrenstein, interview by Seymour P. Lachman, 2005.

56. Creelan and Moulton, *The New York State Legislative Process*, p. 6.

57. Ibid., p. 13.

58. Ibid., p. 13.

59. Ibid., p. 3.

60. Ibid., p. 7.

61. Ibid., p. 3.

62. Greg David, "The Root Cause of Albany's Dysfunction," *Crain's New York Business*, "Greg David on NY" (blog), June 28, 2015, http://www.crainsnewyork.com/article/20150628/S01/150629906/the-root-cause-of-albanys-dysfunction.

63. Warren Anderson, interview by Seymour P Lachman, 2005.

64. Ibid.

65. Ibid.

66. Al Baker, "How Some Popular Bills Die Slowly and Quietly in Albany," *New York Times*, June 16, 2005.

67. Ibid.

68. Michael Cooper, "Congress Passes Bill Nullifying a State Law, and Making It Easier to Lease Cars in New York," *New York Times*, Aug. 4, 2005.

69. Baker, "How Some Popular Bills Die."

70. Jonathan P. Hicks, "Feisty Opposition for Popular Republican Congressman," *New York Times*, Oct. 30, 2004; Daniel L. Feldman and Gerald Benjamin, *Tales from the Sausage Factory* (Albany, NY: Excelsior Editions, SUNY Press, 2010), p. 89; George De Stefano, " 'A burning hatred for the ruling class': Frank Barbaro's Radical Life, from the (Brooklyn) Docks to the (New York) Supreme Court," 2007, http://members.authorsguild.net/gdestefano/files/Barbaro_Italian_Passages.pdf, pp. 1, 16.

71. Martin C. Evans, "Battle in War against Hate," *Newsday*, Apr. 15, 2000, p. A19; Richard Perez-Pena, "State Senate to Pass Bill on Hate Crime," *New York Times*, June 7, 2000, p. B1; Anti-Defamation League, "ADL Hails New York State Senate's Passage of Hate Crimes Bill," news release, June 7, 2000.

72. Evans, "Battle in War against Hate," p. A19; Perez-Pena, "State Senate to Pass Bill on Hate Crime," p. B1; Anti-Defamation League, "ADL Hails New York State Senate's Passage of Hate Crimes Bill."

73. Hate Crimes Act of 2000 (Chapter 107, NYS Public Laws of 2000); "Attacking Hate Crimes," editorial, *New York Times*, June 9, 2000; Raymond Hernandez, "Pataki Signs Bill Raising Penalties in Hate Crimes," *New York Times*, July 11, 2000; New York State Division of Criminal Justice Services, "Law File Changes—Hate Crimes Act of 2000," http://www.criminaljustice.ny.gov/crimnet/clf/hatecrimesact2000.pdf.

74. Richard Pérez-Peña, "State Will Require Coverage of Treatment for Infertility," *New York Times*, May 17, 2002.

75. Azi Paybarah, "A History of Delays: Why New York's Budget Is So Late So Often," *WNYC News*, "Politics" (blog), June 22, 2010, http://www.wnyc.org/story/68686-new-yorks-budget-late/.

76. Al Baker, "Spitzer Says Albany Budget May Be on Time but It Ducks Crucial Problems," *New York Times*, Apr. 7, 2005.

77. Al Baker, "In Albany's Budget Race, Nonprofits' Progress Is Slow," *New York Times*, Mar. 30, 2005.

78. Al Baker, "Albany Passes Budget on Time, a First since 1984," *New York Times*, Apr. 1, 2005.

Chapter 5
In a Lofty Place

1. Hugh Carey, interview with Seymour P. Lachman, 2005.

2. Bennett Liebman, " 'Three Men in a Room' and Albany—Where Did the Phrase Come From?," in *Government Reform* (a project of the Government Law Center at Albany Law School), Mar. 11, 2015, https://governmentreform.wordpress.com/2015/03/11/three-men-in-a-room-and-albany-where-did-the-phrase-come-from/.

3. Richard Norton Smith, *Thomas E. Dewey and His Times* (New York: Simon and Schuster, 1982), p. 373.

4. Ibid., p. 374.

5. Carey interview.

6. Gerald Benjamin, "Reform in New York: The Budget, the Legislature and the Governance Process," Background Paper for Citizens Budget Commission Conference on "Fixing New York State's Fiscal Practices," Nov.13–14, 2003, http://www.cbcny.org/sites/default/files/report_reformnys_11102003.pdf, p. 15.

7. R. Smith, *Thomas E. Dewey and His Times*, pp. 352–354.

8. Robert B. Ward, *New York State Government*, 2nd ed. (Albany, NY: Rockefeller Institute Press, 2006), pp. 375–377.

9. Edward P. Kohn, " 'A Most Revolting State of Affairs': Theodore Roosevelt's Aldermanic Bill and the New York Assembly City Investigating

Committee of 1884," *American Nineteenth Century History*, 10:1 (2009), DOI: 10.1080/14664650802299909, http://dx.doi.org/10.1080/14664650802299909, pp. 77–92.

10. Brad K. Berner, ed., *The Spanish-American War: A Documentary History with Commentaries* (Madison, NJ: Fairleigh Dickenson University Press, 2014), p. 132.

11. Amy H. Sturgis, *Presidents from Hayes through McKinley, 1877–1901: Debating the Issues in Pro and Con Primary Documents*, The President's Position: Debating the Issues (Westport, CT: Greenwood Press, 2003), p. 208.

12. John Stauffer and Benjamin Soskis, *The Battle Hymn of the Republic: A Biography of the Song that Marches On* (New York: Oxford University Press, 2013), p. 145.

13. The landmark legislation was named after assembly floor leader Sherman Moreland, progressive Republican of Chemung, New York, with whom Hughes worked "diligently . . . on legislation to help the chief executive learn how the administrative heads were running their departments and whether they possessed the necessary ability," resulting in speedy passage of the Moreland Act, writes Robert F. Wesser in his biography *Charles Evans Hughes: Politics and Reform in New York: 1905–1910* (Ithaca, NY: Cornell University Press, 1967), p. 141.

14. Richard L. McCormick and Samuel P. Hayes, "The Progressive Era: Liberal or Conservative?," in *Interpretations of American History: Patterns and Perspectives, Vol. II: Since 1877–*, edited by Gerald N. Grob and George Athan Billias, 6th ed. (New York: Free Press, 1992), p. 263. The first edition was published in 1967.

15. See Wesser, chap. XI, "Direct Primary Fight," and chap. XII, "The Direct Primary and the Republican Party Battle of 1910."

16. Michael Stokes Paulsen and Luke Paulsen, *The Constitution: An Introduction* (New York: Basic Books, 2015), see p. 214 material on William Howard Taft, the only individual ever to serve as both president and chief justice, and who named Hughes to his first term on the high court in 1910.

17. Ward, *New York State Government*, p. 116.

18. Ibid., p. 114.

19. Sanny Hakim, "Hevesi, Jailed for Corruption, Is Given Parole; Ex-Aide Isn't," *New York Times*, Nov. 16, 2012, p. A28.

20. Elliott Robert Barkan, *Making It in America: A Sourcebook on Eminent Ethnic Americans* (Santa Barbara, CA: ABC–CLIO), p. 350; Christopher M. Finan, *Alfred E. Smith: The Happy Warrior*, 1st ed. (New York: Hill and Wang, 2002), pp. 9–11; Al Smith with his father, Alfred Smith (formerly Ferraro), uncle Peter Mulvihill, and cousin Tommy Mulvihill (photograph), http://collections. mcny.org/Collection/[Al-Smith,-with-his-father,-uncle-and-cousin.]-24UAKVM-DRME.html.

21. A. Smith, *Up to Now.*

22. The Robert E. Slayton biography is titled *Empire Statesman: The Rise and Redemption of Alfred E. Smith* (New York: Free Press, 2007).

23. An excellent account of the 1911 fire and the efforts of Smith and Wagner are found in the book *Triangle: The Fire that Changed America*, by David von Drehle, (New York: Atlantic Monthly Press, 2003).

24. Francell Lee Schrader, *Man of Honor* (San Joe, CA: Writers Club Press, 2002), p. 79.

25. Robert A. Caro, *The Power Broker: Robert Moses and the Fall of New York* (New York: Viking Press, 1975), p. 96.

26. Joseph Francis Zimmerman, *The Government and Politics of New York State*, 2nd ed. (Albany, NY: SUNY Press, 2008), pp 166–175.

27. Caro, pp. 96–97.

28. Warren Moscow, *Politics of the Empire State* (New York: Knopf, 1948), p. 11.

29. Slayton, p. 16.

30. Alfred E. Smith, *Public Papers of Alfred E. Smith, Governor, 1920* (Albany, NY: Lyon, 1921), p. 369.

31. Matthew Josephson and Hannah Josephson, *Al Smith: Hero of the Cities: A Political Portrait Drawing on the Papers of Frances Perkins* (New York: Houghton Mifflin, 1969), p. 471.

32. Anderson interview.

33. Kenneth S. Davis, *FDR: The New York Years, 1928–1933*, vol. 2 (New York: Random House, 1985), p. 81.

34. James David Barber, *The Pulse of Politics: Electing President in the Media Age* (New Brunswick, NJ, Transaction Publishers, 1992; 2nd ed., 2007), p. 246.

35. Allan Nevins, *Herbert H. Lehman and His Era* (New York: Scribner, 1963), p. 1.

36. Ibid., p. 166.

37. Ibid.

38. Thomas E. Dewey, *Public Papers of Thomas E. Dewey: Fifty-first Governor of the State of New York, 1950* (Albany, NY: Williams Press, 1951), p. 776.

39. R. Smith, *Thomas E. Dewey and His Times*, pp. 443–448; Richard Norton Smith, "The Gangbuster as Governor," in *A Legacy of Leadership: Governors and American History*, ed. Clayton McClure Brooks (Philadelphia, University of Pennsylvania Press, 2008), p. 76.

40. Thomas E. Dewey, *Public Papers of Thomas E. Dewey: Fifty-first Governor of the State of New York, 1946* (Albany, NY: Williams Press, 1947), p. 668.

41. R. Smith, *Thomas E. Dewey and His Times*, p. 362.

42. R. Smith, "The Governor as Gangbuster," p. 71.

43. Seymour P. Lachman and Robert Polner, *The Man Who Saved New York: Hugh Carey and the Great Fiscal Crisis of 1975* (Albany, NY: SUNY Press: 2010), pp 175–177.

44. R. Smith, "The Governor as Gangbuster," p. 75.

45. Robert H. Connery and Gerald Benjamin, *Rockefeller of New York: Executive Power in the Statehouse* (Ithaca, NY: Cornell University Press, 1979), p. 36.

46. Connery and Benjamin, *Rockefeller of New York*, p. 272.

47. Joseph E. Persico, *The Imperial Rockefeller: A Biography of Nelson A. Rockefeller* (New York: Simon & Schuster, 1982), p. 144.

48. Ibid., p. 145.

49. Ibid., pp. 223–246.

50. Ibid., pp. 56, 215.

51. Ibid., p. 202; Paul Goldberger, *On the Rise: Architecture and Design in a Postmodern Age* (New York: Times Books, 1983).

52. Persico, *The Imperial Rockefeller*, pp. 207–211.

53. Lachman and Polner, *The Man Who Saved New York*.

54. Elizabeth Kolbert, "Cuomo Seeking Fordham Dean for Ethics Panel," *New York Times*, Apr. 16, 1987.

55. "Juffe Balks Crime Quiz Here; Is Jailed on Contempt Charge," *Brooklyn Eagle*, Oct. 3, 1938, p. 2.

56. John D. Feerick, "Reflections on Chairing the New York State Commission on Government Integrity," *Fordham Urban Law Journal* vol. 18, no. 2 (1990): p. 161.

57. "Gov. Andrew Cuomo's Eulogy for his Father Mario Cuomo," transcript published online by the *Wall Street Journal*, Jan. 6, 2015, http://blogs.wsj.com/metropolis/2015/01/06/transcript-gov-andrew-cuomos-eulogy-for-his-father-mario-cuomo/

Chapter 6
The Great Gerrymander

1. Ken Lovett, "Skelos Conviction Could Beef Up Influence of Senate IDC," *New York Daily News*, Daily Politics" (blog), Dec. 14, 2015, http://www.nydailynews.com/blogs/dailypolitics/skelos-conviction-beef-influence-senate-idc-blog-entry-1.2464691.

2. Lovett, "Independent Democratic Conference Tells State Sen. Malcolm Smith."

3. Tony Farina, "Democrats Settle on Heastie as New Speaker," *Niagara Falls Reporter*, Feb. 3, 2015.

4. Sasha Abramsky, "The Redistricting Wars," *The Nation*, Dec. 11, 2003.

5. *Reynolds v. Sims*, 377 U.S. 533 (1964).

6. Emily Barasch, "The Twisted History of Gerrymandering in American Politics," *The Atlantic*, Sept. 19, 2012, http://www.theatlantic.com/politics/archive/2012/09/the-twisted-history-of-gerrymandering-in-american-politics/262369/#slide1.

7. Ed Cook, "Legislative Guide to Redistricting in Iowa," Legislative Services Agency, Dec. 2007, https://www.legis.iowa.gov/docs/Central/Guides/redist.pdf; Tracy Jan, "Iowa Keeping Partisanship Off the Map," *Boston Globe*, Dec. 8, 2013.

8. Zimmerman, *The Government and Politics of New York State*, pp. 89–90.

9. Ibid., p. 89.

10. Legislative Task Force on Demographic Research and Reapportionment, Map of Senate District 22; Legislative Task Force on Demographic Research and Reapportionment, Map of Senate District 23.

11. Joseph Berger, "Change in Party Leaning Is No Surprise to Constituents," *New York Times*, Dec. 4, 2012, p. A28.

12. "Phantom Constituents in the Census," editorial, *New York Times*, Sept. 26, 2015; Roland Nicholson Jr., "Where Prisoners Count," letter to the editor, *New York Times*, Oct. 2, 2005; "Phantom Voters, Thanks to the Census," editorial, *New York Times*, Dec. 27, 2005.

13. Stephen Ceasar, "Inmate Residency Law May Remap State Politics," *New York Times*, Aug. 7, 2010, p. A14.

14. Cook, "Legislative Guide to Redistricting in Iowa"; Jan, "Iowa Keeping Partisanship Off the Map."

15. *Arizona State Legislature v. Arizona Independent Redistricting Commission*, 576 U.S. ___ (2005); Mark Sherman (Associated Press), "Justices Uphold Arizona's System for Redistricting," June 29, 2015.

16. Cook, "Legislative Guide to Redistricting in Iowa;" Jan, "Iowa Keeping Partisanship Off the Map."

17. Chap. 45, NYS Public Laws of 1978.

18. *Rodriguez v. Pataki*, 308 F. Supp. 2d 346 (S.D.N.Y. 2004); Bill Hammond, "Inside the Albany Gerrymandering Machine: How N.Y. Pols Rig the Game," *New York Daily News*, Sept. 27, 2011.

19. Ibid.

20. Ibid.

21. Andrew C. White, "New York State Senate Proposed Maps (updated)," *Daily Kos*, Jan 27, 2012, http://www.dailykos.com/story/2012/1/27/1059070/-.

22. Edward V. Schneier, John Brian Murtaugh, and Antoinette Pole, *New York Politics: A Tale of Two States*, 2nd ed. (Armonk, NY: Sharpe, 2009), p. 89.

23. New York State Board of Elections, "Form of Submission of Proposal Number One, An Amendment: Revising State's Redistricting Procedure," 2014, http://www.elections.ny.gov/NYSBOE/Elections/2014/Proposals/ProposalOneFinal.pdf.

24. Justin Levitt. All about Redistricting: New York, http://redistricting.lls.edu/states-NY.php, retrieved Sept. 19, 2016.

Chapter 7
Lobbyists and Legislators Gone Wild

1. Nicholas Confessore, Sarah Cohen, and Karen Yourish, "A Wealthy Few Lead in Giving to Campaigns," *New York Times*, Aug. 2, 2015, p. A1.

2. Michael Cooper, "Political Memo: In Albany, the Two Parties Land in Adjoining Ballrooms," *New York Times*, Feb. 20, 2005.

3. Ibid.

4. Kenneth Lovett, "New York Lobby Is Packed to Rafters," *New York Post*, Oct. 13, 2006.

5. "Take Down Albany's 'For Sale' Sign," editorial, *New York Daily News*, June 12, 2005; "Ken Bruno Quits as Lobbyist," *North Country Gazette*, Dec. 1, 2005.

6. Greg B. Smith, "Brooklyn Condos Build Anger: Gov's Ex-Aide on Developer's Team," *New York Daily News*, July 24, 2005.

7. Ibid.

8. Ibid.

9. Ibid.

10. Ibid.

11. Greg B. Smith, "NYC Buildings Show Connection between Albany Corruption and Real Estate Industry, with Developers Saving Millions on Taxes," *New York Daily News*, May 9, 2015.

12. Ibid.

13. Ibid.

14. Ibid.

15. Andrew J. Hawkins, "Manhattan Democrat to Introduce Pied-à-Terre Tax Bill," *Crain's New York Business*, "The Insider" (blog), Sept. 22, 2014, http://www.crainsnewyork.com/article/20140922/BLOGS04/140929984/manhattan-democrat-to-introduce-pied-terre-tax-bill.

16. Ibid.

17. Commission to Investigate Public Corruption, *Preliminary Report*, p. 33.

18. Bruce Lambert, "Former Chairman of MTA Blocked Investigations, Assemblyman Says," *New York Times*, May 17, 2003; Wayne Barrett, "The Wizard of Al D'Amato: The Former U.S. Senator and Current Powerhouse Lobbyist Has His Hooks Everywhere, Including in New Senate Boss John Flanagan," *New York Daily News*, June 14, 2015.

19. Joint Commission on Public Ethics, *2012 Annual Report*, Mar. 28, 2013, http://www.jcope.ny.gov/pubs/POL/2012%20FINAL%20ANNUAL%20REPORT.pdf, p. 8.

20. Barrett, "The Wizard of Al D'Amato."

21. Ibid.

22. Ibid.

23. Krueger interview with Polner.

24. Ibid.

25. P. Healy, "Minority Party Lawmakers Sue"; Medina, "Censorship Is Alleged in Suit against Leaders in Albany."

26. David, "The Root Cause of Albany's Dysfunction."

27. *Urban Justice Ctr. v. Pataki*, Complaint, 2005, http://www.lizkrueger.com/rulescomplaint.pdf, p. 8.

28. *Urban Justice Ctr. v. Pataki*, Complaint, pp. 8–9.

29. *Urban Justice Ctr. v Pataki*, 2005 NY Slip Op 25523 [10 Misc 3d 939], Nov. 22, 2005, J. Solomon, Supreme Court, New York County.

30. James Nani, "Assemblyman Thomas Kirwan of Newburgh Dies at 78," *Times Herald-Record* (Middletown, NY) Nov. 29, 2011, http://www.recordonline.com/article/20111129/NEWS/111129825/0/SEARCH.

31. Frank Lynn, "Panel, Ending Long Inquiry, Urges Legislation on Ethics," *New York Times*, Sept. 19, 1990; "Excerpts: An Ethics Panel Ends Its Work, and It's Angry," *New York Times*, Sept. 23, 1990.

32. Josefa Velasquez, "Outside Groups Spent $14M on State Senate in General Election," *Capital New York*, Nov. 3, 2014, http://www.capitalnewyork.com/article/albany/2014/11/8555858/outside-groups-spent-14m-state-senate-general-election.

33. "A Way Back to Democracy," editorial, *Times Union* (Albany, NY), Sept. 24, 2015.

34. Chisun Lee, Katherine Valde, Benjamin T. Brickner, Douglas Keith, *Secret Spending in the States*, Brennan Center for Justice at New York University School of Law, June 26, 2016.

35. New York State Board of Elections, "Contribution Limits."

36. "New York's 'Housekeeping' Money," editorial, *New York Times*, Oct. 11, 2011, p. A26.

37. Blair Horner, Rachel Leon, et al., *Over the Top: Corporations Exceeding the Limits of New York State Campaign Finance Law*, Common Cause New York/New York Public Interest Research Group, Apr. 2003, http://www.

commoncause.org/states/new-york/research-and-reports/NY_060909_Report_
Corporations_Exceed_Limits_April_1993.pdf; "How to Miss the Miscreants,"
editorial, *New York Times*, June 12, 2005.

38. Horner, Leon, et al., "Over the Top"; "How to Miss the Miscreants,"
editorial, *New York Times*.

39. "The Crooked Path to Albany," editorial, *New York Daily News*,
Feb.9, 2003, http://www.nydailynews.com/archives/opinions/crooked-path-albany-
article-1.673136.

40. "An Unwelcome Record," editorial, *New York Times*, July 20, 1996.

41. Kenneth Lovett, "Gov. Cuomo Using State Democratic Party to Raise
Money to Promote His Agenda, a Departure from Reliance on a Secret Lobbying
Committee," *New York Daily News*, Feb. 25, 2013,

42. Liam Pleven, "Power Lunch (and Dinner); Senators Use Campaign
Funds to Dig in after Swearing off Lobbyists," *Newsday*, Aug. 7, 2000, p. A03.

43. Susanne Craig and Thomas Kaplan, "Campaign Donations in Albany
Go to Legal Fees," *New York Times*, Aug. 4, 2015, p. A1.

44. Barbara Ross and Greg B. Smith, "Say Pol Pocketed 137G Velella and
Dad Charged with Giving Contracts for Bribes," *New York Daily News*, May 10,
2002.

45. Sabrina Tavernise and Janon Fisher, "It's Back to Jail for Velella, 3
Months after His Disputed Release," *New York Times*, Dec. 28, 2004.

46. Michael Cooper, "Fellow Senators Help Pay for Velella Defense," *New
York Times*, Apr. 20, 2004.

47. Richard Schwartz, "Generous to a Fault: Here's How Your Tax Dollars
Buy the Pols Power and Perks," *New York Daily News*, Aug. 26, 2004.

48. Jennifer Steinhauer and Mike McIntire, "Mayor Seeks Investigation in
Velella Case," *New York Times*, Oct. 1, 2004.

49. New York State Board of Elections, Advisory Opinions, 1989 Opinion
#1, Mar. 31, 1989; Barbara Ross and Bob Kappstatter, "Spare Ol' Fella Velella?
Lawyer Says He's Too Frail to Be Tried with Son," *New York Daily News*, Apr. 20,
2004.

50. "Lawmakers' Audacity," editorial, *Democrat and Chronicle* (Rochester,
NY), Apr. 30, 2004, p. 12A.

51. Liz Krueger, "Former Senator Guy Velella: Convicted Felon,
$80,000-a-Year Public Pensioner," *Gotham Gazette*, Oct. 25, 2004.

52. Michael Gormley, "At Least 13 Former State Officials Convicted of Corruption Eligible for Pensions," *Newsday*, Aug. 6, 2015.

53. Ibid.

54. Ibid.

55. Blair Horner, interview by Seymour P. Lachman and Robert Polner,
2005.

56. Blair Horner and Michelle Stern, "Blowing Away the Smokescreen: The Case against Big Tobacco," New York Public Interest Research Group, Mar. 2003.

57. Ibid.

58. Ibid.

59. Joanna Dearlove and Stanton A. Glantz, "Tobacco Industry Political Influence and Tobacco Policy Making in New York 1983–1999," Institute for Health Policy Studies, School of Medicine, University of California, San Francisco, Feb. 1, 2000, http://escholarship.org/uc/item/2t45x412.

60. Clifford J. Levy, "Tobacco Giant Spends Heavily around Albany," New York Times, July 27, 1999.

61. Ibid.

62. Raymond Hernandez, "In New York, a Record Fine over Lobbying," New York Times, Nov. 13, 1999.

63. Horner and Stern, "Blowing Away the Smokescreen."

64. Michael Slackman, "Case of Former SUNY Official Points to Ethics Law Loophole," New York Times, Feb. 25, 2005.

65. Greg B. Smith, "The Back-Room Billions: News Finds Capitol Insiders Clean Up," New York Daily News, June 12, 2005.

66. Ibid.

67. Bill Mahoney, Eliza Shapiro, and Jessica Bakeman, "Charter Groups Top Unions in Lobbying, Campaign Spending," Capital New York, Feb. 20, 2015, http://www.capitalnewyork.com/article/albany/2015/02/8562581/charter-groups-top-unions-lobbying-campaign-spending.

68. Fredric U. Dicker, "Dads, Don't Let Your Girls Be Interns: DA," New York Post, May 14, 2004; "What's Going on There?," editorial, New York Times, May 21, 2004.

69. Dicker, "Dads, Don't Let Your Girls Be Interns."

70. Kenneth Lovett, "Ex-Staffer Says Top Shelly Aide Raped Her and Silver Did Nothing about It," New York Daily News, June 25, 2008.

71. Danny Hakim, "2 Women Received $32,000 from Assemblyman, beyond Money from State," New York Times, Aug. 29, 2012.

72. Jacob Gershman, "Speaker Admits Mistake," Wall Street Journal, Aug. 29 2012, p. A17; David King, "Silver Regrets 'Confidential' Lopez Settlement," Gotham Gazette, "The Wonkster" (blog), Aug. 28, 2012, http://www.gothamgazette.com/blogs/wonkster/2012/08/28/silver-regrets-confidential-lopez-settlement/.

73. Joint Commission on Public Ethics, Substantial Basis Investigation Report.

74. McKinley, "Lopez Fined $330,000 by Panel over Harassment of Women."

75. Laura Kusisto, "Vito Lopez Loses Council Election," Wall Street Journal, Sept. 11, 2013, p. A20.

76. Rich Calder, "Ex-Vito Lopez Aides Accept $580K Settlement with State," New York Post, Feb. 5, 2015.

Chapter 8
The Overcoat Development Corporation

1. *Compañía General de Tabacos de Filipinas v. Collector of Internal Revenue*, 275 U.S. 87 (1927) at 100.

2. Zimmerman, *The Government and Politics of New York State*, pp. 134–135; Glenn Pasanen and Gail Robinson, "Public Authorities," *Gotham Gazette*, Apr. 12, 2004, http://www.gothamgazette.com/index.php/public-safety/2389-public-authorities.

3. Thomas P. DiNapoli, *Public Authorities by the Numbers*, New York State Comptroller, Office of Budget and Policy Analysis, Dec. 2014, http://www.osc.state.ny.us/reports/pubauth/PA_by_the_numbers_12_2014.pdf, p. 6.

4. Alan G. Hevesi, *Public Authorities in New York State: Accelerating Momentum to Achieve Reform*, New York State Comptroller, Office of Budget and Policy Analysis, Feb. 2005, https://www.osc.state.ny.us/reports/pubauth/pubauthoritiesreform.pdf.

5. Henry Stern of Manhattan memorably dismissed the New York City Council in this way while running, unsuccessfully, for a seat on the body in 1965, saying, "The Council is less than a rubber stamp, because a rubber stamp at least leaves an impression." Kramer, Michael. "Why Not Abolish the City Council?" The City Politic, *New York*, Sept. 28, 1981, p. 21.

6. Demos, "Demos Welcomes Former New York State Assemblyman and Renowned Reformer Richard Brodsky as Senior Fellow," news release, Apr. 26, 2011, http://www.demos.org/press-release/demos-welcomes-former-new-york-state-assemblyman-and-renowned-reformer-richard-brodsky.

7. Lydia Polgreen, "Renewed Scrutiny for the Sale of the State's Canal Property," *New York Times*, Oct. 4, 2003.

8. Eliot Spitzer and Jill Konviser-Levine, "A Joint Investigation into the Contract between the New York State Canal Corporation and Richard A. Hutchens CC, LLC," New York State, Office of the Inspector General, Nov. 2004, http://www.ig.state.ny.us/pdfs/Joint%20Investigation%20Into%20Ethical%20Lapses%20at%20State%20Canal%20Corporation,%20November%202004.pdf, p. 14.

9. Ibid., pp. 8–9.

10. Ibid., p. 9.

11. Ibid., p. 16.

12. Ibid., pp. 10, 16–61.

13. Ibid.

14. Ibid.

15. Ibid.

16. Ibid.

17. Chamber of Commerce of the State of New York, *The Plan of the Port Authority of New York for Future Port Development: Public Opinion upon*

Its Adoption as Expressed by Commercial and Civic Organizations and the Press Together with a Few Facts Regarding the World's Greatest Port, New York, 1922.

18. Caro's *The Power Broker* offers the seminal examination of Robert Moses's decades on impact of New York City and New York State. See pp. 623–631 for a discussion of the power of public authorities.

19. New York State Temporary Commission on Coordination of State Activities, *Staff Report on Public Authorities*, Mar. 21, 1956; Ward, *New York State Government*, pp. 284–285.

20. Zimmerman, *The Government and Politics of New York State*, p. 175.

21. New York State Commission on Government Integrity, *Underground Government: Preliminary Report on Authorities and Other Public Corporations*, Apr. 26, 1990. This has been republished in *Government Ethics Reform for the 1990s: The Collected Reports of the New York State Commission on Government Integrity*, Bruce A. Green, ed. (New York: Fordham University Press, 1991) chap. 11, pp. 340–378.

22. Dan Barry, "About New York: The Cold Facts of Officialdom, Albany-Style," *New York Times*, Mar. 20, 2004.

23. Office of the New York State Comptroller, New York Local Government Assistance Corporation, http://www.osc.state.ny.us/pension/debtlgac.htm, retrieved Sept. 19, 2016.

24. DiNapoli, *Public Authorities by the Numbers*.

25. See Seymour P. Lachman and Robert Polner, *The Man Who Saved New York: Hugh Carey and the Great Fiscal Crisis of 1975* (Albany, NY: Excelsior Editions, SUNY Press, 2010), pp. 75–122, for a full account of the 1975 fiscal crisis.

26. Ibid.

27. DiNapoli, *Public Authorities by the Numbers*.

28. Ibid.

29. Tom Topousis, "N.Y.'s Jets Set to Land—* Stadium Plan Takes Flight * Would Anchor Olympics," *New York Post*, Mar. 26, 2004; Lynn Zinser, "London Wins 2012 Olympics; New York Lags," *New York Times*, July 7, 2007.

30. Errol A. Cockfield Jr, "Scrutiny for Stadium Funding," *Newsday*, May 31, 2005.

31. Blair Golson, "Jets Stadium Foes Have Big Problem with Dolan Family," *New York Observer*, Nov. 22, 2004.

32. Charles V. Bagli, "Jets and Rivals Increase Bids for Railyards," *New York Times*, Mar. 22, 2005; Charles V. Bagli, "Transit and Labor Groups Sue MTA over Railyards," *New York Times*, Apr. 19, 2005.

33. Randy Kennedy, "Hevesi Says MTA Moved Millions to Simulate a Deficit," *New York Times*, Apr. 23, 2003.

34. Charles V. Bagli, "Jets' Offer of Additional $40 Million Seems to Save West Side Stadium Plan, at Least for Now," *New York Times*, Apr. 14, 2005.

35. Bagli, "Jets and Rivals Increase Bids for Railyards;" Bagli, "Jets' Offer of Additional $40 Million."

36. Michael Saul, "Jets Clear For Takeoff! No Contest as MTA Picks Gang Green Stadium Plan 'New Yorkers Will Be the Big Winners if This Project Becomes Reality'—Mayor Bloomberg," *New York Daily News*, Apr. 1, 2005.

37. Joe Mahoney and Michael Saul, "W. Side Story: No Way!: State Board Kills Plan for Jets Stadium," *New York Daily News*, June 7, 2005.

38. Bagli, "Transit and Labor Groups Sue MTA over Railyards."

39. Silver designated himself to represent the assembly majority while the other three leaders appointed trusted members of their conference. Silver's replacement as speaker, Carl Heastie, designated Brooklyn Assemblyman James Brennan, the chair of the Committee on Corporations, Authorities and Commissions.

40. Charles V. Bagli and Michael Cooper, "Olympic Bid Hurt as New York Fails in West Side Stadium Quest," *New York Times*, June 7, 2005; Chris Smith, "The City Politic: The Stadium Catbird Seat," *New York*, May 16, 2005.

41. Al Baker, "New York State to Shine Light into Shadows," *New York Times*, June 25, 2005.

42. Danny Hakim and Jennifer Medina, "Deal in Albany on Budget Gives New School Aid," *New York Times*, Mar. 29, 2006.

43. DiNapoli, *Public Authorities by the Numbers*.

Chapter 9
Other People's Money

1. "What's the big secret?," editorial, *Times Union* (Albany, NY), June 13, 2013, Jimmy Vielkind "JCOPE Reviewers Meet with Commission Critics," *Politico New York*, Aug. 20, 2015; "More Silence from JCOPE," editorial, *Times Union* (Albany, NY), Oct. 20, 2015.

2. "Albany's No-Can-Do Watchdog: The Joint Commission on Public Ethics Needs More than a New Director," editorial, *New York Daily News*, Aug. 10 2015.

3. Yee, "Who's Taking on Ethics in Albany?"

4. Lavine, "After Skelos and Silver, How to Save Albany"; Yee, "Who's Taking on Ethics in Albany?"

5. Stephen Farrell, "Planet Albany" (video), *New York Times*, Mar. 26, 2014, http://www.nytimes.com/video/nyregion/100000002790103/planet-albany.html.

6. Secret, "Ex-State Senator Guilty of Theft from Nonprofit"; Katz, "Ex-Queens State Sen. Shirley Huntley Gets Year and a Day."

7. Golding, "Seabrook Guilty of Funneling $1.5M"; Gearty, "Hiram Monserrate Sentenced to 2 Years."

8. Commission to Investigate Public Corruption, *Preliminary Report*, p. 22.

9. Ibid.

10. Ibid., p. 35.

11. Ibid., p. 38.

12. Ibid.

13. Ibid., p. 41.

14. "Kirwan Bill Would Mandate Overtime Pay for Legislative Employees," MidHudsonNews.com, Sept. 22, 2005, http://www.midhudsonnews.com/News/Archive/leg_staff_OT-22Sep05.htm.

15. Ibid.

16. Wayne Barrett, "The Albany Glacier," *Village Voice*, Nov. 28, 2000.

17. Ibid.

18. Mary Louise Mallick, telephone interview by Robert Polner, May 28, 2015.

19. Ibid.

20. Ibid.

21. E. J. McMahon, "Legislators Still Aim to Sweeten Public Pensions," *Fiscalwatch Memo*, New York Fiscal Watch, July 15, 2005, http://www.nyfiscalwatch.com/html/fwm_2005-07.html.

22. E. J. McMahon, "Plenty of Public Pension Sweeteners Pending in State Legislature," *Public Payroll Watch*, no. 4, Empire Center for Public Policy, June 2009, http://www.empirecenter.org/wp-content/uploads/2009/06/payroll-watch-4.pdf.

23. Richard Pérez-Peña, "Critics Fault Lobbyists' Work for Pataki," *New York Times*, Nov. 25, 2001.

24. Ibid.

25. Common Cause New York, "Why Should You Care about Campaign Finance and Lobby Reform?," fact sheet, 2004, http://www.commoncause.org/factsheets/NY_093004_Factsheet_CTD_Power_Industry_Lobby.pdf.

26. "Maisto Overview," Education Law Center, http://www.edlawcenter.org/cases/maisto-overview/maisto-overview2.html; Nina Schutzman and Joseph Spector, "School Spending Rises as Enrollment and Staff Drop," *Democrat and Chronicle* (Rochester, NY), http://www.democratandchronicle.com/story/news/local/2016/05/11/new-york-school-spending-court-cases-per-pupil/84203572/.

27. Michael Cooper, "Bid to Change Budget Process Is Rejected," *New York Times*, Nov. 9, 2005.

28. Zimmerman, *The Government and Politics of New York State*, p. 139; "Balancing Budget Powers in New York," Philip Weinberg Forum, Nelson A. Rockefeller Institute of Government, Mar. 23, 2005, http://www.rockinst.org/pdf/public_policy_forums/2005-03-23-the_philip_weinberg_forum_balancing_budget_powers_in_new_york.pdf, p. 5.

29. "Balancing Budget Powers in New York," p. 4.

30. Ibid.

31. Henry J. Kaiser Family Foundation, "Total Medicaid Spending," http://kff.org/medicaid/state-indicator/total-medicaid-spending, retrieved Sept. 19, 2016. For fiscal year 2014, New York spent $54,204,075,597, Florida spent $20,425,755,781, and Texas spent $20,425,755,781, .

32. Clifford J. Levy and Michael Luo, "New York Medicaid Fraud May Reach into Billions," *New York Times*, July 18, 2005; Clifford J. Levy and Michael Luo, "Governor Adds Muscle to Curb Medicaid Fraud," *New York Times*, July 20, 2005.

33. Levy and Luo, "Governor Adds Muscle to Curb Medicaid Fraud."

34. Lane, "Albany's Travesty of Democracy."

35. Thomas P. DiNapoli, *Medicaid in New York: The Continuing Challenge to Improve Care and Control Costs*, New York State Comptroller, Office of Budget and Policy Analysis, Mar. 2015, https://www.osc.state.ny.us/reports/health/medicaid_2015.pdf, p. 6.

36. Al Baker, "In Albany's Budget Race, Nonprofits' Progress Is Slow," *New York Times*, Mar. 30, 2005.

37. Fredric U. Dicker, "Shocking Peek Behind Scenes—Foulmouthed Tirades, Patronage Bids Revealed in 'Illegal' Phone Recordings of Gov, Libby and Others," *New York Post*, Aug. 22, 2005.

38. Michael Cooper, "Pataki Asks for U.S. Inquiry into Tapes of Conversations," *New York Times*, Aug. 23, 2005.

39. "Opening Pandora's Tape," editorial, *New York Times,* Aug. 28, 2005 (The Opinion Pages, Westchester and Long Island editions).

Chapter 10
The Road to Reforming a Failed State

1. Vivian Yee, "Who's Taking on Ethics in Albany?"

2. Kaplan, "Renaming the Ethics Bill"; Joan Gralla and Dan Burns, "New York Cuts Pension Benefits for Public Workers," *Reuters*, Mar. 15, 2012, http://www.reuters.com/article/us-newyork-pensions-idUSBRE82E0OF20120315.

3. Cuomo Breaks a Promise by Halting the Moreland Corruption Investigation," editorial, *Buffalo News*, Apr. 14, 2014; "Handling of Moreland Commission an Embarrassment for Gov. Cuomo." editorial, *Post-Standard* (Syracuse, NY), July 27, 2014; "Gov. Cuomo's Moreland Mess: He Did It for Us," editorial, *New York Post*, July 30, 2014.

4. Scott Stringer and Jeremy Creelan, "How to Make Albany Behave," op-ed, *New York Times*, Nov. 7, 2004.

5. Cooper, "Legislators Short on Time."

6. McAndrew, "One-Third of CNY's State Legislators Facing No Opponent."

7. New York State Commission on Government Integrity "Restoring the Public Trust: A Blueprint for Government Integrity," *Fordham Urban Law Journal*, 18:2 (1990), pp. 177–84.

8. "The Albany Money Machine: Campaign Financing for New York State Legislative Races" in *Government Ethics Reform for the 1990s: The Collected Reports of the New York State Commission on Government Integrity*, Bruce A. Green, ed. (New York: Fordham University Press, 1991), chap. 3.

9. Mark Berkey-Gerard, "Albany's Dysfunction," *Gotham Gazette*, July 20, 2004, http://www.gothamgazette.com/index.php/open-government/2482-albanys-dysfunction.

10. "Who Should Redraw the Political Map? Redistricting in New York, Presented by Roman Hedges and Blair Horner," Public Policy Forum, Nelson A. Rockefeller Institute of Government, May 19, 2006, http://www.rockinst.org/pdf/public_policy_forums/2006-05-19-public_policy_forum_who_should_redraw_the_political_map_redistricting_in_new_york_presented_by_roman_hedges_and_blair_horner.pdf.

11. State public authorities spent approximately $38.1 billion according to the 2014 New York. State Comptroller's report (DiNapoli, *Public Authorities by the Numbers*, p. 5) while the state budget for fiscal year 2013–14 was $140.4 billion (Thomas P. DiNapoli, *Report on the State Fiscal Year 2013–14 Enacted Budget and Financial Plan*, New York State Comptroller, Office of Budget and Policy Analysis, July 2013, http://www.osc.state.ny.us/reports/budget/2013/financial_plan0713.pdf, p. 5).

12. Steven Malanga, "Empire Burlesque," Empire Center for Public Policy, *City Journal*, Mar. 11, 2008, http://www.city-journal.org/html/empire-burlesque-10370.html.

13. "Term Limits and Democracy: Out with the Old," *Economist*, March 16, 2006.

14. "Cuomo Looks Back—and Ahead," *New York Sun*, May 21, 2003; Associated Press, "Cuomo: A State Constitutional Convention a Chance for Reform," *Saratogian*, Jan. 15, 2015.

15. "Perspectives on New York Governmental Reform," Philip Weinberg Forum, Nelson A. Rockefeller Institute of Government, November 9, 2004, http://www.rockinst.org/pdf/public_policy_forums/2004-11-09-the_philip_weinberg_forum_perspectives_on_new_york_governmental_reform.pdf. p. 21.

16. Richard Brodsky, telephone interview with Seymour P. Lachman, Sept. 19, 2016.

17. "Call a Constitutional Conventions," (editorial), *New York Times*, Oct. 28, 1997; Nicholas Confessore, "As Voter Disgust with Albany Rises, So

Do Calls for a New Constitution," *New York Times*, Aug. 24, 2009, p. A17; Associated Press, "Cuomo: A State Constitutional Convention a Chance for Reform."

18. Peter Goldmark, telephone interview with Seymour P. Lachman, Dec. 2, 2015.

19. Ravitch interview.

20. Richard Dollinger, interview with Seymour P. Lachman, 2005.

21. Zimmerman, *The Government and Politics of New York State*, pp. 37–49, 130–131.

22. Ibid., p. 44.

23. Jennie Drage Bowser, "Constitutions: Amend with Care," *State Legislatures*, Sept. 2015, p. 17.

24. McAndrew, "One-Third of CNY's State Legislators Facing No Opponent."

25. Carl Hulse, "Rep. Israel of New York Won't Seek Re-election," *New York Times*, Jan. 6, 2016, p. A15.

26. Ida A. Brudnick, "Congressional Salaries and Allowances: In Brief," Congressional Research Service, CRS Report 7-5700, RL30064, Dec. 30, 2014, p. 2.

27. Matthew Chayes, "Mayor de Blasio Signs Bills Giving Raises to Elected Officials," *Newsday*, Feb. 19, 2016.

28. Errol Louis, "The Full-Time Legislature Fraud: Members of The N.Y. Senate and Assembly Already Arguably Get Paid Too Much to Do Too Little," *New York Daily News*, Jan. 12, 2016.

29. Richard Brodsky, "How Not to Reform Albany Ethics: A Former Assemblyman Presents His Prescription," *New York Daily News*, Dec. 4, 2015.

30. Kenneth Lovett, "Gov. Cuomo Hits Back on Convicted Lawmakers Like Dean Skelos Getting Tax-Payer Pensions, Calls It 'Terrible' and 'Insulting,'" *New York Daily News*, Feb. 18, 2016.

31. Chapter 111, NYS Public Laws of 1995.

32. Kenneth Lovett, "Exclusive: Double-Dipping Albany Politicians Collect Pensions While Still on State Salaries," Oct. 26, 2015.

33. New York Public Interest Research Group, "Blueprint for Reform: NYPIRG's Recommendations to the Moreland Commission to Investigate Public Corruption," Nov. 2013, http://www.nypirg.org/pubs/goodgov/2013.11.24BlueprinttoMorelandCommission.pdf, p. 1; see also New York State Board of Elections, Campaign Finance Contribution Limit Page, http://www.elections.ny.gov/CFContributionLimits.html

34. Teri Weaver, "DeFrancisco: Lots of Talk, but Little Change in Albany Following Skelos' Conviction," *Post-Standard* (Syracuse, NY), Dec. 12, 2015; Kenneth Lovett, "Head in the Sand," *New York Daily News*, Dec. 13, 2015.

35. "Siena College Poll: Albany Corruption Is Serious Problem, 89 Percent of NYers Say; 2/3 Say Serious Problem with Legislators from Their Area; Majority: (1) Full Time State Legislature; (2) No Pay Raise," Siena Research Institute, Feb. 1, 2016, https://www.siena.edu/assets/files/news/SNY_February_2016_Poll_Release_--_FINAL.pdf.

36. Preet Bharara, interview with Tom Allon in "In Interview, Bharara Says, 'Putting Corrupt Politicians in Jail May Be Necessary, but It's Not Sufficient.'" *City and State*, Sept. 14, 2016. http://cityandstateny.com/articles/politics/new-york-state-articles/in-interview,-preet-bharara-says-public-corruption-on-albany-culture.html.

37. Louis D. Brandeis, *Other People's Money—and How Bankers Use It* (New York: Stokes, 1914), p. 92.

38. Peter Goldmark, email to Seymour P. Lachman, April 24, 2016.

39. George Santayana, *The Life of Reason, or the Phases of Human Progress: Introduction and Reason in Common Sense* (New York: Scribner, 1906), p. 284.

Selected Biography

Ackerman, Kenneth D. *Boss Tweed: The Rise and Fall of the Corrupt Pol Who Conceived the Soul of Modern New York*. Falls Church, VA: Carroll and Graf, 2005.

Berle, Peter A. A. *Does the Citizen Stand a Chance?* Woodbury, NY: Barron's Educational Series, 1974.

Benjamin, Gerald, with T. Norman Hurd (eds.). *Making Experience Count: Managing Modern New York in the Carey Era*. Albany, NY: Rockefeller Institute Press, 1985.

Benjamin, Gerald, with T. Norman Hurd (eds.). *Rockefeller in Retrospect: The Governor's New York Legacy*. Albany, NY: Rockefeller Institute Press, 1984.

Brads, H. W. *Theodore Roosevelt: The Last Romantic*. New York: Basic Books, 1997.

Caro, Robert A. *The Power Broker: Robert Moses and the Fall of New York*. New York: Knopf, 1974.

Chayes, Sarah. *Thieves of State: Why Corruption Threatens Global Security*. New York: Norton, 2015.

Connery, Robert H., and Gerald Benjamin, *Rockefeller of New York: Executive Power in the Statehouse*. Ithaca, NY: Cornell University Press, 1979.

Creelan, Jeremy M. and Laura M. Moulton. *The New York State Legislative Process: An Evaluation and Blueprint for Reform*. New York: Brennan Center for Justice, New York University School of Law, 2004.

Cuomo, Mario. *Diaries of Mario Cuomo: The Campaign for Governor*. New York: Random House, 1984.

Davis, Kenneth S. *FDR: The New York Years 1928–1933: A History*. New York: Random House, 1985.

DiNapoli, Thomas P. *Public Authorities by the Numbers*. New York State Comptroller, Office of Budget and Policy Analysis, Dec. 2014.

Ellis, David M., James A. Frost, Harold C. Syrett, and Harry F. Carman. *A History of New York State*. Ithaca, NY: Cornell University Press, 1967.

Feldman, Daniel L., and Gerald Benjamin. *Tales from the Sausage Factory: Making Laws in New York State*. Albany, NY: SUNY Press, 2010.

Handlin, Oscar. *Al Smith and His America*. New York: Little, Brown, 1958.

Lachman, Seymour P., and Robert Polner. *The Man Who Saved New York: Hugh Carey and the Great Fiscal Crisis of 1975*. Albany, NY: SUNY Press, 2010.

Lachman, Seymour P., with Robert Polner. *Three Men in a Room: The Inside Story of Power and Betrayal in an American Statehouse*. New York: New Press, 2006.

Lerner, Michael A. *Dry Manhattan: Prohibition in New York City*. Cambridge, MA: Harvard University Press, 2007.

Lessig, Lawrence. *Republic Lost: How Money Corrupts Congress, and a Plan to Stop It, rpt. ed.* New York: Twelve, 2012.

McElvaine, Robert S. *Mario Cuomo: A Biography*. New York: Scribner, 1988.

McEneny, John J. *Albany: Capital City on the Hudson: An Illustrated History*. Portland, ME: Windsor, 1981.

Moscow, Warren. *Politics in the Empire State*. New York: Knopf, 1948.

Nevins, Allan. *Herbert H. Lehman and His Era*. New York: Scribner, 1963.

Newfield, Jack, and Wayne Barrett. *City for Sale: Ed Koch and the Betrayal of New York*. New York: HarperCollins, 1988.

New York State Commission to Investigate Public Corruption. *Preliminary Report*. Kathleen Rice, Milton Williams Jr., and William Fitzpatrick, cochairs, Dec. 2, 2013.

Norden, Lawrence, David E. Pozen, and Bethany L. Foster. *Unfinished Business: New York State Legislative Reform 2006 Update*. New York: Brennan Center for Justice. New York University School of Law, 2006.

Persico, Joseph E. *The Imperial Rockefeller: A Biography of Nelson A. Rockefeller*. New York: Simon & Schuster, 1982.

Ravitch, Richard. *So Much to Do: A Full Life of Business, Politics, and Confronting Fiscal Crises*. New York: Hatchette, 2014.

Rosenman, Samuel I. *Working with Roosevelt*. New York: Harper, 1952.

Schneier, Edward V., John Brian Murtaugh, and Antoinette Pole. *New York Politics: A Tale of Two States*, 2nd ed. Armonk, NY: Sharpe, 2009.

Slayton, Robert A., *Empire Statesman: The Rise and Redemption of Al Smith*. New York: Free Press, 2001.

Smith, Alfred E. *Up to Now: An Autobiography*. New York: Viking Press, 1929.

Smith, Richard Norton, *Thomas E. Dewey and His Time: The First Full-Scale Biography of the Maker of the Modern Republican Party*. New York: Simon & Schuster, 1982.

Stein, Leon, *The Triangle Fire*. New York: Carroll and Graf, 1962.

Stengel, Andrew, Lawrence Norden, and Laura Seago. *Still Broken: New York State Legislative Reform 2008 Update*. New York: Brennan Center for Justice. New York University School of Law, 2009.

Teachout, Zephyr. *Corruption in America: From Benjamin Franklin's Snuff Box to Citizens United*. Cambridge, MA: Harvard University Press, 2014.

Von Drehle, David. *Triangle: The Fire that Changed America*. New York: Atlantic Monthly, 2003.

Ward, Robert B. *New York State Government: What It Does, How It Works*. 2nd ed. Albany, NY: Rockefeller Institute Press, 2006.

Wesser, Robert F. *Charles Evans Hughes: Politics and Reform in New York: 1905–1910*. Ithaca, NY: Cornell University Press, 2009.

Zimmerman, Joseph F. *The Government and Politics of New York State*. 2nd ed. Albany, NY: SUNY Press, 2008.

Index